LIBRARY OF HEBREW BIBLE/
OLD TESTAMENT STUDIES

544

Formerly Journal for the Study of the Old Testament Supplement Series

FOCUSING BIBLICAL STUDIES:
THE CRUCIAL NATURE OF THE PERSIAN
AND HELLENISTIC PERIODS

Essays in Honor of Douglas A. Knight

edited by

Jon L. Berquist
Alice Hunt

t &t clark

Published by T & T Clark International
A Continuum imprint
80 Maiden Lane, New York, NY 10038
The Tower Building, 11 York Road, London SE1 7NX

www.continuumbooks.com

Visit the T & T Clark blog at www.tandtclarkblog.com

© Jon L. Berquist, Alice Hunt, and Contributors, 2012

Library of Congress Cataloging-in-Publication Data
A catalog record for this book is available from the Library of Congress.

ISBN: HB: 978-0-567-62894-7

Typeset and copy-edited by Forthcoming Publications Ltd. (www.forthpub.com)
Printed and bound in the United States of America

CONTENTS

ABBREVIATIONS

AB	Anchor Bible
ABD	*The Anchor Bible Dictionary*. Edited by David Noel Freedman. 6 vols. New York, 1992
AfO	Archiv für Orientforschung
AJSL	*American Journal of Semitic Languages and Literature*
AnBib	Analecta biblica
ANET	*Ancient Near Eastern Texts Relating to the Old Testament*. Edited by J. B. Pritchard. 3d ed. Princeton, 1969
BA	*Biblical Archaeologist*
BAR	*Biblical Archaeology Review*
BASOR	*Bulletin of the American Schools of Oriental Research*
BASORSup	Bulletin of the American Schools of Oriental Research: Supplement Series
Bib	*Biblica*
BibInt	*Biblical Interpretation*
BJRL	*Bulletin of the John Rylands University Library of Manchester*
BK	*Bibel und Kirche*
BMI	The Bible and Its Modern Interpreters
BR	*Bible Review*
BWANT	Beiträge zur Wissenschaft vom Alten und Neuen Testament
BZ	*Biblische Zeitschrift*
BZAW	Beihefte zur Zeitschrift für die alttestamentliche Wissenschaft
CBQ	*Catholic Biblical Quarterly*
CBQMS	Catholic Biblical Quarterly Monograph Series
DSM-IV	*Diagnostic and Statistical Manual of Mental Disorders*. 4th ed. Washington: American Psychiatric Association, 1995
FOTL	Forms of the Old Testament Literature
FRLANT	Forschungen zur Religion und Literatur des Alten und Neuen Testaments
HeyJ	*Heythrop Journal*
HO	Handbook of Oriental Studies series
IEJ	*Israel Exploration Journal*
IRT	Issues in Religion and Theology
JAAR	*Journal of the American Academy of Religion*
JAOS	*Journal of the American Oriental Society*
JBL	*Journal of Biblical Literature*
JBQ	*Jewish Bible Quarterly*
JBR	*Journal of Bible and Religion*

JCS	*Journal of Cuneiform Studies*
JHS	*Journal of Hellenic Studies*
JNES	*Journal of Near Eastern Studies*
JNSL	*Journal of Northwest Semitic Languages*
JSOT	*Journal for the Study of the Old Testament*
JSOTSup	Journal for the Study of the Old Testament: Supplement Series
JSS	*Journal of Semitic Studies*
JTSA	*Journal of Theology for Southern Africa*
Jud	*Judaica*
LAI	Library of Ancient Israel
LHBOTS	Library of Hebrew Bible/Old Testament Studies
NAB	New American Bible
NCB	New Century Bible
NIB	*New Interpreter's Bible*
NIV	New International Version
NLB	New Life Bible
NRSV	New Revised Standard Version
OBO	Orbis biblicus et orientalis
OLA	Orientalia Lovaniensia analecta
OTL	Old Testament Library
OtSt	*Oudtestamentische Studiën*
PEQ	*Palestine Exploration Quarterly*
RA	*Revue d'assyriologie et d'archeology orientale*
RB	*Revue biblique*
REB	Revised English Bible
SBL	Society of Biblical Literature
SBLMS	Society of Biblical Literature Monograph Series
SBLWAW	Society of Biblical Literature Writings from the Ancient World
SBT	Studies in Biblical Theology
SJOT	*Scandinavian Journal of the Old Testament*
SPAW	Sitzungsberichte der preussischen Akademie der Wissenschaften
SWBA	Social World of Biblical Antiquity
TDNT	*Theological Dictionary of the New Testament.* Edited by Gerhard Kittel and Gerhard Friedrich. Translated by Geoffrey W. Bromiley. 10 vols. Grand Rapids, 1964–
THAT	*Theologisches Handwörterbuch zum Alten Testament.* Edited by Ernst Jenni and Claus Westermann. Munich, 1971–76
TynBul	*Tyndale Bulletin*
UF	*Ugarit-Forschungen*
VT	*Vetus Testamentum*
VTSup	Supplements to Vetus Testamentum
WTJ	*Westminster Theological Journal*
ZAW	*Zeitschrift für die alttestamentliche Wissenschaft*

LIST OF CONTRIBUTORS

Cheryl B. Anderson, Garrett-Evangelical Theological Seminary, Evanston, Ill., USA

Deborah Appler, Moravian Theological Seminary, Bethlehem, Pa., USA

Annalisa Azzoni, Vanderbilt University, Nashville, Tenn., USA

Jon L. Berquist, Disciples Seminary Foundation, Claremont, Calif., USA

James L. Crenshaw, Duke University, Durham, N.C., USA

Philip R. Davies, University of Sheffield, Sheffield, UK

Israel Finkelstein, Tel Aviv University, Tel Aviv, Israel

Norman Gottwald, Pacific School of Religion, Berkeley, Calif., USA

Peter J. Haas, Case Western Reserve University, Cleveland, Ohio, USA

Alice Hunt, Chicago Theological Seminary, Chicago, Ill., USA

Jennifer L. Koosed, Albright College, Reading, Pa., USA

Neils Peter Lemche, Copenhagen University, Copenhagen, Denmark

Herbert R. Marbury, Vanderbilt University, Nashville, Tenn., USA

David Penchansky, University of St. Thomas, St. Paul, Minn., USA

Jack M. Sasson, Vanderbilt University, Nashville, Tenn., USA

Ken Stone, Chicago Theological Seminary, Chicago, Ill., USA

Kristin A. Swanson, Luther College, Decorah, Iowa, USA

Robert R. Wilson, Yale University, New Haven, Conn., USA

INTRODUCTION

Alice Hunt

Professor Douglas A. Knight—teacher, colleague, scholar, activist, nurturer, advocate, friend—honored by this volume, continues to move the world of biblical studies, and particularly that of Hebrew Bible studies, toward greater justice and mercy. Known by his friends, colleagues, and students as a scholar *extraordinaire*, he is the kind of thinker who works quietly and intensely on a significant issue and then publishes his research in a way that makes clear the way forward for the field. His widely used *Rediscovering the Traditions of Israel: The Development of the Traditio-Historical Research of the Old Testament, with Special Consideration of Scandinavian Contributions* certainly made that mark. His recent work, *Law, Power, and Justice in Ancient Israel*, promises to do the same. In all his writings (see the complete list following this introduction), Knight proves himself to be an exacting scholar, taking equal care with the complexities of historical work and the intricacies of weaving together traditions, philosophical approaches, and social contexts. The precision of Knight's thought and his desire to showcase scholars' voices so that they may be in conversation with others has made Knight one of the most respected editors, as shown by his six edited volumes and his editorial leadership with some of the most important and highly innovative series of recent decades. Douglas A. Knight keeps setting trends and forging new pathways in biblical studies, not only with his own careful scholarship but also in the ways he brings scholars into conversation with each other.

In his teaching as well as in his research and his guild work, Knight builds bridges between worlds. His encouragement of dialogue between Scandinavian and U.S. biblical scholarship certainly stands as an example, but it is his work over the last twenty years in opening up the social world of ancient Israel and the ancient Near East that continues to bear fruit in the academy. His impact on historiographical studies deserves recognition as well; Knight consistently engages the traditions of scholarship while concurrently insisting that biblical studies not rest on its laurels, and he consistently asks the *next* question based on all the cultural, sociological, historical, philosophical, and religious evidence available today.

This Festschrift is offered with great respect and appreciation in honor of Douglas A. Knight on the occasion of his seventieth birthday. It contains essays from various venues of biblical scholarship that his work has shaped—history, hermeneutics, sociology, archaeology, theory. The range of issues considered by the contributors points to Knight's wide-ranging influence, the freedom he allowed students, and his attention to issues larger than exegesis or parts of the canon. We hope that this collection contributes to the focusing of biblical studies as it represents the recognition of this influential scholar. The volume is comprised of essays by Knight's colleagues—some of them long-time friends and collaborators, others of them former students-turned-colleagues. All of them have written out of deep respect and affection for Douglas A. Knight.

Jack M. Sasson examines the tenth commandment, which prohibits coveting, suggesting several different interpretive avenues. He explores the commandment's two recensions, one in Exodus and one in Deuteronomy, and looks at the question of intent versus action as he also focuses on prohibitions against coveting in ancient Near Eastern contexts in an attempt to discern the meaning of the tenth commandment.

Philip R. Davies proposes a "History of Judah" as a genre that rejects the notion of the nation of Israel as a single historical entity and instead makes a case for the separate origins of Judah and Israel. He examines archaeological, epigraphic, and biblical evidence that provide clues to Judah's origins, arguing that each type of evidence independently supports the claim of Judah's independent beginnings. He suggests that, although Judah and Israel shared a similar culture and were linked to one another by proximity and time period, it is through cultural memory rather any reliable history that the identities of Israel and Judah should be considered as an integrated whole.

Niels Peter Lemche explores the formation of biblical collective memory and the composition of biblical historiography, asking how context helped to form particular cultural understandings found in the Old Testament and contributed to the dynamics that influenced biblical authors. He points, particularly, to the conflict between the survival of Northern traditions with scattered worship sites and the seemingly contradictory biblical emphasis on Jerusalem with importance placed on temple worship alone. He discusses potential explanations for the survival of traditions about Israel, highlights the dominant role of the land and its production as a piece of cultural memory, and draws on Shechem as a key site for this discussion.

In earlier work, Israel Finkelstein has posited that Persian-period Jerusalem covered an area between 2 and 2.5 hectares and that the wall referenced in Neh 3 and the List of Returnees found in Ezra and Nehemiah can be dated to the late Hellenistic period. Here, he responds to critics of these suggestions by asserting the importance of sound methodology in field archaeology and in the interface between archaeology and the biblical texts.

Pointing to an increasing interest in animal studies beyond its traditional home in biological sciences and to the richness of interdisciplinary biblical interpretation, Ken Stone examines animal symbolism in the Hebrew Bible. He emphasizes the importance of historical specificity and socio-political circumstance as components of the zoological gaze and uses the example of jackals and ostriches found in exilic and post-exilic portions of the Isaiah scroll to explore the ways that the animal imagery reflects the different concerns and contexts of these passages. Noting the various ways in which relationships of animals to humans and to God appear in the text, Stone concludes by suggesting that further study of this topic has significant ethical relevance.

By examining the Genesis creation stories and other ancient Near Eastern primordial accounts, Annalisa Azzoni critiques what she identifies as a contemporary inability to engage textual multiplicity and complexity of meaning. She discusses inconsistencies in the Genesis creation accounts, highlighting the importance of translation and the way that the worldview of the biblical authors differed from today's understandings. Throughout, Azzoni asserts that the biblical writers creatively constructed narratives that were meaningful to their specific culture and time, an important understanding to bring to contemporary engagement with the text.

Kristin A. Swanson suggests that the book of Judges is a satirical commentary on Ezra's leadership decisions and offers a perspective on the debates concerning identity and community during the Persian period. She identifies three main sections of Judges that parody leadership: leadership during the conquest in which Judah parodies Joshua; leadership during wars with neighboring enemies in which Ehud, Gideon, and Samson parody David, Moses, and Samuel; and the absence of leadership in which the story of the Levite and his concubine parodies the story of the messengers in Gen 19. Swanson argues that reading Judges as a satirical commentary on Ezra's leadership problematizes the question of the identity of the other and the exclusion of foreign women described in Neh 8–10 and Ezra 9–10.

Robert R. Wilson gives an overview of recent scholarship concerning the composition of exilic- and Persian-period prophetic literature and text production in ancient Israel, summarizing work on this topic done by Philip R. Davies, William Schniedewind, David Carr, and others. Consensus exists on several major issues, including that literate scribes were producers of biblical texts and would have been members of an elite class because of their high education level, rare in ancient Israel. Additionally, scribes were associated with either the temple or the government and their work served the interests of their elite employers. Still, major problems remain unresolved, including questions about the interaction between oral and written literature of the time and the location of scribal activity during the exilic and Persian periods. Wilson concludes by suggesting that the diversity of views represented in prophetic material from this time suggests that scribal writings, rather than promoting a unified position of elite leadership, represented various political and religious perspectives of the time.

Deborah Appler describes the oppressive nature of Nebuchadnezzar's reign and the Persian Empire, including the predatory policies under which its subjects suffered. She connects these extreme levels of economic oppression to the hardships experienced by the two-thirds world in the present day, paralleling the colonizing empire and the global market economy. She examines the language of resistance to Persia's sovereignty in Dan 4 alongside the langue of resistance to imperialism of a contemporary Indian activist, Vandana Shiva. Both Dan 4 and Shiva's texts are written for those in power with the intent to further political change, offering liberatory hope and resistance to the oppressed as well as reproach to oppressors.

Cheryl B. Anderson uses feminist, womanist, queer, and postcolonial work to critique dominant portrayals of Ruth and Esther that interpret these women as exemplary models of loyalty, faithfulness, and commitment. She points out ways in which these texts can serve to maintain oppressive systems and asks how to read them as models of formation for God's people while avoiding the negative consequences that she identifies. She concludes by offering a reading strategy that utilizes thematic, intertextual, and contextual methods to ask new questions about exclusion, inclusion, and redemption.

Herbert R. Marbury investigates the prohibitions in Ezra and Nehemiah against intermarriage between returning exiles and the peoples of the lands, looking at theological, anthropological, and imperial explanations for this separatist rhetoric and blurring lines between the three. He studies the social context out of which this rhetoric may have emerged in order to argue for the importance of economic considerations as key factors in developing an ideology of separation. Marbury concludes by drawing present-day connections, pointing to the overlap of rhetoric in contemporary political and religious spheres and asking about the benefits and the costs of these influences.

James L. Crenshaw's intertextual reading of Ps 39 and Qoheleth begins by emphasizing the warnings against loose speech and the powers of the tongue that characterize international wisdom literature. In Ps 39, the poet's solution to two realities of his time, the brevity of human existence and the punishment of *yhwh*, is silence and withdrawal which lead to further agitation. Like Qoheleth, the poet of Ps 39 understands the human condition as *hebel*, and Crenshaw writes that the poet's remarkable request for relief rises out of this understanding. Crenshaw examines the structure and content of Ps 39, highlights similarities between this and other Psalms, and points out resemblances between Ps 39 and Qoheleth.

Norman Gottwald's close examination of Eccl 5:8-9 looks for extrabiblical connections that help to examine the ideologies present in these verses and in the book of Ecclesiastes. He selects these verses because they lack historically identified reference points and do not have obvious connections to external social and political data. He discusses the roles of the officials in v. 8 and the systems in which they may be operating and names the challenges of translating v. 9. He describes the social placement and ideology of Qoheleth's work, and connects Qoheleth's views of God as a removed authority to the unpredictability and distance of human authorities. Gottwald concludes by emphasizing the importance of social-scientific inquiry that looks for correspondence between the social world and the text, even when immediate connections are lacking.

Four different versions of Saul's death and/or burial in the Hebrew Bible illustrate the different ideologies at work in these varied accounts. Jennifer L. Koosed describes ways in which the Chronicler's narrative is shaped by the trauma of matricide and patricide as well as by the Babylonian destruction and exile. Drawing on psychoanalytic theories of repression and disassociation and traumatic memory studies of the relationship between trauma and representation, Koosed interprets Saul's death as an expression of trauma, both imprinted in the Chronicler's account and repressed from conscious awareness. In her interpretation, the collective anxiety and fragility of the Israelite people is acted out on the body of Saul.

Contrasting his own theories with the work of Alexander Di Lella, who characterizes the Wisdom of Solomon as a progressive response to Hellenistic culture, David Penchansky asserts that Pseudo-Solomon demonstrates a conserving impulse based in assertions of the importance of authority and tradition. Pseudo-Solomon promotes the concept of divine retribution, condemning doubt and suppressing questions, in order to support ideas of reward and punishment in the afterlife. In contrast to the elevation of human experience and the universalism found in the Hebrew wisdom texts of Job, Proverbs, and Qoheleth, Pseudo-Solomon elevates Jewish exceptionalism and the theological assertion that God enforces justice, rewarding the righteous and punishing the wicked.

Peter J. Haas focuses on the Community Rule and the Damascus Document of the Dead Sea Scrolls, examining the way that religious practices of the Qumran community parallel Greek and Greco-Roman mystery religions. The mythical story of Demeter and her daughter Persephone forms the basis of the Elysian mystery cult which has similar rituals as those described in Dead Sea Scroll documents. Both reenact the founding myths of their communities through their religious practices. Both include an invitation for believers to enter the community, an initiation ceremony, ritualistic recitations, and a formulaic response from the community ("amen," for example). Though not enough evidence exists to draw absolute parallels between the Scroll community and mystery religions of the time, Haas suggests that the community was significantly influenced by mystery religions such as that of the Eleusians.

Jon L. Berquist closes the volume by reflecting on the possible trajectories of current and future biblical studies that can and should flourish based on the legacy of Douglas A. Knight.

As a whole, this volume honors Knight's significant and still growing body of work. This volume is also intended to provide a focus—a provocation—not for the future of biblical studies but for biblical studies of the future.

PUBLICATIONS OF DOUGLAS A. KNIGHT

Books

1973　*Rediscovering the Traditions of Israel: The Development of the Traditio-Histori-cal Research of the Old Testament, with Special Consideration of Scandinavian Contributions*. Society of Biblical Literature Dissertation Series 9. Missoula, Montana: Society of Biblical Literature. 452 pp. Revised ed. Missoula: Society of Biblical Literature and Scholars Press, 1975. 454 pp. Reissued. Missoula: Scholars Press, 1979. 3d, exp. and reset ed.: *Rediscovering the Traditions of Israel*. Studies in Biblical Literature 16. Atlanta: Society of Biblical Literature, 2006. Leiden: Brill, 2006. 378 pp.

1977　*Tradition and Theology in the Old Testament* (editor). Philadelphia: Fortress. London: SPCK. 351 pp. French translation: *Tradition et théologie dans l'Ancien Testament*. Translated J. Prignaud, with a preface by Jacques Briend. Lectio divina 108. Paris: Cerf/Desclée, 1982. 354 pp. Repr. Ed.: The Biblical Seminar Series 11. Sheffield: JSOT, 1990. Repr. Ed.: Atlanta: Society of Biblical Literature, 2007.

1982　*Humanizing America's Iconic Book: Society of Biblical Literature Centennial Addresses 1980* (co-editor with Gene M. Tucker). Society of Biblical Literature, Biblical Scholarship in North America 6. Chico: Scholars Press. 186 pp.

1983　*Julius Wellhausen and His Prolegomena to the History of Israel* (editor). Semeia 25. Chico, Calif.: Scholars Press. 164 pp.

1985　*The Hebrew Bible and Its Modern Interpreters* (co-editor with Gene M. Tucker). BMI 1. Chico: Scholars Press. Philadelphia: Fortress. 543 pp. Korean translation: *Hiibru sung syo wa hyundai eyi ha suc sa dul*. Translated Park Mun Jae. Seoul: Christian Digest (Park Myung Gon), 1998. 714 pp.

1989　*Justice and the Holy: Essays in Honor of Walter Harrelson* (co-editor with Peter J. Paris). Homage Series 12. Atlanta: Scholars Press. 348 pp.

1995　*Ethics and Politics in the Hebrew Bible* (editor). Semeia 66. Atlanta: Scholars Press. 184 pp.

2011　*Law, Power, and Justice in Ancient Israel*. LAI 9. Louisville: Westminster John Knox. 326 pp.

2011　*The Meaning of the Bible: What the Jewish Scriptures and Christian Old Testament Can Teach Us* (co-authored with Amy-Jill Levine). New York: HarperOne. 495 pp.

Articles in Academic Journals, Books, and Dictionaries

1974　"The Understanding of 'Sitz im Leben' in Form Criticism." Pages 105–25 in *Society of Biblical Literature 1974 Seminar Papers*. Edited by George MacRae, vol. 1. Cambridge: Society of Biblical Literature.

1977   "Revelation Through Tradition." Pages 143–80 in *Tradition and Theology in the Old Testament*. Edited by Douglas A. Knight. Philadelphia: Fortress. London: SPCK. French translation: "La révélation par la tradition." Pages 153–91 in *Tradition et théologie dans l'Ancien Testament*. Edited by Douglas A. Knight. Paris: Cerf/Desclée, 1982.

1977   "Tradition and Theology." Pages 1–8 in *Tradition and Theology in the Old Testament*. Edited by Douglas A. Knight. Philadelphia: Fortress. London: SPCK. French translation: "Tradition et théologie." Pages 11–19 in *Tradition et théologie dans l'Ancien Testament*. Edited by Douglas A. Knight. Paris: Cerf/Desclée, 1982.

1980   "Canon and the History of Tradition: A Critique of Brevard S. Childs' *Introduction to the Old Testament as Scripture*." *Horizons in Biblical Theology* 2: 127–49.

1980   "Jeremiah and the Dimensions of the Moral Life." Pages 87–105 in *The Divine Helmsman: Studies on God's Control of Human Events, Presented to Lou H. Silberman*. Edited by James L. Crenshaw and Samuel Sandmel. New York: Ktav.

1980   "Why Study the Bible?" (co-authored with Walter Brueggemann). *Bulletin of the Council on the Study of Religion* 11: 76–81.

1982   "Old Testament Ethics." *The Christian Century* 99: 55–59.

1982   "Wellhausen and the Interpretation of Israel's Literature." Pages 21–36 in *Julius Wellhausen and His Prolegomena to the History of Israel*. Edited by Douglas A. Knight. Semeia 25. Chico, Calif.: Scholars Press.

1985   "Cosmogony and Order in the Hebrew Tradition." Pages 133–57 in *Cosmogony and Ethical Order: New Studies in Comparative Ethics*. Edited by Robin W. Lovin and Frank E. Reynolds. Chicago: University of Chicago Press.

1985   "Editors' Preface" (co-authored with Gene M. Tucker). Pages xiii–xxi in *The Hebrew Bible and Its Modern Interpreters*. Edited by Douglas A. Knight and Gene M. Tucker. BMI 1. Chico: Scholars Press. Philadelphia: Fortress. Korean translation 1998.

1985   "Ethics" (pages 283–85) and "Oral Materials, Sources and Traditions" (pages 732–33). *Harper's Bible Dictionary*. Edited by Paul J. Achtemeier. San Francisco: Harper & Row.

1985   "Moral Values and Literary Traditions: The Case of the Succession Narrative (2 Samuel 9–20. 1 Kings 1–2)." Pages 7–23 in *Biblical Hermeneutics in Jewish Moral Discourse*. Edited by Peter J. Haas. Semeia 34. Atlanta: Scholars Press.

1985   "The Pentateuch." Pages 263–96 in *The Hebrew Bible and Its Modern Interpreters*. Edited by Douglas A. Knight and Gene M. Tucker. BMI 1. Chico: Scholars Press. Philadelphia: Fortress. Korean translation 1998.

1989   "The Ethics of Human Life in the Hebrew Bible." Pages 65–88 in *Justice and the Holy: Essays in Honor of Walter Harrelson*. Edited by Douglas A. Knight and Peter J. Paris. Homage Series 12. Atlanta: Scholars Press.

1990   "Ancient Israelite Cosmology: Images and Evaluations." Pages 29–46 in *The Church and Contemporary Cosmology: Proceedings of a Consultation of the Presbyterian Church (U.S.A.)*. Edited by James B. Miller and Kenneth E. McCall. Pittsburgh: Carnegie Mellon University.

1990   "Cosmology" (pages 175–76). "Ethics in the Old Testament" (pages 267–70). "Family" (pages 294–95). "Genre, Old Testament" (pages 322–23). "Sources, Literary" (pages 852–53). "Tradition in the Old Testament" (pages 927–28). *Mercer Dictionary of the Bible*. Edited by Watson E. Mills. Macon: Mercer University Press.

1992   "Foreword to the Reprint Edition" (co-authored with Robert K. Gnuse). Pages xxi–
       xxviii in Sigmund Mowinckel, *The Psalms in Israel's Worship.* The Biblical
       Seminar Series 14. Sheffield: Sheffield Academic.

1992   "Tradition History." Pages 633–38 in vol. 6 of *Anchor Bible Dictionary.* Edited by
       David Noel Freedman. Garden City: Doubleday.

1993   "Hebrews" (Pages 273–74). "Idols, Idolatry" (pages 297–98). *The Oxford
       Companion to the Bible.* Edited by Bruce M. Metzger and Michael D. Coogan.
       New York: Oxford University Press.

1994   "Foreword." Pages v–xvi in Julius Wellhausen's *Prolegomena to the History of
       Israel.* Scholars Press Reprints and Translations Series 17. Atlanta: Scholars Press.

1994   "The Social Basis of Morality and Religion in Ancient Israel." Pages 151–69 in
       Language, Theology, and the Bible: Essays in Honour of James Barr. Edited by
       Samuel E. Balentine and John Barton. Oxford: Clarendon.

1995   "Deuteronomy and the Deuteronomists." Pages 61–79 in *Old Testament
       Interpretation: Past, Present, and Future: Essays in Honor of Gene M. Tucker.*
       Edited by James Luther Mays, David L. Petersen, and Kent Harold Richards.
       Nashville: Abingdon.

1995   "Ethics, Ancient Israel, and the Hebrew Bible." Pages 1–8 in *Ethics and Politics in
       the Hebrew Bible.* Semeia 66. Atlanta: Scholars Press.

1995   "Political Rights and Powers in Monarchic Israel." Pages 93–117 in *Ethics and
       Politics in the Hebrew Bible.* Semeia 66. Atlanta: Scholars Press.

1996   "Herrens bud—elitens interesser? Lov, makt, og rettferdighet i Det gamle testa-
       mente." *Norsk teologisk tidsskrift* 97: 235–45.

1998   "Har gammeltestamentlig tradisjonshistorie en fremtid?" *Tidsskrift for teologi og
       kirke* 69: 263–77.

1999   "James Barr." Pages 98–99 in vol. 1. of *Dictionary of Biblical Interpretation.*
       Edited by John H. Hayes. 2 vols. Nashville: Abingdon.

2000   "Village Law and the Book of the Covenant." Pages 163–79 in *"A Wise and
       Discerning Mind": Essays in Honor of Burke O. Long.* Edited by Saul M. Olyan
       and Robert C. Culley. Brown Judaic Studies 325. Providence: Brown University
       Press.

2000   "Whose Agony? Whose Ecstasy? The Politics of Deuteronomic Law." Pages
       97–112 in *Shall Not the Judge of All the Earth Do What Is Right? Studies on the
       Nature of God in Tribute to James L. Crenshaw.* Edited by David Penchansky and
       Paul L. Redditt. Winona Lake: Eisenbrauns.

2002   "Academic Freedom and the Plight of German Theological Studies." Pages 29–35 in
       *Faith, Truth, and Freedom: The Expulsion of Professor Gerd Lüdemann from the
       Theology Faculty at Göttingen University.* Edited by Jacob Neusner. Binghamton,
       N.Y.: Global. Also published in *Religion* 32 (2002): 107–12.

2002   "Joshua 22 and the Ideology of Space." Pages 51–63 in *"Imagining" Biblical
       Worlds: Studies in Spatial, Social, and Historical Constructs in Honor of James
       W. Flanagan.* Edited by David M. Gunn and Paula M. McNutt. Journal for the
       Study of the Old Testament: Supplement Series 359. Sheffield: Sheffield Academic.

2003   "The Book of Joshua: Introduction, Commentary, Excursus." Pages 303–41 in
       *The New Interpreter's Study Bible: New Revised Standard Version with the
       Apocrypha.* Edited by Walter J. Harrelson. Nashville: Abingdon. Korean
       translation by Dal Joon Won. Nashville: Abingdon, 2008. 357–99 pp.

2004   "Foreword." Pages ix–xi in *Methods of Biblical Interpretation*. (Excerpted from the *Dictionary of Biblical Interpretation*. Edited by John H. Hayes.) Nashville: Abingdon.

2005   "Erobring og okkupasjon: Krig ifølge Josvaboken." Pages 259–68 in *Historie og Konstruktion: Festskrift til Niels Peter Lemche i anledning af 60 års fødselsdagen den 6. september 2005*. Edited by Mogens Müller and Thomas L. Thompson. Copenhagen: Museum Tusculanums Forlag, Københavns Universitet.

2008   "James Barr." *Proceedings of the American Philosophical Society* 153, no. 3: 385–90.

2009   "Traditio-Historical Criticism: The Development of the Covenant Code." Pages 97–116 in *Method Matters: Essays on the Interpretation of the Hebrew Bible in Honor of David L. Petersen*. Edited by Joel M. LeMon and Kent Harold Richards. Society of Biblical Literature Resources for Biblical Study 56. Atlanta: Society of Biblical Literature. Leiden: Brill.

2010   "Conquest and Culture: Joshua's Battles." Pages 261–72 in *Crossing Textual Boundaries: A Festschrift in Honor of Professor Archie Chi Chung Lee for His Sixtieth Birthday*. Edited by Lung Kwong Lo, Nancy N. H. Tan, Ying Zhang, and Kwong Ping Li. Hong Kong: The Divinity School of Chung Chi College, The Chinese University of Hong Kong.

2010   "Politics and Biblical Scholarship in the United States." Pages 83–100 in *Foster Biblical Scholarship: Essays in Honor of Kent Harold Richards*. Edited by Frank Ritchel Ames and Charles William Miller. Society of Biblical Scholarship: Biblical Scholarship in North America 24. Atlanta: Society of Biblical Scholarship. Leiden: Brill.

Reviews

Book reviews published in *Hebrew Studies*, *Interpretation*, *Journal of Biblical Literature*, *Journal of the American Academy of Religion*, *Journal of Religion*, *Religious Studies Review*, *Theological Education*, and *Bible Review*.

Volumes Selected and Edited as Series Editor

1975   James L. Crenshaw. *Hymnic Affirmation of Divine Justice: The Doxologies of Amos and Related Texts in the Old Testament*. SBLDS 24. Missoula: Scholars Press. 190 pp.

1975   Frank Moore Cross, Jr., and David Noel Freedman. *Studies in Ancient Yahwistic Poetry*. SBLDS 21. Missoula: Scholars Press. 198 pp.

1976   Bruce C. Birch. *The Rise of the Israelite Monarchy: The Growth and Development of 1 Samuel 7–15*. SBLDS 27. Missoula: Scholars Press. 181 pp.

1977   Frank S. Frick, *The City in Ancient Israel*. SBLDS 36. Missoula: Scholars Press. 296 pp.

1977   Lester L. Grabbe. *Comparative Philology and the Text of Job: A Study in Methodology*. SBLDS 34. Missoula: Scholars Press. 243 pp.

1977   Leo G. Perdue. *Wisdom and Cult: A Critical Analysis of the Views of Cult in the Wisdom Literatures of Israel and the Ancient Near East*. SBLDS 30. Missoula: Scholars Press. 403 pp.

1977   Alden L. Thompson. *Responsibility for Evil in the Theodicy of IV Ezra: A Study Illustrating the Significance of Form and Structure for the Meaning of the Book.* SBLDS 29. Missoula: Scholars Press. 410 pp.

1978   Harold R. (Chaim) Cohen. *Biblical Hapax Legomena in the Light of Akkadian and Ugaritic.* SBLDS 37. Missoula: Scholars Press. 201 pp.

1978   Richard S. Tomback. *A Comparative Semitic Lexicon of the Phoenician and Punic Languages.* SBLDS 32. Missoula: Scholars Press. 381 pp.

1978   John Bradley White. *A Study of the Language of Love in the Song of Songs and Ancient Egyptian Poetry.* SBLDS 38. Missoula: Scholars Press. 217 pp.

1979   Sandra Beth Berg. *The Book of Esther: Motifs, Themes and Structure.* SBLDS 44. Missoula: Scholars Press. 232 pp.

1980   Rifat Sonsino. *Motive Clauses in Hebrew Law: Biblical Forms and Near Eastern Parallels.* SBLDS 45. Chico: Scholars Press. 355 pp.

1983   James L. Crenshaw, ed. *Theodicy in the Old Testament.* IRT 4. Philadelphia: Fortress. London: SPCK. 175 pp.

1983   Paul D. Hanson, ed. *Visionaries and their Apocalypses.* IRT 2. Philadelphia: Fortress. London: SPCK. 175 pp.

1984   Bernhard W. Anderson, ed. *Creation in the Old Testament.* IRT 6. Philadelphia: Fortress. London: SPCK. 192 pp.

1985   Douglas A. Knight and Gene M. Tucker, eds. *The Hebrew Bible and Its Modern Interpreters.* BMI 1. Chico: Scholars Press. Philadelphia: Fortress. 543 pp.

1986   Robert A. Kraft and George W. E. Nickelsburg, eds. *Early Judaism and Its Modern Interpreters.* BMI 2. Atlanta: Scholars Press. Philadelphia: Fortress. 512 pp.

1987   David L. Petersen, ed. *Prophecy in Israel: Search for an Identity.* IRT 10. Philadelphia: Fortress. London: SPCK. 189 pp.

1989   Eldon Jay Epp and George W. MacRae, eds. *The New Testament and Its Modern Interpreters.* BMI 3. Atlanta: Scholars Press. Philadelphia: Fortress. 633 pp.

1995   Joseph Blenkinsopp, *Sage, Priest, Prophet: Religious and Intellectual Leadership in Ancient Israel.* LAI 1. Louisville: Westminster John Knox. 202 pp.

1997   Susan Niditch, *Oral World and Written Word: Ancient Israelite Literature.* LAI 2. Louisville: Westminster John Knox, 1996. London: SPCK. 170 pp.

1998   Philip R. Davies, *Scribes and Schools: The Canonization of the Hebrew Scriptures.* LAI 3. Louisville: Westminster John Knox. London: SPCK. 219 pp.

1998   Niels Peter Lemche, *The Israelites in History and Tradition.* LAI 4. Louisville: Westminster John Knox. London: SPCK. 255 pp.

1999   Paula M. McNutt, *Reconstructing the Society of Ancient Israel.* LAI 5. Louisville: Westminster John Knox. London: SPCK. 284 pp.

2000   Norman K. Gottwald, *The Politics of Ancient Israel.* LAI 7. Louisville: Westminster John Knox. 383 pp.

2000   Patrick D. Miller, *The Religion of Ancient Israel.* LAI 6. Louisville: Westminster John Knox. London: SPCK. 355 pp.

2001   Philip J. King and Lawrence E. Stager, *Life in Biblical Israel.* LAI 8. Louisville and London: Westminster John Knox. 463 pp.

2011   *Law, Power, and Justice in Ancient Israel.* LAI 9. Louisville: Westminster John Knox. 326 pp.

Translations

1976   Albrecht Alt, "Solomonic Wisdom." Pages 102–12 in *Studies in Ancient Israelite Wisdom*. Edited by James L. Crenshaw. New York: Ktav.

1977   Hartmut Gese, "Tradition and Biblical Theology." Pages 301–26 in *Tradition and Theology in the Old Testament*. Edited by Douglas A. Knight. Philadelphia: Fortress. London: SPCK.

1977   Rudolf Smend, "Tradition and History: A Complex Relation." Pages 49–68 in *Tradition and Theology in the Old Testament*. Edited by Douglas A. Knight. Philadelphia: Fortress. London: SPCK.

1977   Odil Hannes Steck, "Theological Streams of Tradition." Pages 183–214 in *Tradition and Theology in the Old Testament*. Edited by Douglas A. Knight. Philadelphia: Fortress. London: SPCK.

1977   Walther Zimmerli, "Prophetic Proclamation and Reinterpretation." Pages 69–100 in *Tradition and Theology in the Old Testament*. Edited by Douglas A. Knight. Philadelphia: Fortress. London: SPCK.

Miscellany

1976   "Index of Subjects" (with Fred Guttman, Douglas Hawthorne, Bruce Naidoff, and Noel Osborn). Pages 114–21 in Ronald J. Williams, *Hebrew Syntax: An Outline*. 2d ed. Toronto: University of Toronto Press.

1983   "Israel: Images of an Ancient Land." *Vanderbilt Alumnus* 68, no. 3 (Spring): 24–28.

1986   Photographs of Israel and Sinai. Pages 15, 20, 83, 123, 156, 157, 261, 263, 271, and 444 in James L. Crenshaw, *Story and Faith: A Guide to the Old Testament*. New York: Macmillan. London: Collier Macmillan.

1998   "Whither Thou Goest…: Biblical Studies near the Turn of the Millennium." *The Spire* 20, no. 1 (Summer): 7–8.

2001   Photographs. Pages 136 and 137 in Philip J. King and Lawrence E. Stager, *Life in Biblical Israel*. LAI 8. Louisville: Westminster John Knox.

2006   "Intelligent Design: Unbiblical and Unscientific." *Vanderbilt Magazine* 87, no. 1 (Spring): 40–42.

Part I

HISTORY AND CONTEXTS

ANOTHER LOOK AT THE TENTH COMMANDMENT

Jack M. Sasson

His men, his house and his cattle,
I'm tempted not, though all is great.
But let's imagine that his maid
Is beautiful... I've lost the battle!
—Pushkin, *The Tenth Commandment*[1]

You may not *hand over* to a citizen of Kaniš or to a *hapirum* the home of a merchant's widow (literally, "of a merchant, a widow"). You may not covet the fine home, fine slave, fine handmaid, fine field, or fine orchard of any Assur citizen; you may not appropriate (it) by force or give (it) to your follower.[2]

These injunctions occur in an agreement that leaders at Assur wished to impose on the ruler of Kaniš where a large colony of Assyrian merchants kept families. They are written on a recently (2000) found Kültepe 1b tablet that dates to around 1800 B.C.E. (Middle Chronology). While the first clause exhibits difficulties, the second is rare among Near Eastern

---

1. Available (April 2008) at http://www.electroniclibrary21.ru/literature/pushkin/en-01.shtml.

Klaas R. Veenhof kindly allowed access to his study on the Old Assyrian treaties, for which I am very grateful. It is now available as Klaas R. Veenhof, "The Old Assyrian Period," in *Mesopotamia: The Old Assyrian Period* (ed. Markus Wäfler; Fribourg: Academic Press, 2008), 183–215.

2. *Ana bēt tamkarim almattim mer'e Kaniš u ḫapīram lā tuššuruni [tù-šu-ru-ni] ana bētim damqim urdim damqim amtim damiqtim eqlim damqim kirîm damqim ša mer'e Aššur šumšu ēnēka lā tanaššiuma ina emūqi lā tēṭṭerunima ana urdīka lā taddununi* (Kt 006/k6: 61–68, cited from C. Günbatti, "Two Treaties Texts Found at Kültepe," in *Assyria and Beyond: Studies Presented to Mogens Trolle Larsen* [ed. J. G. Dercksen; Leiden: The Netherlands Institute for the Near East, 2004], 252; see also Veysel Donbaz, "An Old Assyrian Treaty from Kültepe," *JCS* 57 [2005]: 65). For the difficult use of *waššurum* + *ana*, see Veenhof, "The Old Assyrian Period," 192–93. For the first phrase, see Donbaz, "An Old Assyrian Treaty," 65, who offers, "You shall not deliver a citizen of Kanesh or an outsider into the house of an (Assyrian) merchant or widow."

contractual agreements in matching the spirit and intent of the Tenth Commandment (hereafter "the C10"), forbidding coveting. Their language is equally categorical: in the use of prohibitives as verbal forms, in the inclusive coverage of objects that must not be desired, and in personalizing the potential target. This association is actually the gist of a study I am offering in full admiration and friendship to Doug Knight, a wonderful colleague and a connoisseur in all matters legal and ancient. The rest of the essay, as they say, is commentary. He need not accept its conclusion; but let me hope he will find it stimulating.

The Tenth Commandment

It cannot be said that the C10, with its prohibition against coveting, has lacked scholarly attention.[3] Oddities make it stand out from the others. First, it is the only commandment that applies only to men; for whereas Hebrew women can despise God and parents, desecrate the Sabbath, murder, be adulterous, and likely also bear false witness, they cannot hope to own the property or the spouses of others.[4] Second, the C10 has come to us in two recensions with significant differences, as we shall see below. Third, when Jeremiah charges Israel with theft, murder, adultery, and perjury (7:9–10), he follows closely on the Decalogue but omits the C10, hinting that the C10 came late to the sequence.[5] Finally, the

---

3. Several monographs on the Decalogue are available, some veering readily into the hortatory. Among those I found the most useful are J. J. Stamm and M. E. Andrews, *The Ten Commandments in Recent Research* (SBT, 2d Series 2; Naperville, Ill.: Allenson, 1967), which has a good exposition of (mostly Christian) scholarship, and Anthony Phillips, *Ancient Israel's Criminal Law: A New Approach to the Decalogue* (New York: Schocken, 1970). Because this commandment is also unique among the others to duplicate the crucial verb either exactly (at Exod 20:17) or synonymously (at Deut 5:21), Syrian, Roman Catholics and Lutherans allocate the material to two separate injunctions. The scheme for having just ten injunctions is preserved by treating as the First Commandment material that Jews and most Protestants allocate to the First and Second. On the Syrian tradition, see M. D. Koster, "Numbering of the Ten Commandments," *VT* 30 (1980): 469, 472. The Samaritans count it as the ninth commandment, the tenth having to do with setting up an altar on Mt Gerizim (Samaritan Exod 20:17; Deut 5:21).

4. Whereas throughout the verbs are couched in the second person masculine, there is nothing about the other commandments that cannot be applied by extension to women. The C10, however, addresses desire for spouses and property that in Israel's legal formulations (perhaps not as much in real life) can only be held by men.

5. Jer 7:9–10: "Will you steal (*gānōv*), murder (*raṣōaḥ*), and commit adultery (*nāʾōf*) as well as swear falsely (*hiššāveʾaʿ*), sacrifice to Baal, and follow other gods

prohibition seems to be about intent rather than undertaking, an issue we shall also soon discuss. For at least these reasons, there is a vast literature on translating its core verbs, on clarifying its goals, on judging its antiquity, and on locating it within Near Eastern legal or social traditions. These issues are rarely pursued independently from each other.

Two Recensions

The Hebrew text of C10 is registered in two recensions, one in Exodus (Exod), the other in Deuteronomy (Deut). Moreover, each has two sets of Masoretic accents:[6]

Exod 20:14	*Deut 5:21*
לא תחמד בית רעך	ולא תחמד אשת רעך ס
לא־תחמד אשת רעך ועבדו ואמתו	ולא תתאוה בית רעך שדהו ועבדו
ושורו וחמרו וכל אשר לרעך: פ	ואמתו שורו וחמרו וכל אשר לרעך: ס

You must not covet (οὐκ ἐπιθυμήσεις) your neighbor's house [LXX: wife]. You must not covet (οὐκ ἐπιθυμήσεις) your neighbor's wife [LXX: house], or his male slave, or his female slave, or his ox, or his ass [LXX: or any of his cattle], or anything that is your neighbor's.

You must also not covet (οὐκ ἐπιθυμήσεις) your neighbor's wife [*Samar.*: house]. You must also not desire (οὐκ ἐπιθυμήσεις) your neighbor's house [*Samar.*: wife]; his field, or his male slave, or his female slave; his ox, or his ass, [LXX: or any of his cattle], or anything that is your neighbor's.

about whom you know nothing, but then come, stand before me in this temple that is consecrated to me to say, 'We are safe, and so may continue to commit disgraces'?" The HB sequence is corrected in the LXX to match those in Exod and Deut: murder, adultery, theft, and swearing falsely. To a lesser extent, Hos 4:2 may also be relevant, giving the following sequence: imprecation, deception, murder, and theft. See Christopher Levin, "Der Dekalog am Sinai," *VT* 35 (1985): 169–72. K.-D. Schunck, "Das 9. und 10. Gebot—jüngstes Glied des Dekalogs," *ZAW* 96 (1984): 104–9, finds thematic correlation between prohibition of theft and coveting and suggests that they belong to the later stages of the Decalogue's development.

6. Most HB editions display the "Lower Accent" tradition. Yet there exists also an "Upper Accent" trope that is used by most congregations only on Succoth; this has a disjunction under the negative adverb *lōʾ* in C9 and 10, but not in C6–8. The Zohar makes much of the difference; see Daniel C. Matt, *The Zohar: Pritzker Edition*, vol. 4 (Stanford: Stanford University Press, 2007), 533–34 and n. 607. Whether or not the reference to nations coveting Israel's land in Exod 34:14 is a rehearsal of the C10 is not of immediate interest here. A list of variants is to be found in Moshe Weinfeld, *Deuteronomy 1–11: A New Translation with Introduction and Commentary* (AB 5; New York: Doubleday, 1991), 283–84.

In Exodus, *ḥāmad* is repeated twice, without a conjunction between the clauses, hinting that the neighbor's estate, *bayit*, in the first clause is developed in the second to include his wife, slaves, edible and draught animals.[7] Beginning with "You must not murder" (5:20) of the Hebrew (but not of the Greek) Decalogue in Deuteronomy, conjunctions link the prohibitions suggesting breaches of equal gravity. Again, in the Hebrew of the Deuteronomic edition (but not in any other recension, including Qumran's), two different verbs are at stake, *ḥāmad*, when the object specifically is a neighbor's wife, but *hitʾavvê* (*hitpael* of *ʾāvâ*) when it concerns his *bayit*, "estate," defined as in Exodus, but excluding the wife.[8] The two sequences are joined by a conjunction, strongly intimating that for the Deuteronomist the two prohibitions were separate.

The distinction between the two controlling verbs is subtle, and there are many opinions on their difference as well as on establishing precedence for one over the other.[9] Because several derivatives of the root *ḥmd* seem to describe qualities inherent to an object (flora, animals, persons) that makes it desirable, to "*ḥāmad*" something is taken to mean submission to base motivations, especially when the incitement for doing so is powerful.[10] The appeal is to self-control. In contrast, the drive that makes people *hitʾavvê* something is normally internal to those individuals, the object of their desires not necessarily distinguished by intrinsic

7. This observation is noted in traditional Jewish exegesis, and picked up by many commentators. The argument of Phillips, *Ancient Israel's Criminal Law*, 149, that *bayit* cannot be a collective "for there is no mention of children, and animals can hardly be reckoned part of the household" is too ingenious. Worth noting is that the Greek version reverses the order, first forbidding the wanting of a neighbor's wife before coveting his house. This order is likely influenced by the sequence in the Deuteronomic recension. We notice that only movable property is cited in the Exodus version.

8. For a harmony of diverse readings, see Sidnie Ann White, "The All Souls Deuteronomy and the Decalogue," *JBL* 109 (1990): 203–6. White does not resist the urge to reconstruct the original of a segment of it.

9. A tight review is offered in Henri Cazelles, "Les Origines du Décalogue," in *W. F. Albright Volume* (Eretz Israel 9; Jerusalem: Jerusalem Exploration Society, 1969), 14–19.

10. Note Deut 7:25, "You shall consign the images of their gods to the fire; you shall not covet the silver and gold on them and keep it for yourselves, lest you be ensnared thereby; for that is abhorrent to the LORD your God." Weinfeld, *Deuteronomy*, 316–17, has a good discussion on the difference between *ḥāmad* and *hitʾavvê*. Any good biblical dictionary will have a discussion on these terms, *sub voci*. See also Schunck, "Das 9. und 10. Gebot," 104–9, who does worry, however, that focusing the C10 only on intent may devalue healthy human drives, falsely assigning them to sinning.

merits, though there may indeed be many. The verbal form (*hitpael*) itself conveys a reflexive act, with the self (*nefeš*) often the subject. That act is not necessarily blameworthy and it is only the context that reveals whether those displaying this urge are commended ("Desire realized is sweet to the soul," Prov 23:19) or disparaged ("Do not share the meal of an envious man or desire his dainties," Prov 23:6).

The gist of this observation is that the C10 in Exodus is throughout warning against moral lapses and the collapse of discipline while that of Deuteronomy is doing the same only when there is lust for someone's wife.[11] In its second exposition, the C10 of Deuteronomy is calling against the greed.[12]

Intent or Action?

In traditional Jewish exegesis, however, the debate has not unduly centered on calibrating the distinction between the verbs; rather, it has focused on whether the offense of *ḥāmad* (and to lesser extent *hit'avvê*) is about intent, where no damaging wrong is necessarily at stake, or about commission, when offenses are carried out that might require legal redress.[13] The issue emerges naturally because the other nine prohibitions seem directed toward controlling undesirable actions rather than suppressing intention. This assessment applies even about positive instructions, such as on observing the Sabbath day or honoring parents; for proof of negligence can come from community reports and specific punishment can be inferred through legal analogy. It has not helped that the sixteen HB contexts in which *ḥāmad* occurs allow for opposite positions on the matter. In some passages (ours plus Exod 34:24; Ps 68:17), *ḥāmad* is the only verb controlling the action, so giving the impression

---

11. It is interesting that Philo treats the biblical dietary laws under the C10, because they urge self-restraint.

12. See already William L. Moran, "Conclusion of the Decalogue, Ex 20:17–Dt 5:21," *CBL* 29 (1967): 548 n. 18.

13. The history of the debate has generated a large bibliography and I mention only recent studies that examine earlier opinions: for the rabbinic argumentation on either position, see Alexander Rofé, "The Tenth Commandment in the Light of Four Deuteronomic Laws," and Moshe Greenberg, "The Decalogue Tradition Critically Examined" (especially 106–9), both appearing in Ben-Zion Segal, ed., *The Ten Commandments in History and Tradition* (Jerusalem: Magnes, 1990). Greenberg shows that contemporary scholarship unknowingly rehearses the same issues as raised in rabbinic and medieval literature. The debate within Western scholarship is covered in most responsible commentaries to Exodus and to Deuteronomy, often with bibliography.

that intent is what is faulted. In most other contexts, however, it is followed by mentions of taking, capturing, or the like, so shifting the offense to a concrete undertaking, such as stealing or abusing another person's property. Inspecting Semitic lexicons to pinpoint a meaning for the verb is not useful here, for none of the attestations of *ḥmd in Semitic languages expresses physical or injurious acts.[14] Also complicating the matter is that when intent is a prelude to a required act, Hebrew tends to describe it through activities, both negative and affirmative. The whole of Ps 15 has that tenor, but rehearsed succinctly in Ps 24:4, where the paired question "Who may ascend the mountain of the LORD? Who may stand in His holy place? " is answered "He who has clean hands and a pure heart, who has not taken a false oath by me or sworn deceitfully."[15]

Interpreting the C10

How to tackle the problem of a commandment that would legislate intent has yielded a number of interpretive avenues, and I offer representative proposals for three positions:

(1) *The C10 is fundamentally about abuse of power.* For Phillips, among others, the Decalogue serves as a criminal code of sorts, so that any provision in it must be prosecutable.[16] Originally it was about the abuse of property, but due to the reform of Jehoshaphat (2 Chr 19:5), judges were made to replace local elders and the commandment became redundant "since it was not the purpose of the criminal law to protect property itself."[17] The commandment was nevertheless kept, spiritualized by substituting *ḥāmad* for a verb that originally denoted taking possession of a home. Rather than proposing a substitution of verbs, Nielsen simply claims that the verb *ḥāmad* does double-duty, with the intent of motivating action to fulfill a premeditated desire.[18] Somewhat similar is Aaron, who relies on accommodating translations of Deut 7:25 and Josh 7:21 to

14.   Erhard Gerstenberger, "חמד *ḥmd* begehren," *THAT* 1 (1971): 579–81.

15.   Isa 33:14–16 and Mic 6:8 are often cited as additional illustrations.

16.   Anthony Phillips, *Ancient Israel's Criminal Law: A New Approach to the Decalogue* (New York: Schocken, 1970), 149–52.

17.   Ibid., 151.

18.   Eduard Nielsen, *The Ten Commandments in New Perspective: A Traditio-historical Approach* (SBT 2d Series 7; Naperville, Ill.: A. R. Allenson, 1968), 101–5. Similarly, Ralph Marcus and I. J. Gelb, "The Phoenician Stele Inscription from Cilicia," *JNES* 8 (1949): 116–20, claim that the "covet" in the Phoenician inscription of Azatiwada needs to be translated, as in the Bible, "To lay covetous hands on [something/someone]."

suggest "confiscating" or "taking possession" for the C10 *ḥāmad* of Exodus, allegedly because biblical laws "do not relate to psychological states."[19]

Essentially the same concretizing goal is reached by those proceeding with a new meaning for the verb *ḥāmad*. Lang proposes that the verb is about appropriating what is not one's own.[20] For him, the C10 itself was meant to save wives from falling into the hands of others when their spouses were taken captive in wars. Weinberg has it both ways by stretching *ḥāmad* into two acts fused into one, "you shall not plan to appropriate."[21] While a specific action is condemned, intent remains firmly fixed in the meaning of the verb. Long ago, Moran had objected to such approaches: "The mere fact that a verb like *ḥāmad* occasionally clearly implies some act of seizure or the like, is not to be understood in the sense that such an act belongs to its proper denotation: rather, such implications are shared by all verbs of desiring, which accordingly cannot be distinguished on the basis of 'inferiority'."[22]

(2) *The C10 explores issues that are internal to Israelite laws.* Coveting and its consequence are readily featured in biblical narratives where we read about Eve desiring the forbidden fruit, Achan coveting spoils of war, David lusting for Bathsheba, and Ahab craving Naboth's vineyard. Jeremiah 35 (vv. 6–7) records how Rechabites explained their origins: an ancestor imposed a series of apodictically couched obligations such as the avoidance of wine, permanent housing, and agricultural pursuits.[23]

19. David H. Aaron, *Etched in Stone: The Emergence of the Decalogue* (New York: T&T Clark International, 2006), 306–12. By contrast, the Deuteronomist who "did entertain psychological categories" (ibid., 310), clarified an ambiguous law by using a form of a verb that is inherently psychological, *hitʾavveh*. Aside from its light investment in philology, Aaron's position assumes priority of Exod over Deut. The issue of priority is fearsomely debated and is beyond the present study's main focus.

20. Bernhard Lang, "'Du sollst nicht nach der Frau eines anderen verlangen': eine neue Deutung des 9 und 10 Gebots," *ZAW* 93 (1981): 216–24.

21. Weinfeld, *Deuteronomy 1–11*, 316. Similarly, in the notes to Exod 20:14 [= 20:17], *The Jewish Study Bible* (ed. Adele Berlin and Marc Zvi Brettler; Oxford: Oxford University Press, 2004), proposes "do not scheme to acquire (your neighbor's house)."

22. Moran, "Conclusion of the Decalogue," 548.

23. "We will not drink wine, for our ancestor, Jonadab son of Rechab, commanded us: 'You shall never drink wine, either you or your children. Nor shall you build houses or sow fields or plant vineyards, nor shall you own such things; but you shall live in tents all your days, so that you may live long upon the land where you sojourn.'"

Gerstenberger has suggested that the terms of the Decalogue drew inspiration from tribal morality and wisdom.[24] Weinfeld has them based on sworn allegiances kings drew from their subjects.[25] Similarly, the C10 and other provisions in the Decalogue can be explained as acceptance among individuals of specific principles, divine formulations notwithstanding. Mowinckel imagined them declaimed periodically at cultic occasions.[26] For Weinfeld, however, the C10 was left up to God, because it was undetectable by humans, hence also unenforceable.[27]

More to the point, Cassuto thinks that in prohibiting the coveting of another person's spouse, the C10 actually creates a first defense against the seventh commandment not to commit adultery.[28] Rofé finds illustrative echoes of the Deut C10 in other statutes warning of trespass against a neighbor (Deut 19:14; 23:25–26; 24:10–11).[29] Matlock, inspired by Vasholz, thinks that the levirate laws of Deut 25:5–10 are exception to the C10 where a *levir* needs to desire a brother's widow to produce an heir, a rather modern application of what was meant to be a mechanical act.[30] There is also much discussion about the coveting of a dowry; yet dowry is never an issue in Hebrew laws.

(3) *The C10 in ancient Near Easter contexts.* Law 25 in Hammurabi's collection stipulates on-site burning for those who steal property they covet when helping to extinguish a fire. The punishment is for committing the theft; yet the spontaneity with which justice is to be achieved suggests a linkage between coveting and the crime it prompted. There is

24. Erhard Gerstensberger, "Covenant and Commandment," *JBL* 84 (1965): 38–51.

25. Moshe Weinfeld, "The Origin of the Apodictic Law: An Overlooked Source," *VT* 23 (1973): 70–71. We now have many such examples in the Mari archives; see Jean-Marie Durand, "Précurseurs syriens aux protocoles néo-assyriens. Considérations sur la vie politique aux Bords-de-l'Euphrate," in *Marchands, Diplomates et Empereurs. Études sur la civilisation mésopotamienne offertes à Paul Garelli* (ed. D. Charpin and F. Joannès; Paris: Éditions Recherche sur les Civilisations, 1991), 13–72.

26. Sigmund Mowinckel, "Zur Geschichte der Dekalogue," *ZAW* 55 (1937): 218–35.

27. Weinfeld, *Deuteronomy 1–11*, 248–49.

28. U. Cassuto, *A Commentary on the Book of Exodus* (Jerusalem: Magnes, 1967), 248–49.

29. Rofé, "The Tenth Commandment."

30. Michael D. Matlock, "The Tenth Commandment," *JSOT* 31 (2007): 295–310; R. Ivan Vasholz, "You Shall Not Covet Your Neighbor's Wife," *WTJ* 49 (1987): 397–403.

also implication that the fire was set to give occasion for the theft.[31] Beyond this case, however, coveting is missing from ancient Near Eastern legal collections—so much so, that the offense is not cited in Westbrook's fine recent handbook on the subject.[32]

Failing to locate Mesopotamian analogues for the C10, a reasonable alternative has been to locate manifestation of this most human of traits in other documents. In wisdom literature, there are a fair amount of references to it as a moral or ethical lapse, and especially so in confessional statements.[33] Some ancient myths, among them Ugarit's Aqhat, shape plots around it, with Anat strongly desiring Aqhat's bow, concretely or metaphorically. In fact, Cyrus Gordon once suggested that the C10 was formulated to reject Canaanite ideology because in a major myth Baal is said to covet (*ḥmd*) a field.[34] More intriguing is the *qal*

31. "If a fire breaks out at a freeman's home and a man striving to extinguish it covets furnishings belonging to the homeowner then takes them, that man will be cast into that very fire."

32. Raymond Westbrook, ed., *A History of Ancient Near Eastern Law* (2 vols.; Leiden: Brill, 2003).

33. Among many examples from Egypt, see H. W. Fairman, "Worship and Festivals in an Egyptian Temple," *BJRL* 37 (1954): 201; Nili Shupak, "A New Source for the Study of the Judiciary and Law of Ancient Egypt: 'The Tale of the Eloquent Peasant,'" *JNES* 51 (1992): 15; and P. Walcot, "Hesiod and the Instructions of Onchsheshonqy," *JNES* 21 (1962): 217. The Book of the Dead is an especially rich thesaurus for self-reproach that includes wanton desire. For Mesopotamia, see Wilfred G. Lambert, "dingir.šà.dib.ba Incantations," *JNES* 33 (1974): 283–85: "I coveted your abundant property (*ana makkūrīka rapši attaši pānīya*)," says a king, "my desire was for your precious silver (*ana kaspīka šūquri lalûwa illiku*)" (lines 141–42), as well as Lambert, *Babylonian Wisdom Literature* (Oxford: Clarendon, 1960), 102:86, 130:88, 146:1. In scholarship, ancient Near Eastern evocations of the C10 multiply when *ḥāmad* is said to reflect an abusive act rather than an intent to potentially commit a crime, with scholars citing such texts as Šurpu ii:47–48 ("He entered his neighbor's house; he approached his colleague's wife"; see Erica Reiner, *Šurpu: A Collection of Sumerian and Akkadian Incantations* [AfO 11; Graz: Im Selbstverlage des Herausgebers, 1958], 14) and the oath the rebel Tefnakht took in allegiance to Pharaoh Piy(ankhy) ("I will not disobey the King's command. I will not trust aside his majesty's words. I will not do wrong to count without your knowledge…" Miriam Lichtheim, *Ancient Egyptian Literature*. Vol. 3, *The Late Period* [Berkeley: University of California Press, 1980], 79–80). On all this, see Cazelles, "Les Origines du Décalogue."

34. C. H. Gordon, "A Note on the Tenth Commandment," *JBR* 31 (1963): 208–9. Stamm and Andrews, *Ten Commandments*, 106–7, offer mild objections (what if C10 originated in nomadic times?) to Gordon's thesis. While dismissive, George Wesley Buchanan, "The 'Spiritual' Commandment," *JAAR* 36 (1968): 126–27, bizarrely proposes that the commandment stopped guests from abusing the wife of a host obligated to be obliging.

vaḥōmer (*a fortiori*) lesson Suppiluliumas constructs for a crude brother-in-law, King Haqqana of Hayasa. Mariya, one of Haqqana's relatives, was executed for casting a glance at the maid of an elite palace woman. How more readily would Haqqana face death should he desire a sister, a sister-in-law, or a cousin?[35] Mariya's punishment is for infringement of a sexual taboo; but the crime is a lust that ignores boundaries. This little illustration is itself embedded within the terms of a treaty between Hatti and Hayasa and it is the cue for me to turn to this material.

In political documents and diplomatic letters there are plenty of charges against rulers who covet the territory of others.[36] Some years ago, attention was quickened by the recovery and publication of protocols in which rulers from the ancient Near East forced a palette of commitments on their clients, threatening earthly and divine retaliation upon infraction of loyalty.[37] The Bronze Age Hittite treaties proved

35. Text in Gary Beckman, *Hittite Diplomatic Texts* (SBLWAW 7; Atlanta: Scholars Press, 1999): 31–32. On these prohibitions, see Michel Mazoyer, "Sexualité et Barbarie chez les Hittites," in *Barbares et civilisés dans L'antiquité* (ed. Patrick Guelpa; Paris: L'harmattan, 2005), and C. Karasu, "Some Observations on the Women in the Hittite Texts," in *Anatolia Antica. Studi in memoria di Fiorella Imparati* (ed. S. de Martino and F. Pecchioli Daddi; Eothen 1; Florence: LoGisma, 2000), 419–24. The setting must be the Hittite court where (unmarried?) palace women and their women were sheltered. Tudḫaliyas III himself is said to have caught the libidinous Mariya as he looked out of his window.

36. Most often used someone raises (*našûm*) an organ toward something: if it is the eye or face, the idiom is mostly about greed; if the heart, it is about sexual desire; see CAD N/2, 104–5. Variations include reference to *itaplusum*, "To gaze, stare, at something" (CAD P, 58), and to *ana* [something] *lalûm alākum*, "following one's desire for something" (CAD L, 49). In Mari documents alone, aside from numerous mentions of the same idiom when desiring land, sheep, households, and the like, I have met with *appam šakānum* (ARM 28 100: 10, "a city") and *īnān eli* [X] *danānum* (A.134 = MARI 8 [1997], 355: 11–12, [Charpin MARI 8 5], "belongings").

37. The venerable study by McCarthy is now superseded but can still be read with profit, *Treaty and Covenant: A Study in Form in the Ancient Oriental Documents and in the Old Testament* (Analecta Biblica 21; Rome: Pontifical Biblical Institute, 1963). Relevant are several chapters in Raymond Westbrook, *A History of Ancient Near Eastern Law* (2 vols.; Handbuch der Orientalistik 72; Leiden: E. J. Brill, 2003). Relevant are the following chapters: J. Cooper's treatment of international law of the Third Millennium (241–54): J. Eidem's study of law in the Old Babylonian period (745–52), G. Beckman's review of Late Bronze age law (753–74) and S. Parpola's overview of Neo-Assyrian laws (1047–66). Old Babylonian covenants are surveyed in B. Lafont's "Relations internationales, alliances et diplomatie au temps des royaumes amorrites. Essai de synthèse," *Amurru* 2 (2001); but see also Durand "Précurseurs syriens." For Hittite treaties, see Beckman, *Hittite Diplomatic Texts*. A fine edition of the Assyrian loyalty agreements is Simo Parpola

especially attractive because their structure reminded some scholars of biblical covenants, with God and Israel as the contracting parties. They thus allowed setting into the Late Bronze Age the Sinai covenant, in which the Decalogue was embedded. The comparison, however, was always tentative. The focus in the ancient Near Eastern material was on political infraction, including disloyalty, rebellion, abuse against other clients, or interference in commerce.[38] Gods were there to punish infraction when kings could not.[39] The biblical context, however, when featuring crimes against individuals, invited communal resolution. The Hebrew God was there as inspiration, but not actively to arbitrate.

(4) *The Old Assyrian agreements.*[40] These inconsistencies have led me to inspect newly published agreements found at Kültepe because they offer promising departures from the Late Bronze treaties, from which they differ in gravitating toward commercial goals. We have four such documents so far, although references in letters make it clear that there were many more.[41] As all but one agreement from the Middle Bronze Age, they are one-sided in that they contain terms that the Assyrians wished their Anatolian hosts to pledge.[42] What to make of finding them in the

and Kazuko Watanabe, eds., *Neo-Assyrian Treaties and Loyalty Oaths* (Helsinki: Helsinki University Press, 1988).

38. Henri Cazelles, "Ten Commandments," in *IDBSup*, 876.

39. A major goal for the comparison was to establish, through parallels, a second-millennium context for the Sinai covenant.

40. For an overview on Old Assyrian trading outposts in Anatolia, see Klaas R. Veenhof, "Kanesh: An Assyrian Trading Colony in Anatolia," in *Civilizations of the Ancient Near East* (ed. J. M. Sasson et al.; New York: Scribner, 1995), 859–71, and, in much more depth, Veenhof, "The Old Assyrian Period."

41. See Veenhof, "The Old Assyrian Period," 183–200, with bibliography.

42. The early eighteenth-century *ṣimdatum* (binding agreement) between Šadlaš and Nērebtum (where it was found) is necessarily bilateral as it seeks to solve post-war issues, such as release and compensation of prisoners, and to set measures for preventing future hostilities. See No. 326, published in Samuel Greengus, *Old Babylonian Tablets from Ishchali and Vicinity* (Uitgaven van het Nederlands Historisch-Archaeologisch Instituut te Istanbul 44; Leiden: Nederlands Historisch-Archaeologisch Instituut, 1979), 74–77. The text is widely discussed, among others in F. R. Kraus, *Königliche verfügungen in altbabylonischer Zeit* (Studia et Documenta ad Jura Orientis Antiqui Pertinentia 11; Leiden: Brill, 1984), 90–93; Yuhong Wu, *A Political History of Eshnunna, Mari and Assyria During the Early Old Babylonian Period: From the End of Ur III to the Death of Šamši-Adad* (Changchun, China: Institute of History of Ancient Civilizations, Northeast Normal University, 1994), 53–56; and Lafont, "Relations internationals," 288. Mari documents show that oppositions to proposed terms were not infrequent.

kārum is an issue. They may have been copies, drafts, memoranda, or even rejected proposals.

The earliest of these agreements comes from level II. It opens so abruptly that we may have the second "page" of terms Kaniš is imposing on an Anatolian prince, guaranteeing recuperation of their losses, their exclusivity of trade, and limitation on taxation. A remarkable clause forbids allowing Akkadians to trade; any that come there must be handed over to die. To judge from the final lines that record a colorful symbolic act accompanying the prince's oath, we may be dealing with a report on how the oath was transacted.[43]

The latest of these documents comes from post-Hammurabi Tell Leilan and is labeled a *nīš ilim*, "an oath on a god" (iii: 11–12, 14).[44] The format is close to what we find in Zimri-Lim's archives.[45] With it, the city of Assur wished Til-Abnum of Apum to guarantee the welfare of its merchants as they made their way to and from Kaniš. While badly preserved, this large text (about 220 lines) opens on Til-Abnum swearing on a stack of gods and ends on pledges to turn back entreaty of other rulers, presumably hostile to Assur. Curses, if any, are not preserved.

Of more interest to us are two accords Assur drafted with two Anatolian towns that had *kārum* settlements, up to half a century earlier when the region experienced mercantile and security insecurities. One was with Kaniš (hereafter K) at modern Kültepe, the second with Ḫaḫḫum (hereafter H), on the caravan route close to where the Euphrates was crossed.[46] Both texts have pockets of damage and each has features that discourage grouping them into accommodating category. Unusual for

43. Latest translations are in Cécile Michel, *Correspondance des marchands de Kaniš au début du IIe millénaire avant J.-C.* (Paris: Cerf, 2001), [LAPO 19 87] 150–51, and by K. R. Veenhof, apud Günbatti, "Two Treaties Texts," 250 n. 8. The final lines read, "[The prince] raised his hand (swearing) by Assur, the Storm-god, the Netherworld, and the spirit of his father. He turned over his table and seat; he filled, then emptied, a pot? and his cup. The prince said, [unclear]. [The Assyrians] said, should we reject your [the Anatolians'] oath, may our blood be spilled like (from) a cup." Alternate ending: "[His officers] said, should we reject your [the Assyrians'] oath, may our blood be spilled like (from) a cup."

44. Jesper Eidem, "An Old Assyrian Treaty from Tell Leilan," in Charpin and Joannès, eds., *Marchands, Diplomates*, 185–207.

45. On the treaty between Mari and Ešnunna, see Dominique Charpin, "Un traité entre Zimri Lim de Mari et Ibâl-pî-El II d'Ešnunna," in Charpin and Joannès, eds., *Marchands, Diplomates*, 139–66.

46. For Ḫaḫḫum, see Khaled Nashef, *Die Orts- und Gewässernamen der altassyrischen Zeit* (Répertoire géographique des Textes cuneiforms 4; Beihefte zum Tübinger Atlas des Vorderen Orients, Reihe B, Geisteswissenschaften 7; Weisbaden: Reichert, 1991), 46–47.

Old Assyrian tablets, H is double-columned and at least twice as long as K; but strategic breaks compromise the thread of argument to the extent that Veenhof proposes reversing the sides that Günbattı sets in his original edition. K accents Assyrian privileges; H gravitates towards Anatolian prerogatives. K speaks directly to the ruler; H addresses an oligarchy, with special focus on three officials with rights to skim garments and money from Assyrian caravans. K likely opens on the naming of gods, but they are not there for invocation. K lacks curses, but it does end by warning the ruler, that "these gods, lords of your oath, are watching you (*ilū anniᵖūtum bēl māmītīka idaggalūka*). H seems to forego both the conjuring of gods and the curses, no matter which face is read first. In Günbattı's treatment of it, the final column urges against secret dealings, "from now on and as long as you live";[47] but its significance is difficult to assess.

The import of all this is that we are dealing with protocols with ad-hoc stipulations rather than treaties with pre-shaped patterns. The conditions then current at Ḥaḫḫum and Kaniš controlled the terms; but because of their bad preservation, it is difficult to judge why each gravitates toward different formulations. H is a rich concatenation of apodictic requests, couched as prohibitives (*lā* and a second person imperfect), on which are built asseveratives (*lū* and a second person imperfect). For example, in one column (either the second or the third), a series of them imposes fair administration of justice:

> You may not side[48] with your followers, your handmaids, your slaves, or a Ḥaḫḫum citizen (on) any decision regarding any Assur citizen or member of the *kārum*. You may not give a ruling on the basis of (imposed) contracts; but must do so fairly in accordance with (traditional) Ḥaḫḫum law. You must come fairly to a verdict regarding any Assur citizen, whether handmaid, slave or member of the Ḥaḫḫum *kārum*. (ii [iii]:1–10)

Prohibitions that follow on circumstances or hypothetical contexts and are introduced by *šumma* or *inūmi* do occur as well; but in K they are in preponderance. For example, at lines 39–44 we find, "Should there be shedding of Assyrian blood in your town or land, incurring loss, you then must pay (the standard) blood reparation and we will kill (the murderer). You must not give us a substitute."[49] A dozen circumstantial

---

47. Günbatti, "Two Treaties Texts," col. *iv*: 23.
48. See Veenhof, "The Old Assyrian Period," 203 n. 857.
49. The last clause is wishful, for the Assyrians may not have the facilities to identify the murderer. There is a delicious story from the Mari archives in which Samsi-Addu receives and executes a person other than the one he was pursuing. No doubt the unlucky victim was badly handicapped. On this matter, see Jack M.

constructions occur in K; but there is just one that is clearly apodictic and it deals with coveting. I have quoted it in the introduction and I repeat here: "You may not *hand over* to a citizen of Kaniš or to a *ḫapirum* the home of a merchant's widow. You may not covet the fine home, fine slave, fine handmaid, fine field, or fine orchard of any Assur citizen; you may not appropriate (it) by force or give (it) to your follower."

While the terms of this injunction also strive to limit Anatolian abuse of Assyrians, it differs from the others in moving beyond immediate causes to focus on injustice, its nature and application: By targeting widows, it sharpens the crime's iniquity; by involving vagrant *ḫapirū* no less than local citizens, it broadens its instruments of offense; by focusing on the covetousness of leaders, it isolates its inspiration; by including people and property as objects of desire, it deepens its rapacity; and by allowing servants of leaders as ultimate beneficiaries, it intensifies its arbitrariness and frivolity. While the onus remains on the ruler of Kaniš, involving his servants and his citizens in the prospective misdeed gives the injunction a communal if not also paradigmatic quality. It also invests it with intimacy in personalizing the source of the injustice. Still it differs from the Hebraic formulation of C10 in that its obligations are not internal to a community but are imposed across ethnic identities. There is no sense that the coveting by Anatolians is at all likely to infect the Assyrians living within a *kārum*.[50]

Coveting in Israel

The distance between Anatolia and Israel is vast, geographically, temporally, and culturally, so for me the issue is hardly about borrowing or of even indirect linkage. I think it was useful to bring this material to the discussion on the C10; but let me end on two increasingly speculative suggestions.

First, I note that K confirms previous suggestions that the C10 belongs to a diplomatic rather than a legislative framework. Yet, because in K the injunction is embedded in a one-sided libretto of potential oaths, it

Sasson, "Scruples: Extradition in the Mari Archives," in *Festschrift für Hermann Hunger, zum 65. Geburtstag gewidmet von seinen Freunden, Kollegen, und Schülern* (ed. Gisela Procházka-Eisl; Vienna: Institut für Orientalistik, 2007), 457–58.
   50. Veenhof ("The Old Assyrian Period," 204) has this to say on the stipulation: "[It] reminds the ruler himself of the fact that he shall not covet and seize possessions of the Assyrians…, presumably not as an act of simple greediness, but rather as a way of obtaining what he likes by punishing them or demanding compensation if they misbehave or default."

bears different implication than if it had been found in a Late Bronze treaty or a Neo-Assyrian loyalty-oath. There, stipulations determined the boundary of unacceptable behavior, with gods activating curses against offenders. While gods may not exact punishment speedily or thoroughly enough, by itself the breaking of oaths is sufficient justification for launching hostilities swiftly, unexpectedly, and guiltlessly. As an example, we have Hammurabi of Babylon's rationalization for attacking Larsa because it "scorned the oaths of Šamaš and Marduk."[51]

The Kültepe situation was different. Assyria was distant, militarily undistinguished, and only in fantasy did Sargon punish Purušḫanda. Betraying the weakness of their position, the merchants put the local princes under oaths periodically, placing their hope in the offer of taxes and bribes, and in their acceptance of shakedowns. (Think of Jews in Medieval Europe.) Violations of terms, however, were dealt with individually, with more success when the issues could be solved internally. Here I draw an analogy with the Decalogue. Yahweh's authorship notwithstanding, to me it reads like an invitation to accept unilaterally a list of stipulations, stated as injunctions but bearing on infractions, such as false testimony, stealing, and murdering, that had to find legal resolution elsewhere.

Secondly, I observe that K did not just proscribe coveting, but attached to it a clarification: there must be no consequential gain, privately by the ruler or distributed to his followers. The absence of such a logical amplification is striking in C10 and it should warn us not to stretch *ḥāmad* so elastically as to meld intent and action by offering such translations as "do not scheme to acquire (your neighbor's house)."[52]

But once these observations are made, a most reasonable question remains: "why would such a powerful series of injunctions end on intent rather than action?" I speculate that the verb, with its plunge into the consciousness of the Hebrew, actually cycles us back to the beginning of the Decalogue where the choice of the Hebrew God, while it can be compelled, must be intentional. The Hebrew is expected to reflect on what is available, but still decide in favor of a God that he cannot see, one without the proven accomplishment of the gods in neighboring lands.

There is a telling verse about all this and it occurs in Deut 7:25. God promises victory to his people when faithful. They are to consign the

51. See ARM 26 385: 16'–20'.

52. We may notice too that in contrast with Exodus, where *ḥāmad* occurs twice, Deuteronomy uses two verbs with synonymous meanings, when the choice of another verb could have moved the meaning toward action. The Greek simply repeats the same verb (ἐπιθυμέω) in all four contexts.

images of false gods to the fire and are not to covet (*ḥāmad*) the gold and the silver mounted on them. The fear was contagion, for coveting the body of a foreign god may lead to grasping it; and in doing so there is potential ensnarement (*pen tivvāqēš bô*) and a weakening attachment to the demanding God Israel accepted at Sinai. Coveting, whether from each other or from others, is the test to overcome; perhaps not by Pushkin or by us, but certainly by the ancient Hebrews.

THE ORIGINS OF JUDAH

Philip R. Davies

In this essay for a generous and versatile friend and colleague I want to propose a new genre: a "History of Judah." In my view (and I am not alone in this[1]), we must abandon the notion of a single historical nation called "Israel" in favor of two separate societies and states, each of which needs to be described independently. That their culture (including material culture) was similar in many ways is undoubtedly true; their fortunes were also linked as close neighbors, and, most importantly of all, Judah assumed the identity of Israel at some point, leading to the creation of a cultural memory of single origins. I have recently tried to account for this creation;[2] here I want to focus specifically on Judah and lay the ground for the new genre. Specifically, I want to suggest that if we examine biblical and non-biblical evidence independently, and then correlate it in a critical way, we can reach some fairly solid conclusions.

To begin with, I should emphasize that by "Judah" I refer to the geographical area. We know nothing of the inhabitants of this land in the Iron Age except for names of various tribal elements in the Bible (Calebites, Jebusites, Kenites, Simeonites, etc.: see 1 Chr 2:4 for a collection of such names). The kingdom of Judah, however, is attested in non-biblical sources from the eighth century B.C.E. While a "tribe" of Judah appears in the biblical literature, the kingdom and its successors, the province on Yehud, are also said to contain members of the tribes of Benjamin and Levi, and under the various kingdoms and provinces of Judea that followed we encounter both Levites and Benjaminites. The only stable definition, therefore, is the territory itself. While this can only be defined approximately, the political and social entities that occupied it fluctuate considerably.

---

1. Israel Finkelstein, "State Formation in Israel and Judah: A Contrast in Context, a Contrast in Trajectory," *Near Eastern Archaeology* 62 (1999): 35–62.

2. Philip R. Davies, *The Origins of Biblical Israel* (New York: T&T Clark International, 2007).

How should the evidence be treated? The archaeological data seem to provide the most objective clues, though the evidence is always incomplete and the interpretation often disputed. There are, moreover, limits to what archaeology (excluding epigraphy, which is mostly documentary evidence) can tell us about any history other than that of settlement.[3] There is never any question of direct confirmation between a historical event and the results of excavation or survey without epigraphic evidence. The results of excavation or survey will therefore either *permit* or *disallow* the possibility of a particular historical (as opposed to natural) event having occurred. There will be degrees of "permission," but the words "support" and "confirm" are both inappropriate, though the history of "biblical archaeology" is bedeviled by them. They apply only in the few cases where all but one possible interpretation of archaeological data is ruled out. But in providing the only purely *material* evidence, archaeology offers the best foundation.

Archaeology

As a result of the West Bank surveys commencing in the 1970s and their collation with excavation results,[4] it is now the broad consensus of both archaeologists and historians that in the central Palestinian highlands, the territories later comprising the kingdoms of Israel and Judah, small farming communities began to appear from the beginning of the Iron Age (ca. 1250 B.C.E.). Although there are some disagreements about this population, the material culture points unambiguously to indigenous or neighboring origins, with certain features showing adaptation to the requirements of highland agriculture.[5] The social, geographical, and economic life of these settlements, involving intermarriage, economic cooperation, shared defense, economic self-sufficiency, and lack of extensive contact with neighboring areas, no doubt fostered, over generations,

---

3. Baruch Halpern, "Text and Artifact: Two Monologues," in *The Archaeology of Israel: Constructing the Past, Interpreting the Present* (ed. Neil Asher Silberman and David Small; Sheffield: Sheffield Academic, 1997), 311–40.

4. See Israel Finkelstein, *The Archaeology of the Israelite Settlement* (Jerusalem: Israel Exploration Society, 1988); Finkelstein, ed., *Highlands of Many Cultures: The Southern Samaria Survey: The Sites*, vol. 1 (Tel Aviv: Institute of Archaeology, 1997); Adam Zertal, *The Manasseh Hill Country Survey.* Vol. 1, *The Shechem Syncline* (Leiden: Brill, 2004); Zertal, *The Survey of the Hill Country of Manasseh.* Vol. 2, *The Eastern Valleys and the Fringes of the Desert* (Leiden: Brill, 2007); A. Zertal and N. Mirkam, *The Survey of the Hill Country of Manasseh.* Vol. 3, *From Nahal ʾIron to Nahal Shechem* (Haifa: University of Haifa, 1999).

5. David C. Hopkins, *The Highlands of Canaan* (Sheffield: Almond, 1985).

the growth of an ethnic identity different from that of the city-state systems of Late Bronze Age Canaan, several of which persisted into the Iron Age. From this highland population—and from similar ones that formed in Transjordan at around the same time—emerged political formations whose kin-based social structures probably differed from those of the city-states.[6] However, these villages did not in all cases exist independently of the cities, which also had their own "daughter" villages; interaction (both positive and negative) between the two systems persisted, and the states that were formed here embraced cities and villages alike.[7]

In light of these developments, it is misleading to identify the first highland farmers as "Israelites" or "proto-Israelites" rather than as a major element in a later political configuration. Regardless of the evidence of the Merneptah stela (see below), the kingdom of Israel or "house of Omri" was not a simply a later form of this society but embraced other populations too: whether or not we should regard it as essentially a tribal kingdom or a territorial state, it seems to have exhibited elements of both. More importantly for the purposes of this essay, "Israelite" and "proto-Israelite" is also inapplicable in any sense to the population of what later became the kingdom of Judah, for the farming population of the southern highlands appears to have originated and developed independently from that to the north—and well after the initial settlement there. As Finkelstein puts it:

> Most striking of all is the paucity of occupation in Judah. This is no archaeological accident, but has been substantiated by considerable research. For example, comparing the number of sites in Judah to an equivalent area in Ephraim, we find ten times as many sites in Ephraim! The regions adjacent to the Judean hills reinforce this picture: The upper Shephelah experienced few, if any, attempts at settlement; no Israelite Settlement sites are known in the southern Hebron hills...; and in the Beersheba Valley, Israelite Settlement did not begin until the 11th century BCE—and even then, only on a limited scale.[8]

---

6. For an excellent description, see Mario Liverani, *Israel's History and the History of Israel* (ed. Philip R. Davies; trans. Chiara Peri and Philip R. Davies; BibleWorld; London: Equinox, 2005), 3–21 (originally published as *Oltre la Bibbia: Storia Antica di Israele* [Rome-Bari: Gius, Laterza & Figli Spa, 2003]).

7. Finkelstein (*Archaeology of the Israelite Settlement*) implies little or no contact; the evidence gathered by Zertal's publications (see n. 5, above), however, suggests that there was such contact. The picture of a highland society isolated from the city-state system (and structures) that were still present in the Iron Age should not be overdrawn.

8. Ibid., 326.

Finkelstein comments that since the southern highlands were quite suitable for settlement and there were hardly any other occupants, such a lack of occupation is surprising. Herzog and Singer-Avitz[9] have further examined the evolution of both "Israelite" and "Judean" societies towards statehood and charted their separate histories. For Judah they suggest a long and gradual process of development, beginning in the Shephelah (the lowlands to the west) and the Beersheba Valley from the mid-tenth to late ninth or even mid-eighth century, and divided into two sub-phases. For Israel they divide Iron Age II into three sub-phases. They argue that each society underwent quite different social processes in its transition towards statehood, partly as a result of different environmental factors. In other words, the results of archaeology reveal no single "Israel" (or "proto-Israel") and no common history, but a separate evolution in two neighboring areas. Even if we were to believe that both populations originated from a common population stock,[10] these elements may have included the later "Ammonites" and "Moabites," and a common population origin does not lead directly to a common ethnic identity: the processes that generate such identity (see above) apparently operated independently in all these regions, ultimately leading to distinct political entities. This is not to deny that similarities in religion and language preserved a sense of affinity (as perhaps reflected in the patriarchal genealogies of Genesis); but that is quite a different matter and certainly does not justify considering the inhabitants of Judah and Israel as comprising a single "people." Indeed, in his more recent book with Silberman, Finkelstein has concluded that we must regard each society as distinct:

> [T]he surveys (and the fragmentary historical information) indicated that in each wave of highland settlement, there always seemed to have been *two* distinct societies in the highlands—northern and southern—roughly occupying the areas of the later kingdoms of Judah and Israel.[11]

9. Zeev Herzog and Lily Singer-Avitz, "Redefining the Centre: The Emergence of State in Judah," *TA* 31 (2004): 209–44, and "Sub-Dividing the Iron Age IIA: A Suggested Solution to the Chronological Debate," *TA* 33 (2006): 163–95.

10. Finkelstein, *Archaeology of the Israelite Settlement*, 326.

11. Israel Finkelstein and Neil Asher Silberman, *The Bible Unearthed: Archaeology's New Vision of Ancient Israel and the Origin of Its Sacred Texts* (New York: Free Press, 2001), 153; cf. 153–55. The whole question of agricultural expansion and its relationship to population density, which is sometimes invoked in Israelite settlement, is a thorny one: see, e.g., Esther Boserup, *The Conditions of Agricultural Growth: The Economics of Agrarian Change Under Population Pressure* (Chicago: Aldine, 1965). If she is correct, there is no necessary correlation between an

Liverani makes the same point from a different perspective;[12] Shechem and Jerusalem were the main city-states during the Amarna age. This reflected the topography of the highland region and the consequent boundaries of economic and political influence. Since that pattern is replicated in Iron II (though with Shechem replaced by Samaria), it is reasonable to suggest that in the intervening period the two areas remained separate. Writing of the so-called united monarchy, Finkelstein and Silberman conclude, "there is no archaeological evidence whatsoever that this situation of north and south grew out of an earlier political unity"[13]—to which they could have added "ethnic or social unity." These conclusions are in no way affected by the current debate about chronology, nor about (strongly disputed) claims of "Davidic" structures in Jerusalem. Without an inscription, there is no archaeological way of assigning any structure to a particular king and certainly not to a king regarded as ruling Judah and Israel together (or even Judah). We can therefore leave these issues aside.

We have, at any rate, evidence from inscriptions of two states in central Palestine, and archaeology does permit conclusions about the processes that formed those states and their relative chronology, based on indexes such as population density, public works, and luxury items. On the basis of these, Jamieson-Drake concluded that Judah could not be regarded as having become a state until the eighth century,[14] a conclusion with which Finkelstein concurs;[15] the evidence is that this occurred rather rapidly. The process of state formation in Israel is less straightforward, but Assyrian inscriptions (see below) point to a significant political force by the mid-ninth century. The results of excavations at Megiddo, Jezreel, and Samaria can therefore be interpreted as evidence of an Israelite state at this time. The picture is complicated, however, by the case of Beersheba and Arad, where large-scale fortifications have also been discovered. While some interpret these structures as evidence of a Judahite state in the ninth century, they are not matched by any similar remains in Judah; perhaps they point to the boundaries of Israelite power at this

---

increasing population density in the Ephraimite highlands and an expansion of this population into the Judean highlands.

12. Liverani, *Israel's History and the History of Israel*, 83–89.

13. Finkelstein and Silberman, *The Bible Unearthed*, 158.

14. David W. Jamieson-Drake, *Scribes and Schools in Monarchic Judah: A Socio-Archaeological Approach* (Sheffield: Almond, 1991).

15. Finkelstein, "State Formation in Israel and Judah," 39. See also Finkelstein and Silberman, *The Bible Unearthed*.

time—or to no regional power, but rather to independent cities. Both Moab and Ammon likewise seem to have reached statehood in the ninth century.[16] There seems, then, to have been a gap of about 150 years between the beginnings of a kingdom/state of Israel and a kingdom/state of Judah.[17] The reasons for this lag in development have been summarized by Finkelstein as greater demographic, cultural, and political continuity and openness to neighbors in Israel (and in Ammon and Moab), compared with the insularity in all these respects of Judah—until its participation in the Assyrian sphere of influence.[18] Herzog and Singer-Avitz have elaborated and refined this analysis.[19]

But how do we describe the political configuration of the territory that became the kingdom of Judah before the mid-eighth century? Following the biblical lead, modern historians have always written of "kings" of Judah preceding Ahaz—who, for reasons given below, may have been the first ruler of a kingdom of Judah. The archaeological clues permit (though do not suggest) a short-lived political unification of the two regions, but do not point to Jerusalem as the capital: the political center of gravity was always to the north.

Inscriptions

A number of inscriptions permit more precision to be applied to the archaeological scenario. Merneptah's "Israel stela," often the highlight of discussion about the "origin" of "Israel," is probably irrelevant to the early history of Judah. Even if its reference to "Israel," and as a population element rather than a geographical area, is a correct reading, we have no reason to conclude that the population of Judah is included: indeed, the indications are that southern highlands were sparsely inhabited at the time. The campaign accounts of Sheshonq I (ca. 925 B.C.E.) are likewise of little help: Arad, Beth-Horon, Beth-Shean, Gibeon, Mahanaim, Megiddo, Rehov, and Taanach are mentioned, but no sites in the heartland of Judah. The list is incomplete, however, and should strictly be regarded as of no evidential value for Judah.

---

16. Nadav Na'aman, "King Mesha and the Foundation of the Moabite Monarcy" *IEJ* 47 (1987): 83–92; William J. Fulco, "The ʿAmmān Citadel Inscription: A New Collation," *BASOR* 230 (1978): 39–43.

17. The problem with using the term "kingdom" is that "king" is not a stable description: it could apply to the rulers of city states or clan chiefs. The Assyrians appear to have withheld the title from those they deemed unworthy (see below).

18. Finkelstein, "State Formation in Israel and Judah."

19. Herzog and Singer-Avitz, "Redefining the Centre."

More valuable is the Mesha stela, celebrating the liberation of Moab from subjugation to Israel. Recently, Lemaire has restored one destroyed letter, the first *dalet* in "[D]avid" to provide a complete sentence in the latter part of line 31: "As for Horonen, there lived in it the house of [D]avid" (*whwrnn yšb bh bt [d]wd*).[20] Lemaire takes his conjectured "house of David" to designate the kingdom of Judah. But Lemaire's reading is widely disputed and not generally accepted. Margalit, for example, has supplied *mem* instead of *dalet* here, plus further conjectures and a translation: "Now Horoneyn was occupied at the en[d] of [my pre]decessor['s reign] by [Edom]ites."[21] Bordreuil has also stated that he cannot confirm Lemaire's reading.[22]

If Lemaire *were* correct, the usage might be significant. For while Mesha names both "Omri" and "Israel" it does not call it "house of Omri" as do several Assyrian inscriptions (see below). Accordingly, we might expect him to refer to either "David" or "Judah" if Mesha wished to refer to a kingdom of Judah: the usage "house of David" could therefore be significant. Whether or not Lemaire is correct, we can explore the implications of Mesha's account. First, the stela makes Israel the suzerain and not Judah. Given the geographical position of Moab, to the immediate southeast of Judah, it seems unlikely that Israelite control would have been possible had Judah been a kingdom of any significance—or, alternatively, that if Moab were a vassal, then Judah would have been also. In either case, it is questionable whether Judah had the status of a kingdom—at least in the view of either the Omrides or of Mesha himself. Lemaire's reading, if it were correct, would suggest that Mesha did *not* regard it as such. It would confirm, however, that this "house of David" was an Israelite vassal, obliged to play an assisting role in Israel's subjugation. If we may depart from the strict method and consider at this point the biblical account, we can note that its account of Mesha's rebellion (2 Kgs 3) has "Jehoram the king of Israel" summoning Jehoshaphat the king of Judah to accompany him on his campaign to subdue the rebellion. The account represents Jehoshaphat as a Judahite king and portrays him as an enthusiastic ally: "my people are your people: my horses are your horses" (v. 7). This Judahite version supports the conclusion that Judah participated in the campaign against Mesha

20. André Lemaire, "'House of David' Restored in Moabite Inscription," *BAR* 20 (1994): 30–37.

21. B. Margalit, "Studies in NW Semitic Inscriptions," *UF* 26 (1994): 217–315.

22. Pierre Bordreuil, "A propos de l'inscription de Meshaᶜ: deux notes," in *The World of the Aramaeans*, vol. 3 (ed. P. M. Michèle Daviau, John W. Wevers, and Michael Weigl; Sheffield: Sheffield Academic, 2001), 158–67 (162–63).

and thus makes Lemaire's reading plausible. But it implies that Judah was probably also under Israelite patronage. That a Judahite account would name Jehoshaphat as "king" goes without saying and does not carry much weight.

Like the Mesha stela, the Tel Dan stela also relates to the kingdom of Israel but contains a reading that is (this time more widely) regarded as referring to Judah. In the first fragment of the inscription, the author states that an (unnamed) king of Israel had invaded the territory of his father, but that he had repulsed the invasion. The inscription is by general consent dated to the late ninth or early eighth century, when the archaeological evidence of a major rebuilding phase suggests the city of Dan had come under Aramean control.

There are numerous problems with the arrangement and interpretation of the two portions of the inscription (named A and B). It is not certain that their alignment by Biran and Naveh is correct, or even that the fragments are contiguous and thus *can* be correctly aligned. Hence, we cannot really be sure that the contents of one fragment can be directly related to the contents of the other.[23] In fragment A, the phrase "king of Israel" (*mlk ysrʾl*) is clearly legible, followed by a form of the verb "kill" (*qtl*); and in the next line *bytdwd*, with a *kaph* as the surviving last letter of the preceding word, which Biran and Naveh restore as *[ml]k*. Yet the reading "king of the house of David" which they propose is anomalous. Such a term does not occur anywhere else, including in the Bible. As for the phrase "house of David" itself, that is attested (apart from the possible reading of the Mesha stela—see above) only in biblical texts. Fragment B contains the sequence *]yhw br[*, probably a personal name ending in a Yahwistic theophoric, followed by "son [of]." Biran and Naveh supply *[Amaz]iah son of[Joash*, a conjecture based on biblical data: Amaziah is mentioned in 2 Kgs 12–14 as a monarch of Judah at approximately the time of the events that Biran and Naveh believe to be mentioned in the inscription. But even if a Yahwistic personal name is a probable reading, the inference that this person might be Judahite, or a king, depends entirely on their alignment of the two fragments.

The use by Biran and Naveh of biblical data to supply the name of Amaziah is understandable but problematic because correlations between the inscription and the biblical narrative are difficult. If *bytdwd* alludes to a ruling family in Judah, then perhaps this battle referred to is the one between Bar Hadad II of Aram on the one hand and Ahab of Israel and Jehoshaphat of Judah on the other, described in 1 Kgs 22:29–38; or, as

---

23. See for discussion, George Athas, *The Tel Dan Inscription: A Reappraisal and a New Interpretation* (Sheffield: Sheffield Academic, 2003), 191.

the editors prefer, a battle between Hazael of Aram on the one hand and Joram of Israel assisted by Ahaziah of Judah on the other (2 Kgs 8:28–29; 9:14–16). But according to the biblical narrative, both battles took place at Ramoth-Gilead in Transjordan, not in the vicinity of Dan. According to 1 Kgs 15:16–22 (= 2 Chr 16:1–6) a battle *did* take place between Bar Hadad I of Aram and Baasha of Israel, in which Bar Hadad captured Dan, along with other Israelite cities. However, according to this account Asa, the king of Judah, was on the side of Bar Hadad I against Baasha. Possibly, then, the reference is to a battle that is *not* mentioned in the Bible: Biran and Naveh do not express an opinion on this, but they do conclude that the author of the inscription was Hazael of Damascus. Athas, however, has argued for his successor Bar-Hadad (whom he calls "II").[24]

What are the implications of this inscription for the political status of Judah during the ninth and eighth centuries? Much depends on whether "house of David" is the correct translation of *bytdwd*. There are alternatives, such as a place name; it is worth pointing out that a phrase *ʾrʾl dwdh* does occur in the Mesha stela, and may point to another meaning for *dwd*. In favor of the popular translation is that a number of Aramean kingdoms/states of the time bore the name *Bet-X*, possibly after the name of the ruling family. Additionally, appeal is made to the Assyrian term for the kingdom of Israel, *bit humri(ya)*, "house of Omri." This usage is not invariable: on Shalmaneser III's "Black Obelisk" Jehu "son of Omri" is mentioned and depicted, but his "Kurkh stela" uses the derogatory term "Ahab the Israelite." The Nimrud slab inscription recording Adad-nirari III's expedition to Palestine in 803 mentions Hatti-land, Amurru-land, Tyre, Sidon, [mat]Hu-um-ri (land of Omri), Edom, Philistia, and Aram (but not Judah). Although his "Rimah stela" mentions "Joash of Samaria" and Tiglath-pileser III (743–732) mentions "Menahem of Samaria" together with a list of other north Palestinian and Syrian kingdoms,[25] Sargon II describes his conquest of the of the city of Samaria along with "the whole house of Omri." Whether "house of Omri" represents the kingdom or the dynasty is not always clear and indeed from the Assyrian perspective makes no difference: the two are interchangeable—to defeat the ruler is to defeat the land he controls (Adad-Nirarir's "land of Omri" belongs in a geographical list). The regular

24. Ibid., 263.
25. The reference to *az-ri-a-u* [*ANET ia-u-ha-zi*] [mat]*ia-u-da-a* is seen by a minority of scholars (see, e.g., *ANET*) as a reference to Azariah of Judah; the majority, however, identify the state in question as *Yʾdi*, mentioned in the Zinjirli inscription and located in northern Syria.

Assyrian usage is thus "House of Omri" or "land of Omri," even when the Omride dynasty may have no longer been in existence (as at the time of Sargon) and the name "Samaria" began to be preferred. As already observed, Mesha uses "Omri" and "Israel" interchangeably.

But while this usage provides a plausible analogy to "house of David" as a name for Judah, it is important to bear in mind that Assyrian and Babylonian texts *always* refer to "Judah" by that name, and never use the term "house of David." We are thus left in the Tel Dan inscription, as with the Mesha stela, with a *possible* reference to a "house of David." Unlike the Moabite text we have no one clear biblical narrative of the same events, but several possibilities. And again it may be more convenient to consider these biblical texts at this point. The story in 1 Kgs 22[26] features Jehoshaphat king of Judah and an unnamed king of Israel (the mention of "Ahab" in v. 20 is widely suspected as a later editorial clarification). But like 2 Kgs 3, it implies that Judah (in the person of "king" Jehoshaphat) willingly accedes to a request to provide forces against Aram. Indeed, we find the same formula in v. 4—"my people are your people: my horses are your horses"—and we may suspect that if there is a historical reality behind this response, it constitutes a vassal–client relationship: Judah assists Israel in its own wars when "requested."

The story in 1 Kgs 15 perhaps deserves a brief comment. As already noted, it has no likely connection with the events referred to in the Tel Dan stela. It represents Asa king of Judah as under attack from Baasha of Israel and offering tribute to Ben-Hadad of Damascus to withdraw from supporting Israel, to which the Arameans responded by attacking Israel. The biblical account of the reign of Asa concludes by commenting that "there was war between Asa and King Baasha of Israel all their days." Though it appears to suggest that Judah was under pressure from Israel very soon after the "division" of the kingdoms, there are two difficulties with any kind of historical assessment or interpretation of this story. First, unlike 2 Kgs 3, there is no other account of such events with which we may compare and verify it. Second, the reign of Asa, on the biblical chronology, would have to be assigned to the early ninth century, and this confronts it with archaeological data. The current debate about the chronology of the tenth and ninth centuries, quite apart from the problems of positing a "united monarchy" and thus a "division" make this

---

26. On which see J. Maxwell Miller, "The Rest of the Acts of Jehoahaz (1 Kings 20; 22.1–38)," *ZAW* 80 (1968): 337–42. For a review of scholarship, see Simon John De Vries, *Prophet Against Prophet: The Role of the Micaiah Narrative (1 Kings 22) in the Development of Early Prophetic Tradition* (Grand Rapids: Eerdmans, 1978), 4–10.

period impossible to reconstruct with any confidence. Although, for example, Finkelstein and Silberman comment that "there is no reason to doubt seriously the reliability of the biblical list of Davidic kings who ruled in Jerusalem over the two centuries that followed the time of David and Solomon,"[27] the phrase "no reason to doubt" is strikingly characteristic of the older "biblical archaeology." But there are no reasons to take them seriously, either, as both Brettler[28] and Auld[29] have recently argued. The canonized Judahite history is obliged to supply a complete list of "Davidic" kings, but we are not obliged to accept that list until or unless we have confirmation and certainly not that the names are those of "kings" who "ruled in Jerusalem."

Biblical Evidence

Some biblical evidence relevant to particular episodes has already been discussed. Here we shall consider more widely the biblical presentation of Judah's history, and here we are dealing specifically with *cultural memories*, a particular kind of representation of the past. The main problem with aligning biblical texts with other data is that the texts themselves require intricate interpretation, especially involving questions of dating, context, and purpose. It is only a *critical* assessment of the texts that can be offered as appropriate for historical interpretation. All too often individual bits of data have been extracted as if potential nuggets of "history" and then correlated with contexts suggested, or permitted, by archaeology or by other literary texts. In the case of the origins of Judah, a critical analysis of a range of biblical texts can nevertheless yield some probabilities about at least what was collectively remembered about Judahite origins. This analysis should, of course, be conducted independently of the other evidence already considered.

We can commence such an analysis with the narrative as it stands and not with any reconstructed source or redaction. Here the crucial moment is the point at which a twelve-tribe "Israel" gives way to the two "houses" of Israel and Judah—when Judah assumes a separate identity. This separation becomes fully evident in 1 Samuel, though we can discover

27. Finkelstein and Silberman, *The Bible Unearthed*, 231.

28. Marc Zvi Brettler, "Method in the Application of Biblical Source Material to Historical Writing (with Particular Reference to the Ninth Century B.C.E.)," in *Understanding the History of Israel* (ed. H. G. M. Williamson; Oxford: Oxford University Press for the British Academy, 2007), 305–36.

29. A. Graeme Auld, "Reading Kings on the Divided Monarchy," in Williamson, *Understanding the History of Israel*, 337–43.

traces of it in the preceding narrative, and it brings with it some uncertainty about the "Israel" from which it is separated. Saul is king of an "Israel" that now and then seems to represent the twelve-tribe nation of the Pentateuch. But in 1 Sam 11:8 Saul musters "Israel" and "Judah" separately; they are again distinguished in 17:52 and 18:16. Finally, in 2 Sam 2:4, after Saul's death, David becomes king of Judah. David is presented as the legitimate successor of Saul as king of Israel, and as commander of its armies. But he is also king of Judah, and later thus of a "united monarchy" (to use the common descriptive term), not a single undifferentiated "Israel." This separation is given no explanation. Indeed, in the light of Judg 20–21, where Judah is presented as Israel's leading tribe and Benjamin—from whom Israel's first king is chosen—is set against the remainder, it is incomprehensible that Judah seems to become detached from Israel and that Israel's first king comes from Benjamin!

The separation of Judah and Israel might be explained as the result of the later circumstances of distinct monarchies being retrojected to an earlier period. But why should that countervail the image of a single nation that dominates the Pentateuch and most of Joshua and Judges? And why should the division of that nation into "Judah" and "Israel" be assigned to the time of David rather than totally blamed on Jeroboam's "rebellion"? In fact, the detachment of Judah from Israel is perceptible also in parts of Joshua and Judges, in the form of revisions that secondarily introduce Judah into the history of Israel. Whereas in Genesis–Deuteronomy there are no hints of any separation of Judah from a ten- or eleven-tribe "Israel," nor in the tribal allotments of Josh 13–24, in the stories of conquest the narrative focuses on the territory of Benjamin, with the war-camp based in Gilgal. There is a second campaign encompassing the territory of Judah (Josh 10) preceding an expedition to the north (ch. 11), but both of these are (correctly) seen as supplements to the more focused and elaborate account relating to Gilgal, Jericho, Ai, and Gibeon (5:1–10:15). The separation of Judah extends into Judges, where the Judahite figure of Othniel is again widely interpreted as a secondary intrusion, borrowed from Josh 15:17 (see also Judg 1:13). The first judge to figure in a developed narrative is Ehud from Benjamin. In the early chapters of 1 Samuel, too, where the leading characters are Samuel and Saul, the focus remains in Benjaminite territory, perhaps extended to the "Ephraimite hill" where Samuel, like Joshua, was born (and where Ehud also summons fighters, Judg 3:27). There is, then, a continued narrative focus on a particular territory, mostly that of Benjamin, where "Israel" conquers its land, defends it, and establishes its kingdom, while Judah is represented in this narrative in secondary additions, apart from the general framework of a twelve-tribe nation that dominates the book of Joshua but is less intrusive in Judges (and confined mainly to 1:1–3:6 and chs. 19–21). In the books of Joshua–Judges we can therefore see the collision of two profiles: of an Israelite nation on the one hand and on the other an Israel less clearly defined but centered on Benjamin, and a separate Judah.

After the interlude of "united monarchy," where the separate Israel and Judah are combined into a single political entity, relations between the two kingdoms are characterized largely by subservience on the part of Judah and hostility. I have already suggested that the stories of 1 Kgs 22 and 2 Kgs 3 suggest that the Judahite ruler was a vassal of the Israelite one. But Jehoshaphat's son and successor is named as Jehoram/ Joram, who married the daughter of Ahab (2 Kgs 8:16–18). Ahab's son and successor (after his brother Ahaziah) is also named Joram, however, and Miller's plausible conjecture is that the two kings were one and the same, and that a single king ruled both territories, succeeding his brother-in-law Ahaziah of Israel before being killed.[30] The text has Jehoram of Judah dying and being succeeded by Ahaziah, then both kings being killed by Jehu (2 Kgs 9).[31] On Miller's theory the one king J(eh)oram was killed and the Israelite throne taken by Jehu, who also killed J(eh)oram's son Azariah, leaving Judah ruled by Azariah's queen Athaliah. According to the picture in 2 Kings, she would have been an enemy of Jehu, who was apparently then unable to regain control of Judah.

The story in 2 Kgs 14, according to which Amaziah of Judah challenged Jehoash of Israel to battle, might be understood in this context as a bid for Judahite independence from Israel. But the episode ends in the capture and plunder of Jerusalem. Later, 2 Kgs 16 relates that Ahaz, pressured by both Israel and Aram to join its coalition, appealed for protection to Assyria, which responded with an attack on Damascus (one that no doubt it intended anyway); but the outcome, inevitably, was Judah becoming an Assyrian client, freeing it from any threat from Israel.

If we set aside the Pentateuchal portrait of a twelve-tribe nation of Israel, and the Judahite layers from what are apparently Israelite stories in Joshua and Judges, we can trace a reasonably clear narrative of two separate societies. But in the case of Judah, because the earliest phases of

---

30. J. Maxwell Miller and John H. Hayes, *A History of Ancient Israel and Judah* (Philadelphia: Westminster; London: SCM, 1986), 280–84.

31. Jehu is—suspiciously—the son of a certain Jehoshaphat (2 Kgs 9:14).

Judah's past have been integrated into Israelite stories, we have no independent Judahite account of how the Judean kingdom began. There is almost no Judahite story that relates to the time before David.

I say "almost" because there are two possible exceptions. The story of Gen 38 provides no account of Judah's origins, as distinct from the origin of some of its components. Perhaps significantly, though, it opens by commenting on the separation of Judah "from his brothers" (v. 1), leaving us to speculate that it may reflect—or attempt to reflect—some degree of Judahite independence already in the "patriarchal" era. A second possible exception rests in the once-popular theory that the component tribes of Israel had found their way into Palestine in two independent groups, as represented by different traditions of land entry preserved in the Pentateuch. Half a century ago it was quite widely believed, in the words of Rowley:

> That the Joseph tribes and Judah entered into the possession of their territory in different periods is agreed by a very long line of modern scholars...[32]

The suggestion was not taken to the point of implying separate ethnic identities, however. Rowley stated:

> That all the tribes were of kindred stock, and that those who went into Egypt broke off from their kindred and about a century and a half later came and settled in their midst, is a view which is in substantial agreement with Biblical traditions, when freed from the fictitious unity that has been imposed on them.[33]

De Vaux's *History of Israel* also devoted much space to the analysis of separate tribal land occupation by Israel and Judah[34] and suggested a settlement in Palestine around 1250 B.C.E. for the "southern groups" and 1200 for the "northern groups." But Rowley's assertion of a "common stock" has no argumentation behind it. Recently, elements of this theory have been revived by Blenkinsopp[35] and in the light of the present discussion the notion of separate Judahite and Israelite stories of entry from outside the land should be entertained.

---

32. H. H. Rowley, *From Joseph to Joshua* (London: British Academy, 1950), 140.

33. Ibid., 162–63.

34. Roland de Vaux, *The Early History of Israel* (trans. David Smith; 2 vols.; London: Darton, Longman & Todd, 1978), 441–620.

35. Joseph Blenkinsopp, "The Midianite–Kenite Hypothesis Revisited and the Origins of Judah," *JSOT* 33 (2008): 131–58.

Conclusion: A Provisional History of Judah

I wish to suggest that there is an unusually high degree of correspondence between the archaeological, epigraphic, and biblical evidence about the origins of Judah when each is considered independently. If we place them together, we can reach a very probable conclusion that the origins of Israel and the origins of Judah were separate and indeed remembered as such in Judah. The two societies each began in central Palestine in the Iron Age, along with other societies in Transjordan, and all of them gradually developed into kingdoms. Israel and Judah were close neighbors, but Israel was always more powerful, until the second wave of Assyrian aggression that culminated in the annexation of Samaria as an Assyrian province. Judah itself succumbed to the Neo-Babylonians, probably becoming a province ruled from Mizpah in the territory of Benjamin, a region probably full of Israelite stories, including those of a founding Israelite king called Saul.

Israelite—specifically Benjaminite—stories about the arrival of "Israel" in Palestine, and its fortunes up to the arrival of the first king, Saul, were apparently co-opted in Judah, and in the process Judah was made a member of an Israelite nation. In the case of the Pentateuch, where this portrait is most emphatic, it is arguable (and it has been argued, especially by Hjelm[36]), that the Pentateuchal tradition is essentially a Samaritan one taken over by Judah. However, from the reign of Saul onwards, a different kind of relationship was "remembered." Here Judah is not presented as *part* of a larger "Israel" but as the dominant partner in a political configuration that combines two "houses" of Israel and Judah. The earliest memories of Judah in this narrative are connected to the figure of David, its first "king," and to his Judahite throne the Israelite throne is *added*. The collision of Saul and David in the biblical narrative is now the device whereby the two states are brought together, and not the image of a single nation. The unity established by David is not of a single "Israel" but of a single kingdom comprising two thrones but centered in Jerusalem. In other words, we have in the Bible two different and contradictory mechanisms by which Judah and "Israel" become associated. Needless to say, neither of them can be regarded as historically reliable. Indeed, the succession of Saul by David is a purely historiographical creation and there is no reason to conclude that these two figures, if they were indeed historical, met or were contemporaries; they are, rather, the remembered heroes of two different societies.

36. Ingrid Hjelm, *The Samaritans and Early Judaism: A Literary Analysis* (Sheffield: Sheffield Academic, 2000).

A possible reconstruction of events from all the sources surveyed is that Judah was ruled by a "house of David," vassals of the Israelite ruler. Reflections of this might still be found in the profile of David as the leader of a private army who offered his services to the Philistines as well as to Israel. This profile may shed some light on the leadership of Judah before it achieved statehood. There are clues that the chiefs of the Judahite house soon became clients of the kings of Israel, and perhaps even integrated into the Israelite royal line by marriage, unifying the two kingdoms. The advent of Assyrian power enabled the Judahite ruler in the eighth century to shift from Israelite to Assyrian patronage and thus to enable Judah's sudden rise to statehood, perhaps with a recognized king with nominal independence. This new alignment in turn ushered in a period of increased openness and economic activity that the fall of Samaria accelerated. The culmination of Judah's life as a kingdom was probably the long and prosperous period under Manasseh.[37] Perversely, the verdict of the writers of 2 Kings (and the book of Isaiah) is that Ahaz did wrong to usher in the Assyrians, and Hezekiah and Josiah were the real heroes: the first losing most of his territory and paying a huge tribute, the second dying at the hands of the Pharaoh, and neither achieving much for Judah's economic prosperity or political security.

My own proposed "History of Judah" can thus be divided into two parts—Judah-as-Judah and Judah-as-Israel—for at some point and for reasons I have elaborated elsewhere,[38] the fortunes and the identity of the two populations converged and were integrated. One result of this was the creation in part of the biblical narrative of an Israelite "nation" in which Judah had participated from the outset. In this short essay I have been able only to sketch the sources and arguments upon which a "History of Judah" might be written—one that moreover uses the biblical sources fully and critically but avoids the trap of treating them simply as "history."

37. As argued by E. Axel Knauf, "The Glorious Days of Manasseh," in *Good Kings and Bad Kings* (ed. Lester L. Grabbe; London: T&T Clark International, 2005), 164–88.
38. Davies, *The Origins of Biblical Israel*.

SHECHEM REVISITED:
THE FORMATION OF BIBLICAL COLLECTIVE MEMORY

Niels Peter Lemche

Cultural memory and collective memory are keywords that commonly feature in modern treatments of history. How did the past help to form modern conscience and our understanding of the world? Indeed, in the political landscape of power, the same symbols appear in the most different places culminating in the mall in Washington where we find the dome of the Capitol at one end and the obelisk at the other, symbols originating in ancient Rome, perpetuated over and again in different European contexts.

The approach of the "Copenhagen School of Biblical Studies" has emphasized the character of the Old Testament as a piece of cultural memory: "How Writers Create a Past!"[1] By removing the historical referent—the alleged event behind the biblical story about the past—the focus has changed and placed the author in the center. This approach should not be mistaken as a modern or even postmodern hermeneutical approach to reading biblical texts (although it may help in promoting such readings). It is definitely a "modern," even historical-critical, approach, as it places not the modern reader but the ancient writer at the center of interest and in this way prepares for a better understanding of the literature this writer wrote, including his memory of the past.

So how do we get closer to this writer whose identity will never be known to us? By dating him? Probably not! The dating of biblical texts is most elusive, as there are often several possible options. I illustrated this in a previous study, proposing three different scenarios for the Yahwist writer: an early scenario in the early period of the monarchy; a medium scenario, in the time of, say, Josiah—a very popular option today; and a very late scenario, with at least three possibilities being proposed—the period of the Babylonian Exile, the Persian Period, and the Hellenistic

---

1. Cf. Thomas L. Thompson, *The Bible in History: How Writers Create a Past* (London: Jonathan Cape, 1999).

Period.[2] There is still no external evidence pointing to the date of composition, the Ketef Hinnom Silver amulets being so far the only example of a text known from the Old Testament found in a late Iron Age context.[3] We must, then, look for internal evidence, but what kind of evidence are we looking for? One option would be to concentrate on the information included in our text and decide for the *terminus a quo* and the *terminus ad quem* of this information. Thus it goes without saying that a story about Nebuchadnezzar's conquest of Jerusalem cannot be older than the conquest in question, that is, 597 B.C.E. or 587 B.C.E., although the last date is not attested outside of the Old Testament. Such an example only provides a *terminus a quo*, not a *terminus ad quem*, although this difference is often neglected by students of biblical literature, one example being the date of the Deuteronomistic History proposed on the basis of the information in 2 Kgs 25:27–30, that King Jehoiachin received supplies from the Babylonian court after the death of Nebuchadnezzar in 562 B.C.E. The year 562 B.C.E. can only be a *terminus a quo*, as admitted by Martin Noth, who on the other hand also believed that this date indicates a time frame of the Deuteronomistic History placing it in the middle of the sixth century B.C.E.[4] Now the note in 2 Kgs 25 says that Jehoiachin received these supplies *as long as he lived*, though it is not interested to tell us when he died, which would be the true *terminus a quo*. No *terminus ad quem* is indicated by this note. Nothing really dates this history to the middle of the sixth century B.C.E.

2. Niels Peter Lemche, *Prelude to Israel's Past: Background and Beginnings of Israelite History and Identity* (Peabody, Mass.: Hendrickson, 1998), 220–22. The Exile has been in the focus of the investigations of John Van Seters; on the Yahwist, see especially his *Prologue to History: The Yahwist as Historian in Genesis* (Louisville: Westminster John Knox, 1992). The Persian Period as a time of writing biblical literature has been popular, as, for example, in the studies of Philip R. Davies, while the Hellenistic Period was proposed by this writer in "The Old Testament—a Hellenistic Book?," *SJOT* 7 (1993): 163–93, and reprinted with corrections in *Did Moses Speak Attic? Jewish Historiography and Scripture in the Hellenistic Period* (ed. Lester L. Grabbe; JSOTSup 317; Sheffield: Sheffield Academic, 2001), 287–318.

3. Originally presented to the public by G. Barkay, "The Divine Name Found in Jerusalem," *BARev* 9, no. 2 (1983): 14–19. Analysis and literature (to 1995) is to be found in Johannes Renz, *Handbuch der althebräischen Epigraphik*, vol. 1 (Darmstadt: Wissenschaftliche Buchgesellschaft, 1995), 447–56.

4. Martin Noth, *Überlieferungsgeschichtliche Studien* (Halle: Niemeyer, 1943; repr. Darmstadt: Wissenschaftliche Buchgesellschaft, 1963), 12. Noth's way of presenting his case is typical of the period: "*Wesentlich unter diesen terminus a quo herabzugehen, liegt für uns kein grund vor.*"

Another way would be to concentrate on the author in order to create a profile of this author. This can be done in at least two ways. One way would be to determine the mental status of the author of a biblical book. There is nothing new here. It has been common for several generations of biblical scholars to date Ecclesiastes to the Hellenistic Period because the skepticism expressed by its author is similar to a certain trend within Greek philosophy. However, when we move to the historical literature, the question of the mental setup of the historiographers is more complicated, although it should be possible to demonstrate how these historiographers were acquainted with ancient Near Eastern as well as Greek tradition even though the Greek connection was neglected until a few years ago.[5] In recent years, scholars have attempted to create new connections between biblical and Greek tradition, although such comparative studies have until now with few exceptions mostly concentrated on the oldest extant specimen of Greek historiography represented by Herodotus's *Histories*.[6] The old mania in biblical scholarship to date everything as early as possible is still very powerful.

If a Greek connection can be demonstrated, we definitely have a new *terminus a quo* for the composition of biblical historiography, which will preclude a date to the Iron Age of this literature. A *terminus ad quem* will be the appearance of biblical books in a physical form, such as is the case of the biblical manuscripts found among the Dead Sea Scrolls. Since the book of Isaiah appears as a manuscript in this context in a shape very similar to the Masoretic book of Isaiah, we can establish for certain that the *terminus ad quem* of this book will be the date of the Isaiah scroll, namely, probably the early first century B.C.E. The *terminus a quo* and the *terminus ad quem* for the historiography of the Old Testament would

---

5.   If not to very ancient Greek tradition, as evidenced in some works by Cyrus H. Gordon, in such works as *Before the Bible: The Common Background of Greek and Hebrew Civilizations* (New York: Harper & Row, 1962).

6.   Beginning with John Van Seters, *In Search of History: Historiography in the Ancient World and the Origins of Biblical History* (New Haven: Yale University Press, 1983). On Herodotus and the Old Testament, see Sarah Mandell and David N. Freedman, *The Relationship Between Herodotus' History and Primary History* (South Florida Studies in the History of Judaism 60; Atlanta: Scholars Press, 1993); Flemming A. J. Nielsen, *The Tragedy in History: Herodotus and the Deuteronomistic History* (JSOTSup 251; Sheffield: Sheffield Academic, 1997); Jan-Wim Wesselius, *The Origin of the History of Israel: Herodotus' Histories as Blueprint for the First Books of the Bible* (JSOTSup 345; Sheffield: Sheffield Academic, 2002). An exception is Russell E. Gmirkin, *Berossus and Genesis, Manetho and Exodus: Hellenistic Histories and the Date of the Pentateuch* (LHBOTS 433; New York: T&T Clark, 2006), 8.

in this case be the date of Greek historiography of the fifth century (Herodotus's *Histories* belong to the middle of the fifth century B.C.E.), and the *terminus ad quem* will be most likely the first century B.C.E.

The time of the cultural memory of the historiographer might accordingly be included within these termini, saying that it was made up of ancient Oriental as well as Greek and Hellenistic "memories," and molded into a new synthesis by the historiographer.[7] When the historiographer constructed his past, he included memories of sundry origins: Palestinian, Mesopotamian, Egyptian, and Greek traditions. He did not rewrite either Greek or Oriental traditions; rather, they were combined into a new synthesis which was his cultural memory, the way he understood himself and the world of which he was part. Because his memory was accepted by his readership—otherwise it would hardly have survived—we are also allowed to speak about the collective memory of the society to which the tale of the past was presented.

Now one more step in the reconstruction of the time of the composition of biblical historiography remains, a control of the result so far obtained. Will there be additional evidence for a Hellenistic date of this historiography? The external evidence in the shape of the physical existence of this literature—perhaps not in its final form but certainly in an edition similar to what has been handed down to posterity—is the biblical manuscripts from the library of the Dead Sea Scrolls. The *terminus ad quem* seems to be the first century B.C.E., if we for a moment forget the book of Ezra, which may be even later in the edition that became part of the Hebrew Bible, and Esther, which was not found among the fragments from the caves of Qumran. However, will there be additional internal evidence making the already reached conclusion even more likely?

One way to answer this question about a controlling factor would be to study the direct addresses by the historiographer to his audience, in case such addresses exist. In my *The Old Testament Between Theology and History*,[8] I presented a survey of such addresses and commentaries made by the author, not directly part of the narrative but superposed on it, expressing sentiments which may tell us more about the time and expectation of this author. It is obvious that such elements of the text function

---

7. For an early discussion of these issues, see my "How Does One Date an Expression of Mental History? The Old Testament and Hellenism," in Grabbe, ed., *Did Moses Speak Attic?*, 200–224.

8. Niels P. Lemche, *The Old Testament Between Theology and History: A Critical Survey* (Louisville: Westminster John Knox, 2008).

as guidelines to the readership, explaining the meaning of the narrative, beginning already in the very first chapter of Genesis and continuing until the end of the story in 2 Kings. This has to do with the function of ancient literature as a rhetorical and pedagogical device: ancient prose literature is basically educational rather than plain entertainment.[9] In the Pentateuch and in the Deuteronomistic History such comments follow the progress of the tragic history of biblical Israel from the creation to the destruction of the temple of Jerusalem and the exile of the Israelite people. However, we also find similar addresses to the audience in the Prophets, although the "didactic" aim of these is even more obvious here. The addresses to the audience in the Prophets—very often in the shape of admonitions and invitations to repentance and conversion—also include hopes for the future, especially the return of the people in exile, and here it soon becomes obvious that far more is intended than just a Babylonian exile. A passage such as Hos 11:11—

> His children shall come trembling from the west.
> They shall come trembling like birds from Egypt,
> And like doves from the land of Assyria;
> And I will return them to their homes, says the LORD

—has little meaning in the alleged time of the prophet Hosea (second half of the eighth century B.C.E.). It is speaking about a dispersal that includes "Assyria," that is, Mesopotamia, and Egypt, but also from the west. The only sensible interpretation of this text (and other similar ones) is that it refers to the Jewish dispersal that is the *Diaspora*. They are not addressing a people in exile but a people longing to return home—from everywhere. In the study just mentioned, I aimed at isolating biblical literature as Jewish and diaspora-related. It is also the literature of a religious community, and each section has a role to fulfill: the historical writings explains how this community ended in exile; the Prophets ask for repentance and conversion (this part is the façade to the outside world), while the Psalms (the façade to the inside world) describes the battle between the just and the godless, ending with the total victory of the just and God-fearing community: "Let everything that breathes praise the LORD!" (Ps 150:6)

9. Cf., on this aspect, my "Good and Bad in History: The Greek Connection," in *Rethinking the Foundations: Historiography in the Ancient World and the Bible. Essays in Honour of John Van Seters* (ed. Steven L. McKenzie and Thomas Römer; BZAW 294; Berlin: de Gruyter, 2000), 127–40.

The Deuteronomistic History and Northern Tradition[10]

The collective memory of biblical historiography is made up of traditions from many parts of the ancient world. However, it would be absurd to deny that the memory of the ancient land of Israel did not play a dominant role. Everything centers on this land of the forefathers, a land lost and to be regained some day in the future. This is part of the exilic mind governing the composition of many biblical books, aiming at the return to the country. Here a new society will appear, the true people of God bound to God by a new covenant (Jer 31:31–34) on the ruins of the nation of the fathers who sinned and were thrown into exile. In this way, the long history from the beginning of the world to the fall of Jerusalem serves not only as a tragic remembrance for later Jews from the so-called post-exilic period, it also functions as a kind of foundation myth for the Jewish community. This community, consisting of the sons of the fathers who went into exile because of their sins, claims for itself the right to inherit the land of their fathers. In doing so, they ignore any claim formulated by people living in Palestine who were not part of the exilic experience.

One astonishing fact remains about the collective memory of this new Jewish community: the extent of Northern tradition accepted as the past of the Jewish community of Jerusalem and Judah. The presence of the traditions of historical Israel in a narrative that evidently focuses on Jerusalem and its temple as the only legitimate place to worship Yahweh, the God of Israel, has become increasing problematic for many scholars, especially as a late dating of biblical texts has become more popular. We should probably expect a reaction like the one in Chronicles. Here the

---

10.   Although I use the term "Deuteronomistic History" here, I sincerely doubt the existence of such a work. The study of John Van Seters, *The Edited Bible: The Curious History of the "Editor" in Biblical Criticism* (Winona Lake: Eisenbrauns, 2006), making the concept of an editor redundant, seems to exclude the possibility that such an edited history ever existed. The argument becomes even more problematic in light of the different schools opting for various redactions of this history. The argument essentially appears in two versions: a double redaction, including a pre-exilic sketch of the history and an exilic redaction of it (cf. Richard D. Nelson, *The Double Redaction of the Deuteronomistic History* [JSOTSup 18; Sheffield: JSOT, 1981), and a tripartite redaction as argued by the so-called "Göttingen school" (cf. Rudolf Smend, *"Das Gesetz und die Völker: Ein Beitrag zur deuteronomistischen Redaktionsgeschichte,"* in *Probleme biblischer Theologie. Gerhard von Rad zum 70. Geburtstag* [ed. Hans Walter Wolff; Munich: Kaiser, 1971], 494–509, and Walter Dietrich, *Prophetie und Geschichte: Eine redaktionsgeschichtliche Untersuchung zum deuteronomistischen Geschichtswerks* [FRLANT 108; Göttingen: Vandenhoeck & Ruprecht, 1972]).

Chronicler simply obliterates references to Israel in his version of the history of his people, paraphrasing largely the story found in the Deuteronomistic History.

In previous scholarship the Chronicler's attitude to northern tradition was generally seen as a result of his Judean orientation and reflecting sentiments in his society in the post-exilic period. The late pre-exilic or exilic Deuteronomistic History had no problems combining Israelite and Judean tradition into one narrative, or so it was believed. The reason for the presence of these northern elements in the Deuteronomistic History— nobody really asked about their presence in the Pentateuch—was the assumed presence of northern refugees in Jerusalem after the fall of Samaria in 722 B.C.E. At least this was the explanation of the origins of Deuteronomism put forward by Albrecht Alt, and later adopted by the majority of scholars, including also the "middle of the road" approach as found in popular books by Israel Finkelstein and Neil Asher Silberman.[11] As a matter of fact, this stream of refugees is mandatory to any dating of the historiography of the Old Testament to the Iron Age. The demise of the Davidic and Solomonic kingdom will demand a new explanation for the pan-Israelite sentiments of the historical books, as a political unity between the historical states of Israel and Judah never existed.

However, the Old Testament itself is totally silent as to such a move of northerners to Jerusalem after 722 B.C.E. On the contrary, it tells us that the people of ancient Samaria were moved by the Assyrians into exile in Mesopotamia (2 Kgs 17:6) and substituted by settlers from other parts of the Near East (2 Kgs 17:24). The hypothesis about the immigrants from Samaria who brought their tradition to Jerusalem after 722 B.C.E. remains an unfounded assertion and should rather be forgotten.[12]

11. Albrecht Alt, "Die Heimat des Deuteronomiums," in *Kleine Schriften zur Geschichte Israels* (Munich: Beck, 1953), 250–75. On modern use of the theory, see Israel Finkelstein and Neil Asher Silberman, *The Bible Unearthed: Archaeology's New Vision of Ancient Israel and the Origin of Its Sacred Texts* (New York: Free Press, 2001), and *David and Solomon: In Search of the Bible's Sacred Kings and the Roots of the Western Tradition* (New York: Free Press, 2006). The dating of the Deuteronomistic History can be found among other places in *The Bible Unearthed*, 42–43.

12. The increase of the population of Jerusalem at the end of the eighth century (cf., e.g., Finkelstein and Silberman, *The Bible Unearthed*, 243–46) is more likely to be the result of Sennacherib's well-attested destruction of the Judean lands in 701 B.C.E. including the major city of Lachish. For more on this theme, see my "The Deuteronomistic History: Historical Reconsiderations," in *Raising Up a Faithful Exegete: Essays in Honor of Richard D. Nelson* (ed. K. L. Noll and B. Schramm; Winona Lake: Eisenbrauns 2010), 41–50.

Basically, the idea of the time of Josiah as the great period of producing biblical historiography, including the first drafts of the Deuteronomistic History, is based on circular argumentation—one bolstered by an
unfounded assertion about immigrants from the North. This date for the
historiography is based on exactly the same argumentation as was the
previous dating of the Yahwist to the time of King Solomon: the Yahwist
displays an international orientation. Solomon's court is described as
internationally orientated; therefore the Yahwist must belong to Solomon's court; the only evidence we have from Solomon's court is,
however, found in the Old Testament.[13]

Returning to Josiah, it is evident that the historiographer describes him
as a new David, aiming at reestablishing the kingdom of David, including
also the territory of the former state of Israel. The narrative also describes
Josiah as the great reformer of the temple in Jerusalem. Although the
archaeological "leg" in this argumentation seems to be an established
fact—there really was a city here at the end of the sixth century—the rest
of the story is still based on circular argumentation, not always supported
by all versions of the story of biblical Israel. Thus the Chronicler did not
like King Josiah, who is killed because he disobeyed the Lord, and who
was no great reformer—the real reformer was Hezekiah, the hero of the
books of Chronicles (2 Chr 34–35).

However, the assumption that Josiah was following a policy of
reestablishing the Davidic kingdom must deal with the fact that this
kingdom never existed. Josiah had to "invent" a kingdom of David and
turn it into a program for his expansions in the territories of the former
northern kingdom. The only source for Josiah's program is the biblical
narrative in 2 Kgs 22–23, a narrative that is dated according to the expan-
sionist program it includes, meaning that the program of Josiah is based
on the same texts which are dated by it. This hypothesis, which is therefore unfounded and illegitimate, demands much from its readership,
including a complicated theory about the setup of an invented history of
Israel in the time of Josiah. It also has to explain why the Chronicler
entertained such a negative view on Josiah. The hypothesis of Josiah's
period as the time of composition of biblical historiography is simply too
complicated and a house of cards. Worse, it cannot be falsified and it is
unnecessary.

13.   The classic study on this is Gerhard von Rad, "Der Anfang der Geschichts-
schreibung im alten Israel" (1944), in his *Gesammelte Studien zum Alten Testament*
(ThBü 8; Munich: Kaiser, 1958), 148–88.

Although neither a conservative scholar nor a "maximalist," the archaeologist Israel Finkelstein has fallen into the same trap as many biblical scholars—trying to rescue whatever can be saved from "ancient Israel."[14] Furthermore, he has not seen that his argument in favor of Josiah is exactly the same as found in much literature written by his adversaries. As a matter of fact, he has at several occasions criticized fellow archaeologists such as William G. Dever for using exactly the same kind of argumentation to back up his archaeological analyses.[15] Truly, the saying "Why do you see the speck in your neighbor's eye, but do not notice the log in your own eye?" (Matt 7:3) is as valid as ever.

Although standing on the shoulder of much Old Testament scholarship, Finkelstein's reliance on the time of King Josiah as a formative period of biblical historiography has no support from the normal laws of logically founded argumentation. We cannot deny that he might be right, but worse, neither can we disprove it. If a better case can be made for another theory, the link to Josiah's time should be given up.

Shechem Revisited

The present state of investigations in the Jerusalem area and the renewed interest in the events of the sixth and fifth centuries may have presented new opportunities for discussing the survival of northern tradition in the Old Testament. The level of destruction in the former Judean territory and the break of city life in the Jerusalem area also indicate a break of tradition. We are talking about a complete societal break-down as first described by David Jamieson-Drake and vastly expanded and illustrated by Oded Lipschits. The possibility of having to move down to the fourth century B.C.E. before a city-like settlement appeared founded on the ruins of Jerusalem has serious implications.[16] It is also of the uttermost

14. In the present study I am using the terms "biblical Israel," "historical Israel," and "ancient Israel" in the sense proposed by Philip R. Davies: "biblical Israel" is the Israel of the pages of the Old Testament; "historical Israel" is the state of Israel/ the House of Omri/Samaria known to have existed in central Palestine between ca. 900 and 722; "ancient Israel" is the Israel formed in the mind of biblical scholars combining the two other Israels. See Philip R. Davies, *In Search of "Ancient Israel"* (JSOTSup 148; Sheffield: Sheffield Academic, 1992).

15. Most recently (perhaps) in Brian B. Schmidt, ed., *The Quest for the Historical Israel: Debating Archaeology and the History of Early Israel* (Archaeology and Biblical Studies 17; Atlanta: SBL, 2007), 11 and 111.

16. Cf., David Jamieson-Drake, *Scribes and Schools in Monarchic Judah: A Socio-Archaeological Approach* (SWBA 9; Sheffield: Almond, 1991), and Oded Lipschits, *The Fall and Rise of Jerusalem: Judah Under Babylonian Rule* (Winona

importance that the central area of the country, the land of the Samaritans, was not affected by the destructions following the Babylonian conquest. As a consequence, it is to be assumed that the local tradition survived. This is one part of the changing horizon of the so-called post-exilic period. Related to it is the question of the origins of the Samaritan community. When did the break between Jerusalem and Samaria occur, and who caused it to happen? The traditional view has been that Samaria broke with Jerusalem. However, the opposite may have happened, as argued by some scholars, most notably by Ingrid Hjelm.[17] However, the break meant more than just a politico-religious severance of relations between Jerusalem and Gerizim; it also implied the transfer of Samaritan tradition as preserved in the Pentateuch to Jerusalem.

Here Hjelm really builds on an old local tradition, although she may not fully explore it, represented by Eduard Nielsen's thesis from 1955 about Shechem,[18] and here the importance of cultural memory becomes clear. Eduard Nielsen is one of the few surviving members of the "Uppsala school," himself a student of Ivan Engnell, the founder of the "school" and professor at the University of Uppsala. Nielsen follows Engnell's guidelines for a tradition-historical approach to biblical historiography. This school was the subject of the second part of Douglas A. Knight's dissertation on tradition history, displaying Knight's command of the Scandinavian languages.[19] Although many times declared dead and

Lake: Eisenbrauns, 2005), supplemented by Lipschits, "Demographic Changes in Judah Between the Seventh and the Fifth Centuries B.C.E.," in *Judah and the Judeans in the Neo-Babylonian Period* (ed. Oded Lipschits and Joseph Blenkinsopp; Winona Lake: Eisenbrauns, 2003), 323–76; Lipschits, "Achaemenid Imperial Policy, Settlement Processes in Palestine, and the Status of Jerusalem in the Middle of the Fifth Century B.C.E.," in *Judah and the Judeans in the Persian Period* (ed. Oded Lipschits and Manfred Oeming; Winona Lake: Eisenbrauns, 2006), 19–52, and Oded Lipschits and Oren Tal, "The Settlement Archaeology of the Province of Judah: A Case Study," in *Judah and the Judeans in the Fourth Century B.C.E.* (ed. Oded Lipschits, Garry N. Knoppers, and Rainer Albertz; Winona Lake: Eisenbrauns, 2007), 33–52.

17. Ingrid Hjelm, *The Samaritans and Early Judaism: A Literary Analysis* (JSOTSup 303; Sheffield: Sheffield Academic, 2000). On this connection, see also her *Jerusalem's Rise to Sovereignty: Zion and Gerizim in Competition* (JSOTSup 404; London: T&T Clark International, 2004).

18. Eduard Nielsen, *Shechem: A Traditio-Historical Investigation* (2d ed., Copenhagen: Gad, 1959).

19. Douglas A. Knight, "The Scandinavian Debate on Traditio-Historical Problems," in *Rediscovering the Traditions of Israel* (3d ed.; Studies in Biblical Literature 16; Atlanta: SBL, 2006), 165–299.

gone,[20] the basic approach of the Uppsala school might be revitalized as essentially related to the modern concept of collective memory. In its quest for the origins of biblical traditions, the tradition history of the Uppsala school is not very different from modern attempts to analyze modern cultural memory by dissecting it into its various parts. Eduard Nielsen's study on the tradition about Shechem in the Old Testament provides a perfect example of the dynamics of this approach, using the Shechem tradition to reconstruct the ancient history of Israel and the competing traditions that were never totally reconciled when they became part of the literature of the Old Testament. Thus, the competition between Shechem and other holy places—not least of all Jerusalem—is apparent in these traditions.

Of course—as was usual in those days—everything is dated early. The historical basis for Nielsen's study is mainly Martin Noth's reconstruction of Israelite history, including Noth's thesis of an Israelite tribal league in the Period of the Judges.[21] All of this has vanished today, as has the idea of a "Period of the Judges." However, the tension present in the Shechem traditions is still there, as is the search for a new *Sitz im Leben*. Perhaps we find here a clue to the reconstruction of the process that led to the formation of the collective memory of biblical historiography. Nielsen is definitely right that the Shechem tradition plays a significant, if not decisive, role in this process. Supported by Hjelm's recent study of the Zion tradition, it now seems possible to present the contours of a hypothesis about the formation of biblical collective memory as found in the historiography of the Old Testament, with its preponderance of Northern tradition embedded in an outspoken Judaic and Jerusalemite frame.

A Hypothesis About the Formation of Biblical Collective Memory

The two decisive factors to be reconsidered are on one hand the solid tradition about Israel found in the Old Testament, and on the other the favoring of Jerusalem as expressed in the demand for the exclusive

---

20.   Some of the scholars present at the conference at Sandbjerg Manor near Sønderborg in southern Denmark in 1982 (the present author included) may have looked upon the meeting as the funeral for the Uppsala school. The proceedings of the conference were published as Knud Jeppesen and Benedikt Otzen, eds., *The Production of Time: Tradition History in Old Testament Scholarship* (Sheffield: Almond, 1984).

21.   Martin Noth, *Geschichte Israels* (Göttingen: Vandenhoeck & Ruprecht, 1950).

importance of the temple of Jerusalem vis-à-vis all other sanctuaries of the ancient land of Israel. It could in many ways be said that we here have a case of conflicting traditions that are almost impossible to unify. The decision made by the Chronicler to exclude as much as possible of the tradition about the North is a logical one. In many ways it resembles the decision in Neo-Babylonian times to "forget" Assyria, which is now mostly referred to as Subartu, a country from the hoary past. The Chronicler, however, worked on the basis of an already established combination of North and South; he was simply reducing the importance of the North.

The Pentateuch, if not the Hexateuch,[22] speaks strongly in favor of seeing the book of Joshua as the culmination of the story told in the five books of Moses. It is a battleground of pro-Shechemite and anti-Shechemite sentiments, allowing on one side the sons of Jacob to kill the inhabitants of Shechem (Gen 34), and placing on the other side Shechem in the center of the religious tradition. Following the proposal that the Pentateuch (Hexateuch) may originally have been a Samaritan tradition usurped by Jerusalem, it is clear that some major reworking has taken place, centering not least on the activities of Abraham as the founder of the sanctuary in Shechem (Gen 12:6–7), but also as the one who transfers his allegiance to God to the Temple of Jerusalem embodied in the person of Melchizedek (Gen 14:17–24).

In the Deuteronomistic literature, the attitude to Shechem and the north is generally negative, especially if we reckon Joshua as part of a Hexateuch instead of a Deuteronomistic History. In Joshua, Shechem is still the place where the final contract is signed between old Israel and Yahweh (Josh 24). Apart from that, Shechem represents the break-away from Jerusalem (1 Kgs 12).

Summing up the evidence, which is mostly circumstantial, as we have no direct witnesses to the process, we may state: after the Babylonian conquest of the early sixth century B.C.E. Jerusalem and Judah was a wasteland, although not emptied of all inhabitants. The city was in ruins, and it would be centuries before it was rebuilt. The area to the north, especially the Samaritan area, was almost unaffected by the disaster that

22.   The Pentateuch *plus* the book of Joshua, favored by several scholars of the past, including, most notably, Otto Eissfeldt, *Hexateuch-Synopse: Die Erzählung der fünf Bücher Mose und des Buches Joshua mit dem Anfange des Richterbuches* (1922; repr. Darmstadt: Wissenschaftliche Buchgesellschaft, 1962), and Gerhard von Rad, *Das formgeschichtliche Problem des Hexateuch* (BWANT 4/26; Stuttgart: Kohlhammer, 1938; repr. *Gesammelte Studien zum Alten Testament* [Munich: Kaiser, 1960]), 9–86 (page citations are to the reprint edition).

struck Judah. No deportations from this area followed the Babylonian conquest. Although it is likely that the Assyrians substituted the ancient elite of the north with a new one, the majority of the population here descended from the inhabitants of the ancient state of Israel.

When the demographic situation changed in and around Jerusalem, it is likely that immigrants from Mesopotamia—maybe also from other places—had a decisive importance. Although the biblical tradition about Ezra and Nehemiah may be of dubious historical value, it is united in the view that the rebuilding of the city and the remolding of the society was initiated by Jews arriving from the Diaspora. Whether or not there was a temple of Jerusalem in, say, the fifth or fourth century B.C.E.,[23] is unimportant. Yet the tradition of the problems with Samaritan authorities represented by Sanballat (whose Assyrian affiliation seems certain in light of his name, Sinuballit, a classical king name in Assyria) during Nehemiah's reconstructions of the fortifications of Jerusalem (Neh 3:33–4:17)—whether historical or not—may indicate tensions between the society under construction in Jerusalem and Samaria as the authority of the Northern administration was jeopardized by the rebuilding of Jerusalem.

Although a famous letter from Elephantine with a petition to rebuild the local temple of Yahweh refers to Bagoas as the governor of Judah and Sanballat as the governor of Samaria, thus indicating separate administrations of Judah and Samaria towards the end of the fifth century,[24] it is a fair assumption that what was left of Judah after 597/587 B.C.E. was dominated by the North. The decision how to handle Northern tradition would have to be made when a political break occurred between the North and the South, when the South, so to speak, became "independent" (though still part of a major empire, whether Persian or Greek). Following the political break, the diaspora took over in Judah, usurped northern tradition as its own, and denied to accept any local instance as truly "Jewish." The myth of the empty land was a convenient answer to the problem of people living in the land when the rebuilding began: they were foreigners—they must have been since everybody went into exile. And the Samaritan population was unclean because of its foreign origins: Samaria was repopulated by foreign immigrants.

23. For a new vista on the rebuilding of Jerusalem's temple traditionally dated to 516 B.C.E., cf. Diana Edelman, *The Origins of the "Second" Temple: Persian Imperial Policy and the Rebuilding of Jerusalem* (Bible World; London: Equinox, 2005), who dates Zerubbabel's activities to ca. 440 B.C.E.

24. Cowley no. 30 (translation from *ANET*). The letter is generally known as AP30, or Cowley 30, from Arthur Cowley, *Aramaic Papyri from the Fifth Century* (Oxford: Clarendon, 1923), 108–14.

As a matter of fact, the schism between the North and the South found in the collective memory of the Old Testament can easily be explained in light of political, religious, and demographic developments in the Persian and Hellenistic periods. Maybe it is time to re-invent tradition history to study the process, following the lead of Eduard Nielsen's *Shechem*. As already said, Nielsen dated everything a thousand years too early, but in those days everybody did so. It would, however, be interesting to see how an analysis of the Shechem traditions like his would develop in a modern context.

PERSIAN PERIOD JERUSALEM AND YEHUD REJOINDERS*

Israel Finkelstein

In two recent articles on Persian period Yehud, I deal with Jerusalem and Nehemiah's wall,[1] and with the archaeology of the List of Returnees in Ezra and Nehemiah.[2] My main conclusions are:

- Persian-period Jerusalem was a small settlement that covered an area of ca. 2–2.5 hectares, with a population of no more than a few hundred people.
- Over a century of archaeological investigation in Jerusalem has failed to reveal any trace of a city-wall that can be dated to the Persian period or identified as the wall of Nehemiah.
- The description of the construction of the wall in Neh 3 may represent the reality of the erection of the First Wall in the Hasmonean period.
- The archaeology of the places mentioned in the List of Returnees in Ezra (2:1–67) and Nehemiah (7:6–68) seems to show that this text, too, probably represents a Late Hellenistic (second century B.C.E.) rather than a Persian-period reality.

A few recently published articles have taken issue with these observations.[3] In what follows I wish to address the main arguments of

---

* Submitted November 2009. (An earlier version of this essay was published online in the *Journal of Hebrew Scriptures* 9 [2009], Article 24.)

1. Israel Finkelstein, "Jerusalem in the Persian (and Early Hellenistic) Period and the Wall of Nehemiah," *JSOT* 32 (2008): 501–20.

2. Israel Finkelstein, "The Archaeology of the List of Returnees in Ezra and Nehemiah," *PEQ* 140 (2008): 7–16.

3. Ziony Zevit, "Is There an Archaeological Case for Phantom Settlements in the Persian Period?," *PEQ* 141 (2009): 124–37; E. Mazar, "The Wall that Nehemiah Built," *BAR* 35, no. 2 (2009): 24–33, 66; G. Barkay, "Additional View of Jerusalem in Nehemiah Days," in *New Studies in the Archaeology of Jerusalem and Its Region*, vol. 2 (ed. David Amit and Guy D. Stiebel; Jerusalem: Israel Antiquities Authority and the Hebrew University of Jerusalem, 2008), 48–54 (Hebrew); Oded Lipschits, "Persian Period Finds from Jerusalem: Facts and Interpretations," *JHS* 9 (2009): Article 20.

the authors of these studies; my major interest is not the dispute itself, but rather the methodological questions that stand behind the debate, namely, issues related to the methods of field archaeology and the interface between archaeology and the biblical texts.

Albright Revividus, *But No Albright*

Ziony Zevit[4] has contested my treatment of the archaeology (mainly surveys) of sites mentioned in the List of Returnees and defended the dating of the list to the Persian period.

The debate translates into two contrasting attitudes to the reconstruction of the history of Ancient Israel. Zevit—in the footsteps of the Albright School—repeats the biblical testimony in modern language, adapts archaeology when it is useful and rejects it when it stands in his way, and fiercely fights off any attempt to challenge the historicity of the descriptions in the text. I tend to give archaeology a central, independent role and treat the text as a stratified literary work whose layers are embedded with the ideological goals of their authors and the realities of their time.

Zevit's summary of the history of Jerusalem in the Persian period best demonstrates his approach, as described above:

> Some early returnees rebuilt an altar and reinstituted sacrifices to ward off misfortune. Over a year later they got around to setting the foundation for a new temple. Only some years later, during the reign of Darius I, was the temple completed... Jerusalem, however, remained unsettled with her ruined houses and breached walls. It was only during the reign of Artaxerxes I...that Cyrus' original project was completed. Nehemiah, an official in the royal court, turned Jerusalem into a religious and political centre in Yehud...by completing a slapdash wall with some descendents from the first returnee settlers among the labourers...[5]

The reconstruction of the history of ancient Israel should be based on three pillars: archaeology, the biblical text, and ancient Near Eastern records. The latter do not exist for the Persian period, hence Zevit's description is based solely on the biblical text, challenging the archaeological finds. In other words, the quotation above, as well as other statements in the article, should be read as a theological manifesto rather than as modern, critical scientific research.

Zevit's article demonstrates lack of knowledge—and understanding— of archaeological method and techniques:

4. Zevit, "Is There an Archaeological Case?"
5. Ibid., 134.

1. He argues against the reliability of archaeological surveys: "Surveys are simply surveys. The accidental origin of what surveyors pick up somewhat randomly cannot be used to determine the actual nature of a site..."[6] In a properly conducted survey finds are not picked up "randomly" and the results are not arbitrary. This has been demonstrated by the best and brightest of American archaeology (none belonging to the biblical archaeology branch of the profession), who in fact established the basics of the art of modern archaeological surveys: Braidwood in the plain of Antioch,[7] Willey in South America,[8] Adams in Mesopotamia,[9] and others. Survey work, though not devoid of errors, is a highly sophisticated domain of archaeology,[10] and is especially valuable when a large number of sites are examined (and some of them excavated)—exactly the case under discussion here.[11]

2. "Theoretically an historical presence [in the Persian period— I.F.] could be invisible to archaeology."[12] This is a surprising statement. Walls, floors, sherds, stone vessels, metal implements, and other finds do not evaporate. Even faint human activity leaves traces, which can be detected in excavations. Surveys, too, if properly executed, provide a good picture of the settlement history of a site. This is especially true in the highlands, where settlements are usually located on ridges and hills, and thus sherds are eroded to the slopes where they can easily be collected in large numbers.

3. To use Zevit's words again, "surveys are simply surveys." That is, in certain cases mainly when the number of sherds collected

6. Ibid., 131. Incidentally, in the same breath Zevit (ibid., 128) uses the very same surveys to support his reading of Haggai and Zechariah regarding population decline in Yehud in the sixth century B.C.E.

7. Robert J. Braidwood, *Mounds in the Plain of Antioch: An Archeological Survey* (Chicago: University of Chicago Press, 1937).

8. Gordon R. Willey, *Prehistoric Settlement Patterns in the Viru Valley, Peru* (Washington: U.S. Government Print Office, 1953).

9. Robert McCormick Adams, *Heartland Cities: Surveys of Ancient Settlement and Land Use on the Central Floodplain of the Euphrates* (Chicago: University of Chicago Press, 1981).

10. E. B. Banning, *Archaeological Survey* (New York: Kluwer Academic/ Plenum, 2002); James M. Collins and Brian Leigh Molyneaux, *Archaeological Survey* (Walnut Creek, Calif.: Altamira, 2003).

11. Six of the 17 sites of the List of Returnees treated by me were thoroughly excavated.

12. Zevit, "Is There an Archaeological Case?," 125.

is small—they may supply less than a full picture of the settlement history of a given site. This is certainly not true in the case of sites which produce hundreds of sherds: 242 sherds were collected at Anata, 440 at Deir el-ʿAzar (the location of Kirjath Jearim), 243 at Khirbet el-Kafira (the mound of biblical Chephirah), 359 at er-Ram (Ramah), 284 at Jaba (Geba), and 643 at Mukhmas (Michmash).[13] In these cases the results are decisive, even when the evidence is negative; certainly, they cannot be ignored.[14]

4. What Zevit says about the "two partially overlapping Persian periods" (the historical and the archaeological)[15] is trivial. Similar phenomena have been studied long ago regarding other transition periods, for example, from the Roman to Byzantine and from the Byzantine to Early Islamic periods. Similarly, what Zevit states about the transition of pottery traditions between the late Iron II and the sixth century B.C.E.[16] is known to every first-year archaeology student and taken into consideration in every serious research of the period. In any event, the fifth- to fourth-century B.C.E. pottery repertoire is well-known and easy to identify.[17] This repertoire is missing from five of the 17 sites that appear in the List of Returnees and that are discussed in my article, including the *well-excavated* Gibeon and Bethel.

Surprisingly, despite his reservations, Zevit seems to accept the fact that five of the sites mentioned in the List of Returnees were not inhabited in

13. For details, see two chapters in Israel Finkelstein and Uri Dinur, eds., *Archaeological Surveys of the Hill Country of Benjamin* (Jerusalem: Israel Antiquities Authority, 1993), Hebrew with English abstract: Amir Feldstein et al., "Southern Part of the Maps of Ramallah and el-Bireh and Northern Part of the Map of Ein Karem (Sites 141–321)," 133–264, and Uri Dinur and Nurit Feig, "Eastern Part of the Map of Jerusalem," 339–427.

14. When dealing with the location of biblical Anathoth, for example, can one ignore the 242 sherds from the village of Anata only because of what an early scholar claimed in 1936 (Zevit, "Is There an Archaeological Case?," 134), when archaeology was in its infancy? Incidentally, in this case, too, Zevit practices a double standard: on the one hand arguing that surveys cannot supply an accurate picture of the settlement history of a site; on the other hand criticizing my cautious description of the results in terms of intensive or weak activity (ibid., 131).

15. Ibid., 132.

16. Ibid., 125.

17. Ephraim Stern, *Material Culture of the Land of the Bible in the Persian Period, 538–322 B.C.* (Warminster: Aris & Phillips, 1982); Oded Lipschits, *The Fall and Rise of Jerusalem* (Winona Lake: Eisenbrauns, 2005), 193–203.

the Persian period. His logic of solving the problem is as follows: the returnees settled in all places mentioned in the list in the late sixth century B.C.E., but a few decades later (and I should add—during a peaceful, empire-dominated period), they abandoned five of them, including the two highly important sites of Gibeon and Bethel. This acrobatic hypothesis, aimed at saving Zevit's simplistic reading of the text, does not seem to me to be a viable historical option.

Zevit's discussion of geographical history shows how hypothetical his method is compared to the solid, conservative method of archaeological survey. Following is his logic regarding the location of Senaah, which appears in the list (Neh 3:35; *possibly* a place rather than a family name—italics mine, I.F.): Senaah *may be* equated with Hassenuah of Neh 11:9 and 1 Chr 9:7, and the latter *may be* associated with Madalsenna of Eusebius, which was *probably* located north of Jericho; this place can *possibly* be equated with Toponym 88 of the Sheshonq I Karnak list (incidentally, this toponym is listed with the Negeb group of sites!), and this in turn *may* tell us that the location of another *possible* place (if not a clan)—Elam—was north of Senaah near Wadi Farah... I counted seven(!) conditions in this single identification. Zevit adds that perhaps "each territory, Senaah and the other Elam, contained some small permanent villages, a scatter of seasonal hamlets, and many range-tied, migratory tent communities..."[18] Yet, there are no settlements, hamlets, or migratory communities in the region mentioned by Zevit; the archaeology of the Jordan Valley north of Jericho does not have them.[19] Here, too, highly hypothetical interpretation rules and the facts of archaeology are ignored.

The identification of Gibbar and Magbish, supposedly named for Persian personalities (supporters of Darius I) with Gibeon and Mizpah[20] is even more far-fetched. We do not know if these are indeed place names; there is no testimony for calling places after Persian personalities; and there is no indication for a change in the name of Gibeon and Mizpah. In short, in these cases the important field of geographical history becomes a farce.

The only merit in Zevit's article is as a case-study of the flaws of the Albrightian attitude to biblical history.

18. Zevit, "Is There an Archaeological Case?," 129.
19. See, e.g., P. Bar-Adon, "The Judaean Desert and the Plain of Jericho," in *Judaea, Samaria and the Golan, Archaeological Survey 1967–1968* (ed. M. Kochavi; Jerusalem: The Archaeological Survey of Israel, 1972), 92–149 (Hebrew).
20. Zevit, "Is There an Archaeological Case?," 129–30.

Nehemiah's Wall in Jerusalem: Built on Quicksand

Eilat Mazar recently announced the discovery in the City of David of a fragment of the wall built by Nehemiah.[21] She refers to the northern tower in Area G (and a section of a wall connected to it on the south), which were first excavated by Macalister and Duncan.[22] The tower has commonly been interpreted as part of the First Wall built in the late Hellenistic (Hasmonean) period.[23]

Mazar bases her dating of the fortification on finds retrieved *under* the tower: two dog burials (with no pottery) were found "directly below the lower course of the tower." A 1.5 meter thick layer uncovered under these burials produced sherds dated to "the end of the sixth and the first half of the fifth centuries B.C.E."[24] Farther down Mazar uncovered a 3 meter thick layer with a large quantity of pottery dating to the late sixth and beginning of the fifth century B.C.E.[25] According to Mazar's logic, these finds date the tower to the middle of the Persian period, which allows her to identify it as part of Nehemiah's wall.

Needless to say, these layers provide no more than a *terminus post quem* for the construction of the tower—later than the sixth/early fifth century B.C.E. The absence of Persian period material here (unless the dog burials belong to this period) means nothing; the wall was constructed on the edge of the ridge, at the top of the steep slope, and it is only logical to assume that it was laid after preparatory work, which could have included a leveling operation. The most logical date for the towers and the wall is the late Hellenistic (Hasmonean) period. This

21. Eilat Mazar, *The Palace of King David: Excavations at the Summit of the City of David, Preliminary Report of Seasons 2005–2007* (Jerusalem: Shoham Academic Research and Publication, 2009), and "The Wall that Nehemiah Built," *BAR* 35, no. 2 (2009): 23–33, 66.

22. R. A. S. Macalister and J. Garrow Duncan, *Excavation on the Hill of Ophel, Jerusalem 1923–1925* (London: Harrison & Sons, 1926).

23. E.g. Kathleen M. Kenyon, *Digging Up Jerusalem* (London: Benn, 1974), 191–95; Yigal Shiloh, *Excavations at the City of David.* Vol. 1, *Interim Report of the First Five Seasons* (Qedem 19; Jerusalem: Institute of Archaeology, 1984), 29–30; G. J. Wightman, *The Walls of Jerusalem: From the Canaanites to the Mamluks* (Sydney: Meditarch, 1993).

24. Similar material was found laid against the northern tower by Kenyon (*Digging Up Jerusalem*, 183) and possibly under the tower by Macalister and Duncan, *Excavation on the Hill of Ophel*, 51.

25. Mazar, *The Palace of King David*, 74–76, and "The Wall that Nehemiah Built."

wall is known from many locations in both the southeastern and southwestern hills.[26]

Similar to Zevit's, Mazar's attitude to the biblical testimony is highly literal and uncritical:

> Decades after the Babylonian destruction of Jerusalem in 586 B.C.E., the city appears to have remained desolate and in ruins. A change occurred with the surrender of the Babylonians to the Persians and the decree of Cyrus, king of Persia, in 538 B.C.E., which allowed exiled Jews to return to Jerusalem and rebuild their temple... In 445 B.C.E., Nehemiah was appointed governor and given the authority from the Persian king to rebuild the walls of Jerusalem. Nehemiah's descriptions reflect the actual appearance of the ruined, and, later, the restored walls of the city.[27]

How Full Is an Empty Glass?

Barkay has recently addressed the question of Persian-period Jerusalem.[28] Indirectly, Barkay agrees with me about the positive evidence, which testifies to a 2–2.5 hectare settlement (2.8 hectares according to Lipschits;[29] see below). But based on his rejection of the negative evidence, Barkay adds almost 10 hectares(!) and argues that in the Persian period Jerusalem covered an area of 12 hectares. In this, he positions himself as the ultra-maximalist of our generation. One can understand how a text scholar reaches a maximalist estimate based solely on the biblical testimony.[30] But how does an archaeologist arrive at such an estimate?[31] Barkay rightly acknowledges that no Persian-period structure

---

26. E.g. Wightman, *The Walls of Jerusalem*; Hillel Geva, "Summary and Discussion of Findings from Areas A, W and X–2," in *Jewish Quarter Excavations in the Old City of Jerusalem*, vol. 2 (ed. Hillel Geva; Jerusalem: Israel Exploration Society, 2003), 529–34.

27. Mazar, *The Palace of King David*, 72. For Mazar's similar literal reading of other biblical material on Jerusalem, see Israel Finkelstein et al., "Has King David's Palace Been Found in Jerusalem?," *TA* 34 (2007): 142–64.

28. Barkay, "Additional View of Jerusalem."

29. Lipschits, "Persian Period Finds from Jerusalem."

30. E.g. Joel Weinberg, *The Citizen–Temple Community* (Sheffield: JSOT, 1992), 43.

31. The large number of Yehud seal impressions noted by Barkay is acknowledged by all scholars and cannot be an argument in the discussion of the size of the settlement. Barkay accepts Eilat Mazar's identification of the northern tower on the eastern slope of the City of David with the wall of Nehemiah: "Recent excavations by Eilat Mazar proved that Macalister and Duncan's northern tower should be dated

or floor has ever been found in Jerusalem,[32] but he says that this is also the situation in the Late Bronze, Iron IIA, Babylonian, and Early Hellenistic periods. He seems to see this as evidence for the possibility that even periods of prosperous settlements can leave no remains, because "the core of the urban area, which was the nucleus of the settlement in these periods, was entirely 'devoured' [*sic*] by the intensive settlement of later periods…" (here and below my translation—I.F.). I have already challenged the notion that walls, vessels, and other finds can disappear, and in any event, I would interpret the situation described by Barkay in the opposite way: in these periods (apart from the finds from the Iron IIA which do indicate a growing settlement[33]) the settlement was indeed poor and limited in size and population.

Barkay claims that the Persian-period pottery is difficult to distinguish from the pottery of the Iron II and Hellenistic periods.[34] This may be true for a limited number of pottery forms, especially when found in a small quantity in a survey. It is certainly not the case in a large-scale survey and in an excavation. Persian-period storage jars, mortaria, cooking pots, juglets, and imported vessels are easy to identify and distinguish from their counterparts in the late Iron II and Hellenistic periods.[35]

Barkay argues that the entire southern part of the Persian-period settlement on the ridge of the City of David was eradicated by the Hasmoneans in the late Hellenistic period, in connection with the construction of the Akra fortress.[36] This is a *hypothesis* based on an *assumption* (the location of the fort here) which is not supported by a single find. It also contradicts all other suggestions for the location of the Akra, which are supported by at least some evidence—archaeological and/or textual.[37]

Barkay's reference to the few finds retrieved in the sifting of earth taken by the *waqf* from the Temple Mount[38] is misleading. He acknowledges that very few Persian-period finds were retrieved, but withholds

---

to the Persian period" (Barkay, "Additional View of Jerusalem," 52). As seen above, this statement gives new meaning to the term "prove" in archaeology.

32. Ibid., 50.

33. Israel Finkelstein, "The Rise of Jerusalem and Judah: The Missing Link," *Levant* 33 (2001): 105–15.

34. Barkay, "Additional View of Jerusalem," 49.

35. See, e.g., the collection of sherds and few vessels in Mazar, *The Palace of King David*, 75.

36. Barkay, "Additional View of Jerusalem," 48.

37. Summary in Oren Tal, *Hellenistic Palestine: Between Orientalism and Hellenism* (Winona Lake: Eisenbrauns, in press).

38. Barkay, "Additional View of Jerusalem," 49.

the full picture of strong evidence for Iron IIB-C and late Hellenistic activity there.[39] The same holds true for the evidence from the vicinity of Jerusalem. Barkay mentions the existence of spots with Persian-period remains,[40] but does not provide the reader with the full set of data: the thorough survey of the Jerusalem countryside revealed 185 Iron II and 140 Hellenistic find spots, compared to 17 Persian-period find spots.[41]

Barkay attacks my proposal to see a Hasmonean reality behind Neh 3. Though I have suggested this with caution, as a possibility, none of *his* arguments stands scholarly scrutiny:

1. Similar to Zevit and E. Mazar, Barkay's point of departure is the acceptance of the geographical material in the book of Nehemiah as a testimony for the Persian period.[42] This, of course, is a circular argument.

2. Barkay rejects the idea that ch. 3 is a later addition to the book of Nehemiah.[43] Yet, text scholars have noted the independent nature of the list in Neh 3 as compared to the rest of the "Nehemiah Memoir"[44] and some understood it as a later addition to the book.[45]

3. Barkay opposes my notion that highlands sites were not fortified in the Persian period and brings the fortification of Stratum I at Lachish as an example of a Persian-period city-wall *in Judah*.[46] But Lachish is not located in the highlands and was not included

---

39. G. Barkay and Y. Zweig, "The Temple Mount Debris Sifting Project: Preliminary Report," in *New Studies on Jerusalem*, vol. 11 (ed. E. Baruch, Z. Greenhut, and A. Faust; Ramat-Gan: Bar Ilan University, 2006), 213–37 (Hebrew).

40. Barkay, "Additional View of Jerusalem," 50.

41. Amos Kloner, *Archaeological Survey of Israel, Survey of Jerusalem: The Northwestern Sector, Introduction and Indices* (Jerusalem: Israel Antiquities Authority, 2003), 19.

42. Barkay, "Additional View of Jerusalem," 51.

43. Ibid.

44. Sigmund Mowinckel, *Studien zu dem Buche Ezra–Nehemia* (Oslo: Universitetsforlaget, 1964), 109–16; H. G. M. Williamson, *Ezra, Nehemiah* (Waco: Word, 1985), 200; Joseph Blenkinsopp, *Ezra/Nehemiah: A Commentary* (Philadelphia: Westminster, 1988), 231, to name a few.

45. E.g. Charles C. Torrey, *The Composition and Historical Value of Ezra–Nehemiah* (Giessen: Ricker, 1896), 37–38, and *Ezra Studies* (Chicago: University of Chicago Press, 1910), 249; Mowinckel, *Studien zu dem Buche Ezra–Nehemiah*, 109–16.

46. Barkay, "Additional View of Jerusalem," 51.

in the territory of Yehud;[47] rather, it was an Achaemenid administrative center.[48]

4. "The list [in Neh 3—I.F.] is clearly of administrative nature, it is technical and boring, composed of names of people and places only... If the list was fictitious and anachronistic, we would have expected that it would disclose an ideological motivation of sort, and that it would be less dry and more interesting."[49] According to this logic the description of the list of Judahite towns in Josh 15—dry, boring, composed of toponyms only, and lacking any apparent ideology—should be dated to the time of Joshua...

5. If the list dates to the Hasmonean period, one would expect it to disclose Greek names.[50] According to this logic, almost no biblical text was written in the Hellenistic period.

6. Some of the names of individuals and families which appear in Neh 3 are mentioned in other chapters of Nehemiah and even in Ezra; they do not appear in sources of other periods,[51] plus, at least ten toponyms which appear in the list are known from earlier sources.[52] These are not arguments, because the compiler of Neh 3 could have taken names of individuals and places from earlier biblical texts.

7. The list of districts of Yehud in Neh 3 "well fits the distribution of the Yehud seal impressions of the Persian period and does not fit the extent of Hasmonean rule at the time when the First Wall was built."[53] This statement is wrong. The overwhelming majority of Persian-period Yehud impressions[54] are concentrated in

---

47. See, e.g., the maps in Stern, *Material Culture of the Land of the Bible*, 247; Lipschits *The Fall and Rise of Jerusalem*, 183.

48. David Ussishkin, "A Synopsis of the Stratigraphical, Chronological, and Historical Issues," in *The Renewed Archaeological Excavations at Lachish (1973–1994)* (ed. David Ussishkin; Tel Aviv: Emery & Claire Yass Publications in Archaeology, 2004), 1:95; Alexander Fantalkin and Oren Tal, "Identifying Achaemenid Imperial Policy at the Southern Frontier of the Fifth Satrapy," in *Judah and the Judeans in the Persian Period* (ed. Oded Lipschits and Manfred Oeming; Winona Lake: Eisenbrauns, 2006), 167–98.

49. Barkay, "Additional View of Jerusalem," 52.

50. Ibid.

51. Ibid.

52. Ibid., 52–53.

53. Ibid., 53.

54. Types 1–12 in David Vanderhooft and Oded Lipschits, "A New Typology of the Yehud Stamp Impressions," *Tel Aviv* 34 (2007): 12–37.

Jerusalem and its immediate surroundings, including Ramat Rahel. No such seal impressions were found at Beth-zur and Qeilah and only a relatively small number was found north of Jerusalem. The list in Neh 3 seems to fit the extent of Hasmonean Judea before it started expanding to the west and north in ca. 140 B.C.E.[55]

8. The list of enemies of Judah—Tobiah the Ammonite, Sanballat the Horonite and Geshem the Arabian (e.g. Neh 2:19; 6:1)—fits only the Persian period.[56] This argument should be seriously considered since: (i) a Sanballat is mentioned in the Elephantine papyri as the Governor of Samaria, and (ii) Gashmu the king of Kedar appears in a fifth-century Aramaic inscription on a silver vessel ostensibly found at Tell el-Maskhuta in the Delta. But the fact that these names appear in the "Nehemiah Memoir" means nothing for the date of Neh 3, considered by most scholars to be an independent source (see the partial list of references above). Moreover, as I will try to show in detail in another place, these names cannot be read in a simplistic way also in regard to the rest of the book of Nehemiah: (a) the name Sanballat is mentioned in the Wadi ed-Daliyeh papyri and by Josephus, *Ant.* 11; both (and probably also Sanballat of the Elephantine papyri) are later than the conventional date given to Nehemiah. (b) The Tobiads appear in extra-biblical texts in the third and second centuries B.C.E.; being a symbol of Hellenistic culture, in Hasmonean times there was good reason to portray them negatively. (c) Geshem is a common Arab name; though there must have been a Qedarite king named Geshem sometime in the Persian period, a Lihyanite (northwest Arabia) king with the same name ruled in the early second century B.C.E.[57] (d) The Ashdodites are also included among the enemies of Yehud in Nehemiah (4:7); there is no logic in seeing Ashdod as a foe before the expansion of the Hasmoneans to the west in the 140s B.C.E., an expansion which brought them closer to the territory of Ashdod. In short, in the case of the enemies of Nehemiah, too, second-century realities could have been mixed with old traditions.

55. Israel Finkelstein, "The Territorial Extent and Demography of Yehud/Judea in the Persian and Early Hellenistic Periods," *RB* 117 (2010): 39–54.

56. Barkay, "Additional View of Jerusalem," 53.

57. Saba Farés-Drappeau, *Dedan et Lihyan: Histoire des Arabes aux confines des pouvoirs perse et hellénistique* (Lyon: Maison de l'orient et de la Méditerranée, 2005), 122–23.

Facts or Hypotheses: What Comes First?

Lipschits also challenges my analysis of the size of Jerusalem and its population in the Persian and Early Hellenistic periods.[58] Lipschits concludes that Jerusalem of the Persian period covered an area of 5 hectares—twice the area that I suggested. This case is different from the ones dealt with above, because Lipschits' reading of the biblical text is critical. Here the dispute is only about the meaning of negative evidence in archaeology.

Lipschits agrees with me that the Persian-period settlement covered *mainly* the central part of the City of David's ridge; we are also not too far apart regarding its size—2.2–5 hectares in my analysis, 2.8–3 hectares in his. Yet, Lipschits and I differ regarding the negative evidence—areas with *no* Persian and Early Hellenistic finds. Lipschits adds the two hectares of the Ophel (between the Temple Mount and Area G) to his calculation and gets a settlement of ca. 5 hectares.

In this case, too, one is faced with a major methodological problem: What should rule—archaeological facts, even negative evidence (also a fact), or hypotheses? Lipschits writes (my comments in italics in brackets):

> The importance of the Ophel hill as the main built-up area in the Persian and Early Hellenistic periods was never discussed in the archaeological and historical research. The reason was the scarcity of finds [*in fact, no finds*] in this area, of about 20 dunams… This is the only flat, easy-to-settle area in the city. Its proximity to the Temple Mount on the one hand and the easy option to fortify it [*no fortification has ever been found*]… made it the preferred option for settlement in the Persian period. In spite of the scarcity of finds [*in fact, no finds*] in this area, the relatively abundance of Persian period finds along its southern slope, its proximity to the Temple Mount, its geographical characteristics and its importance in the Iron Age and post-Persian periods—all these facts [*these are interpretations rather than facts*] indicate that this area should be considered part of the settled area of Jerusalem during the Persian and Early Hellenistic periods. The absence of Persian period finds in the Ophel hill [*here "scarcity of finds" is correctly replaced with "absence of finds"*]… is an indication of the limitations of archaeological research.[59]

A similar case comes from Knauf.[60] He argues that Persian-period Jerusalem had a population of 3000 souls. In his opinion, two reasons

58. Lipschits, "Persian Period Finds from Jerusalem."
59. Ibid., 19–20.
60. E. A. Knauf, "Inside the Walls of Nehemiah's Jerusalem: Naboth's Vineyard," in *The Fire Signals of Lachish: Studies in the Archaeology and History of*

might account for the absence of significant archeological evidence for such an occupation. First, the settlement was spread on a large area (including the southwestern hill); second, the site continued to be inhabited without a crisis until 70 C.E., with very considerable construction activity in the Hellenistic and early Roman periods. Thus, "Persian settlement debris was permanently recycled for 500 years, and every object of possible re-use sifted out. After all, there is little doubt that there was a governor's palace at Jerusalem after 444 B.C.E...."

In this case too, hypotheses—on the population of Jerusalem and the existence of a Persian-period palace there—come before archaeology. I just wish to remind the reader that many years of excavations in the southwestern hill did not yield Persian-period finds and that pottery does not disappear even if later activity damaged old walls.

Needless to say, hypotheses and interpretation, not facts, dictate Lipschits' discussion: there are no finds, but since the area must have been settled according to his logic, there must have been a settlement there. As an archaeologist I cannot accept this line of reasoning.[61] I should repeat: it is impossible that all pottery sherds, walls and other finds—even those representing a meager settlement—have disappeared.

Summary

The present study is about method no less than data. I have dealt with methodological issues such as inconsistencies between archaeology and text; the meaning of negative evidence in archaeology (in surveys and excavations alike); the trustworthiness of a theory built on hypotheses; the pace of change in material culture; the meaning of *terminus post quem* in archaeology, and so on. On the factual level, with the available

Israel in the Late Bronze Age, Iron Age and the Persian Period in Honor of David Ussishkin (ed. Israel Finkelstein and Nadav Na'aman; Winona Lake: Eisenbrauns, 2011), 185–94.

61. Which is also true for Jane M. Cahill, "Jerusalem at the Time of the United Monarchy: The Archaeological Evidence," in *Jerusalem in Bible and Archaeology: The First Temple Period* (ed. Andrew G. Vaughn and Ann E. Killebrew; Atlanta: SBL, 2003), 13–80; Amihai Mazar, "Jerusalem in the 10th Century B.C.E.: The Glass Half Full," in *Essays on Ancient Israel and Its Near Eastern Context: A Tribute to Nadav Na'aman* (ed. Yaira Amit et al.; Winona Lake: Eisenbrauns, 2006), 255–72; and Nadav Na'aman, "When and How Did Jerusalem Become a Great City? The Rise of Jerusalem as Judah's Premier City in the Eighth–Seventh Centuries B.C.E.," *BASOR* 347 (2007): 21–56; regarding latter periods in the history of Jerusalem, see, e.g., Israel Finkelstein, "The Settlement History of Jerusalem in the Eighth and Seventh Centuries BCE," *RB* 115 (2008): 499–515.

data at hand, I see no reason to change my views on the issues: Persian-period Jerusalem covered ca. 2–2.5 hectares, and both the description of the construction of the city-wall in Neh 3 and the List of Returnees in Ezra and Nehemiah probably reflect late Hellenistic (Hasmonean) period realities. Only new data that would change the *archaeological* picture can call for a new interpretation of these texts.

JACKALS AND OSTRICHES HONORING GOD: THE ZOOLOGICAL GAZE IN THE ISAIAH SCROLL

Ken Stone

Introduction

Douglas Knight has long called attention to the importance of interdisciplinary biblical interpretation, noting in particular "the contributions sociology, anthropology, and archaeology can make to our understanding of [biblical] literature and its social world."[1] Having been encouraged by Knight in the past to adopt an interdisciplinary perspective on biblical notions about sex and gender,[2] I would like to explore here the possibility that questions or concepts developed outside the biblical guild might also prove useful for the reexamination of biblical animal symbolism. More specifically, I wish to consider several biblical texts in terms of what I will call "the zoological gaze." Although the phrase, "zoological gaze," might seem equally at home in such diverse fields as biology or art criticism, I have adopted the term from a study by sociologist Adrian Franklin. After summarizing Franklin's approach to "the zoological gaze" below, I will turn to several passages from the Isaiah scroll in order to consider manifestations of "the zoological gaze" in exilic and postexilic biblical literature. My interest does not lie simply with Isaiah,

1. Douglas A. Knight, "Deuteronomy and the Deuteronomists," in *Old Testament Interpretation: Past, Present, and Future: Essays in Honor of Gene M. Tucker* (ed. James Luther Mays, David L. Petersen, and Kent Harold Richards; Nashville: Abingdon, 1995), 76. See also Knight's "Political Rights and Powers in Monarchic Israel," in *Ethics and Politics in the Hebrew Bible* (ed. Douglas A. Knight and Carol Meyers; Semeia 66; Atlanta: Scholars Press, 1994), 93–117.

2. My *Sex, Honor and Power in the Deuteronomistic History* (Sheffield: Sheffield Academic, 1996), had its origins in a dissertation under Douglas Knight's direction. The approach adopted there also informs my *Practicing Safer Texts: Food, Sex and Bible in Queer Perspective* (London: T&T Clark International, 2005), and "Gender Criticism: The Un-Manning of Abimelech," in *Judges and Method: New Approaches in Biblical Studies* (ed. Gale A. Yee; 2d ed.; Minneapolis: Fortress, 2007), 183–201.

however. Rather, I wish to use my brief review of forms taken by the zoological gaze in Isaiah to suggest that sustained attention needs to be given to animal symbolism in biblical scholarship, as now seems to be happening in other areas of contemporary academic discourse.

The Zoological Gaze in Sociohistorical Perspective

Although questions about animal symbolism have not been widespread in biblical scholarship, one can find animals prowling around the edges of the discipline. For example, a number of scholars have examined in detail the systems of animal classification that structure Pentateuchal stipulations for diet and sacrifice.[3] A few monographs can also be found on other animal-related topics, such as Borowski's work on the "use" of animals in Israel or Strawn's study of the lion in biblical and ancient Near Eastern "image and metaphor."[4] Studies of Israel's social-material world rightly deal with questions about "animal husbandry"; and even so obscure a topic as the distribution of pig bones in the archaeological record has made an occasional appearance in the discourse of biblical scholarship.[5] Yet in spite of such scattered examples, animals have not often been a central focus for biblical studies.

Outside of biblical scholarship, however, a growing body of inter-disciplinary writing has begun to explore what Cary Wolfe calls "the pressing relevance of the question of the animal."[6] Whereas disciplinary

3. See, e.g., Jacob Milgrom, *Leviticus 1–16* (AB 3; New York: Doubleday, 1991), 643–742; Walter Houston, *Purity and Monotheism: Clean and Unclean Animals in Biblical Law* (Sheffield: Sheffield Academic, 1993), as well as the influential anthropological observations of Mary Douglas in *Purity and Danger: An Analysis of the Concepts of Pollution and Taboo* (London: Routledge & Kegan Paul, 1966). Cf. Stone, *Practicing Safer Texts*, 46–67.

4. Oded Borowski, *Every Living Thing: Daily Use of Animals in Ancient Israel* (Walnut Creek: Altamira, 1998); Brent A. Strawn, *What Is Stronger than a Lion? Leonine Image and Metaphor in the Hebrew Bible and the Ancient Near East* (Fribourg: Academic Press Fribourg, 2005).

5. See Philip J. King and Lawrence E. Stager, *Life in Biblical Israel* (Louisville: Westminster John Knox, 2002), 112–22; Brian Hesse and Paula Wapnish, "Can Pig Remains Be Used for Ethnic Diagnosis in the Ancient Near East?," in *The Archaeology of Israel: Constructing the Past, Interpreting the Present* (ed. Neil Asher Silberman and David Small; JSOTSup 237; Sheffield: Sheffield Academic, 1997), 238–70.

6. Cary Wolfe, "Introduction," in *Zoontologies: The Question of the Animal* (ed. Cary Wolfe; Minneapolis: University of Minnesota Press, 2003), x. See also Wolfe's *Animal Rites: American Culture, the Discourse of Species, and Posthumanist Theory* (Chicago: University of Chicago Press, 2003).

divisions in the modern university traditionally relegated animals to the biological sciences, it is increasingly common for scholars across the humanities and human sciences to turn their attention to animals as well. This interdisciplinary interest in "animal studies" has just started to influence the study of religion; and only a few biblical scholars seem to have noticed the appearance of such studies.[7] However, one can imagine that greater attention to such research might inspire fresh investigations of biblical texts that deal in one way or another with non-human animals.

It is hardly surprising that this body of interdisciplinary scholarship includes contributions from the social sciences. Indeed, anthropological examinations of animal-related topics served as an early stimulus to the contemporary recognition that, as Claude Lévi-Strauss famously put it, animals are "good to think."[8] However, social-scientific studies of animal-related topics involve certain limitations of perspective that should be noted by those of us who engage such studies. Because sociology and social or cultural anthropology are all defined as modern academic specializations in relation to *human* society and culture, these disciplines are inevitably characterized by what Barbara Noske, herself trained in social anthropology, calls "*a priori* anthropocentrism."[9] The social sciences place humans firmly at the center of research, and so according to anthropologist Tim Ingold they often display "a strangely ambivalent attitude towards non-human animals."[10] Moreover, social-scientific discourse frequently relies upon methodological distinctions

7. In religious studies, see, e.g., Laura Hobgood-Oster, *Holy Dogs and Asses: Animals in the Christian Tradition* (Urbana: University of Illinois Press, 2008); Paul Waldau and Kimberley Patton, eds., *A Communion of Subjects: Animals in Religion, Science and Ethics* (New York: Columbia University Press, 2006); and Ingvild Saelid Gilhus, *Animals, Gods and Humans: Changing Attitudes to Animals in Greek, Roman and Early Christian Ideas* (London: Routledge, 2006). For a more theological perspective, see Stephen H. Webb, *On God and Dogs: A Christian Theology of Compassion for Animals* (New York: Oxford University Press, 1998). In biblical studies, see Heather A. McKay, "Through the Eyes of Horses: Representation of the Horse Family in the Hebrew Bible," in *Sense and Sensitivity: Essays on Reading the Bible in Memory of Robert Carroll* (ed. Alistair G. Hunter and Phillip R. Davies; JSOTSup 348; London: Sheffield Academic, 2002).

8. Claude Lévi-Strauss, *Totemism* (trans. Rodney Needham; Boston: Beacon, 1963), 89.

9. Barbara Noske, *Beyond Boundaries: Humans and Animals* (Montreal: Black Rose, 1997), ix. See also Noske's "Great Apes as Anthropological Subjects: Deconstructing Anthropocentrism," in *The Great Ape Project: Equality Beyond Humanity* (ed. Paola Cavalieri and Peter Singer; London: Fourth Estate, 1993), 258–68.

10. Tim Ingold, "Introduction," in *What Is an Animal?* (ed. Tim Ingold; London: Routledge, 1994), 11.

between society and culture, on one side, and "nature," on the other. Humans and their products (including texts) are then associated with society or culture, while non-human animals are traditionally associated with nature. In truth, the lines between these categories are fluid, as one realizes when reflecting upon the ambiguous status of so-called domesticated animals (a complex category that Noske among others analyzes[11]) or the existence of something similar to cultural transmission and "social traditions" among certain animal species, especially great apes.[12] Indeed, the influential critical theorist Donna Haraway has begun using the neologism, "naturecultures," in her work on relations between humans and other animals as a way of getting at the complexities that are obscured by anthropocentric constructions of boundaries between nature and culture.[13]

For the biblical scholar, however, some degree of methodological anthropocentrism may be required since biblical scholarship deals first of all with human products. After all, when we read biblical texts, we do not meet actual animals. We are dealing instead with literary texts, which are indisputably human creations. To be sure, the humans who wrote biblical texts may have done so after encounters with actual animals. Many Israelites even lived with animals in their houses.[14] Moreover, the significance of the interactions that Israelites had with actual animals is not captured simply by noting that Israelites "used" or lived alongside animals. Who we are as human individuals, and who we become as sociocultural beings, depends in part on the specific animals with which we interact in particular material and historical circumstances. Nevertheless, biblical representations of animals were ultimately produced by human beings. These humans were interpreting things they saw in their own world, including other animals; but they were not only doing that. They were also using those interpretations to deal with specific problems and circumstances faced by the humans themselves.

11. See also Juliet Clutton-Brock, "The Unnatural World: Behavioural Aspects of Humans and Animals in the Process of Domestication," in *Animals and Human Society: Changing Perspectives* (ed. Aubrey Manning and James Serpell; London: Routledge, 1994), 23–35.

12. See, e.g., William C. McGrew, *The Cultured Chimpanzee: Reflections on Cultural Primatology* (Cambridge: Cambridge University Press, 2004); and Noske, "Great Apes as Anthropological Subjects."

13. Donna Haraway, *When Species Meet* (Minneapolis: University of Minnesota Press, 2008).

14. King and Stager, *Life in Biblical Israel*, 34; Paula McNutt, *Reconstructing the Society of Ancient Israel* (Louisville: Westminster John Knox, 1999), 67. Cf. 1 Sam 28:24; Amos 6:4.

The fact that humans view other animals through lenses shaped by human social concerns plays an important role in Adrian Franklin's notion of "the zoological gaze." The sociological study in which Franklin discusses this gaze is focused largely on relations between humans and animals in modernity and postmodernity. However, while Franklin notes that "[l]ooking at animals is considered desirable and pleasurable in all Western societies," he also observes that "this attitude is neither confined to the West nor to the present."[15] Humans across space and time observe animals, but "[p]eople from different cultures and times look at animals in different ways." In order to understand this "changing zoological gaze,"[16] one must take into account the wide range of cultural assumptions and social concerns that shape perceptions of animals in different societies. For, as Franklin points out,

> Animals convey meanings and values that are culturally specific; in viewing animals we cannot escape the cultural context in which that observation takes place. There can be no deep, primordial relationship underlying the zoological gaze since it must always be mediated by culture.[17]

Franklin also notes that since "animals are like us and different, they can be incorporated into discourses of similarity (of me, us, we, etc.) and difference (of they, other, etc.) within the social." On the one hand, this means that even animals which are quite distinct from us can be understood in terms of human norms and frames for perception. In order to illustrate this point, Franklin calls attention to the contemporary passion for watching whales and dolphins. While such marine animals are clearly different from humans, interactions among these animals are often read in terms of perceived similarities to the interactions humans have with one another. Thus modern humans look at whales and dolphins and see such qualities as "family togetherness, nurturing, and even leisure," all of which are valorized in the modern West. Franklin therefore suggests that

> We will go to some lengths to see large marine mammals in the wild but when we see them we are just as likely to say they are just like us... We have always to interpret, to provide the meaning for what we see, and for that we can only draw upon human values, emotions, and interpretations. When we gaze at animals we hold up a mirror to ourselves.[18]

---

15. Adrian Franklin, *Animals and Modern Cultures: A Sociology of Human–Animal Relations in Modernity* (London: Sage, 1999), 62.
16. Ibid., 64.
17. Ibid., 62.
18. Ibid.

On the other hand, our interpretations of animals are not only structured in terms of perceived similarities and differences between humans and other animals. The perception of relations between distinct groups of humans also plays a role in the zoological gaze. During the era of European colonial expansion, for example, "non-Europeans" were often represented by Europeans as "animal-like."[19] Europeans who gazed at exotic animals in menageries could therefore glimpse a dangerous otherness originating from distant lands, which "positively confirmed the civilizing influence and European ordering" of those lands.[20]

Franklin notes as well that changing socio-political circumstances often correlate with changes in the ways in which humans look at animals. During the French Revolution, for example, the liberation of animals from the French royal menagerie symbolized the overthrow of political tyranny.[21] Later, as urbanization increased in nineteenth-century England, efforts were made "to change working-class comportment and behavior" by replacing forms of sport and leisure that urban immigrants brought with them from the countryside with more rational forms of recreation.[22] Such developments shaped the rise of the modern zoo, which came to be associated with "instruction or improvement" of the new urban masses.[23] Today, of course, efforts at conservation and anxieties about ecological change or the global economy are more likely to shape the ways in which we look at animals. In all of these contexts, however, "The zoological gaze is not merely social and cultural, it is also historically specific."[24]

If the zoological gaze is "historically specific," as Franklin suggests, then biblical references to animals will clearly not reflect the same circumstances and concerns that Franklin himself identifies in his discussions of modernity and postmodernity. Animals may be a kind of "blank paper which can be inscribed with any message, and symbolic meaning, that the social wishes," as another sociologist, Keith Tester, argues; but in order to understand such meanings we have to recognize that "animals are not only social, they are also *historical* objects."[25] Thus, the sociological-historical analyses carried out by Franklin, Tester and

19. Ibid., 69.
20. Ibid., 66.
21. Ibid.
22. Ibid., 67.
23. Ibid., 68.
24. Ibid., 69.
25. Keith Tester, *Animals and Society: The Humanity of Animal Rights* (London: Routledge, 1991), 46–47 (emphasis in original).

others may indicate that greater attention should be given to the biblical zoological gaze by scholars who are interested in either biblical symbolism or the social world of ancient Israel. Biblical references to animals are not simply specimens from the "natural" world, caught in textual nets. They are products of an ancient zoological gaze, which saw in animals social symbols that both reflected and responded to the changing contexts and concerns that generated biblical texts.

The Zoological Gaze in the Isaiah Scroll

In order to reflect further on some of the ways in which biblical scholars might explore this "changing zoological gaze" in biblical literature, I want to turn to the Isaiah scroll, and especially its exilic and postexilic portions. As John Olley notes, "Isaiah has the greatest diversity of animal names outside of the food legislation passages in the Torah."[26] However, attempts to interpret Isaiah's references to animals in relation to socio-historical contexts are complicated by the difficulties involved in dating sections of the book. Since a consensus no longer exists around neat, tripartite divisions of Isaiah, broad socio-historical contextualization may be preferable to attempts to tie particular verses to specific dates.

Nevertheless, a few conclusions can still be drawn about the book's likely contexts of origin. Most scholars continue to believe, for example, that some or all of the chapters traditionally referred to as "Deutero-Isaiah" (chs. 40–55) were written during the reign of Cyrus the Persian, who is mentioned by name twice (44:28; 45:1). Hence the chapters can plausibly be read in relation to issues raised for Yehudites living in Babylon by the rise of Persian hegemony, the end of the Babylonian exile, and the beginning of Israel's "Persian Period."[27] These chapters emphasize, among other themes, the sovereignty of YHWH; the impotence of other (especially Babylonian) gods; the selection of Cyrus the Persian by YHWH; the destruction of Babylon; and the fact that God's chosen people Israel, though formerly punished, is now being or is about to be redeemed. The rhetoric of creation (including the conceptualization of YHWH as creator of Israel) plays an important role in the articulation

---

26. John W. Olley, "'The Wolf, the Lamb, and a Little Child': Transforming the Diverse Earth Community in Isaiah," in *The Earth Story in the Psalms and the Prophets* (ed. Norman C. Habel; Sheffield: Sheffield Academic; Cleveland: Pilgrim, 2001), 220.

27. For a useful overview of Deutero-Isaiah and its likely historical context and social location, see Jon L. Berquist, *Judaism in Persia's Shadow: A Social and Historical Approach* (Minneapolis: Fortress, 1995), 29–43.

of these themes, as scholars have long noted.[28] While such rhetoric is not limited to language about animals, animals and animal symbolism do appear at several points in chs. 40–55.

For example, animals as burnt offerings are referred to more than once (e.g. 40:16; 43:23, 24) and the prophet's critique of idolatry includes the observation that Babylonian gods are carried about on animals (46:1). In a more symbolic register, both YHWH (40:11) and Cyrus (44:28) are represented in terms of the "shepherd" imagery that is found throughout the Hebrew Bible. Cyrus is also described as "a bird of prey from the east" (46:11).[29] The earth's inhabitants are compared to grasshoppers (40:22), moths and worms (51:8), while Israel is called a worm and a maggot (41:14)[30] and compared to sheep that have gone astray (53:6).

However, the example of biblical animal imagery that provides me with my primary focus occurs in ch. 43. The well-known oracle found in 43:16–21 focuses on the "new thing" (43:19) that YHWH is about to do or is now doing for Israel. In spite of YHWH's admonition not to "remember the former things, or give heed to the things of old" (43:18), the oracle opens (as does the chapter as a whole [cf. 43:2]) with language that recalls traditions about the exodus from Egypt and God's victory at the Red Sea. YHWH is described as creating "a way in the sea, and a path in the mighty waters" (43:16); and references are made to "chariot and horse, army and power" (43:17). By emphasizing the "new thing" that "springs forth," the prophet indicates that a new journey to Israel rather than the one associated with Moses is here in view. This journey, like the former one, will entail passage through wilderness. And in connection with this passage through wilderness, the prophetic gaze, which claims to mediate a divine gaze, falls upon animals:

> I am making a way in the wilderness,
>   and rivers in the desert.
> The living things of the field will honor me,
>   jackals and ostriches.

28. See, e.g., Thomas W. Mann, "Stars, Sprouts and Streams: The Creative Redeemer of Second Isaiah," in *God Who Creates: Essays in Honor of W. Sibley Towner* (ed. William P. Brown and S. Dean McBride Jr.; Grand Rapids: Eerdmans, 2000); Terence E. Fretheim, *God and World in the Old Testament: A Relational Theology of Creation* (Nashville: Abingdon, 2005), 181–98; Claus Westermann, *Isaiah 40–66: A Commentary* (OTL; Philadelphia: Westminster, 1969), 25 et passim.

29. Translations are my own unless otherwise noted.

30. For "maggot," see Joseph Blenkinsopp, *Isaiah 40–55: A New Translation with Introduction and Commentary* (AB 19A; New York: Doubleday, 2002), 199. NRSV reads "insect."

For I give water in the wilderness,
rivers in the desert,
to give drink to my chosen people,
the people whom I formed for myself
so that they might declare my praise. (43:19b–21)

Here we find a general reference to "living things of the field" who will "honor" YHWH, followed by specific references to jackals and ostriches. The reason these animals will honor God seems straightforward: God will "give water in the wilderness, rivers in the desert," where these animals dwell. But why do jackals and ostriches, in particular, catch the prophet's eye?

Jackals and ostriches appear together in several other biblical texts, including two additional passages from the book of Isaiah itself. While both of these passages are found in Isa 1–39 (and hence in that part of the book traditionally associated with the eighth-century prophet Isaiah), arguments have been made for a later dating for each passage. Isaiah 13, for example, contains an oracle that looks forward to the destruction of Babylon. Although a superscription links this oracle to "Isaiah son of Amoz" (13:1), several considerations, including the reference to attacks on Babylon by the Medes (13:17–18), lead many scholars to read the chapter instead as a product of the sixth century, dating perhaps to "the decade preceding the fall of Babylon to Cyrus in 539 B.C.E., more or less contemporaneous therefore with the anti-Babylonian diatribe in Isa 40–48."[31] Here the poet imagines a time when Babylon will be destroyed "like the overthrowing by God of Sodom and Gomorrah" (13:19). Human inhabitants will no longer be found in the ruins of Babylon. However, the prophet does see in those ruins several other sorts of creatures, including jackals and ostriches:

But wild animals will lie down there,
and its houses will be full of owls.
There ostriches will live,
and there goat-creatures[32] will dance.
Hyenas will cry in its bereaved dwelling places,
and jackals in the pleasant palaces. (13:21–22a)

---

31. Joseph Blenkinsopp, *Isaiah 1–39: A New Translation with Introduction and Commentary* (AB 19; New York: Doubleday, 2000), 277. See also Marvin A. Sweeney, *Isaiah 1–39: With an Introduction to Prophetic Literature* (FOTL; Grand Rapids: Eerdmans, 1996), 231.

32. Though the nature of these creatures, referred to in translations as "satyrs" (so KJV) or "goat demons" (so NRSV), is obscure, something other than simple goats seems to be in view. See Blenkinsopp, *Isaiah 1–39*, 280, 453–54.

As Gene Tucker notes, judgment against Babylon here involves "a return to the 'chaotic' state of the uncultivated and uncultured land."[33] The placement of ostriches and jackals in this scene indicates that both creatures were associated with just such an "uncultured" chaos by the author of this passage.

Jackals and ostriches are found together again in Isa 34:13. Chapters 34 and 35 are usually dated to the post-exilic period, though the precise context(s) for the composition of these two chapters has/have long been a matter for scholarly debate.[34] The oracle in ch. 34 looks forward to the annihilation, not of Babylon (as in chs. 13 and 43), but rather of Edom, which is given an ominous new name, "No Kingdom There" (34:12). Edom is represented as being destroyed under circumstances that sound similar to the fiery destruction of Sodom and Gomorrah (34:9–10), which was mentioned explicitly in ch. 13. In this scene of devastation, described in 34:11 with words (*tohu* and *bohu*) that recall the chaos that precedes God's creative activity in Gen 1:2, human inhabitants are missing. However, other creatures do live in Edom, which has become "a dwelling place for jackals, an abode for ostriches" (34:13) as well as a home to numerous other beasts. Although some of the creatures mentioned in ch. 34 are difficult to identify, they do include, in addition to jackals and ostriches, the hyenas and goat-creatures mentioned in ch. 13, as well as other wild animals and the mysterious Lilith. Again, these specific creatures seem to represent the antithesis to civilization and order. Yet they have been called to the ruins of Edom by the "command," indeed the "spirit," of YHWH (34:16b). God's "hand" has given them Edom as a place to possess "forever, from generation to generation" (34:17). They may be instruments of God's judgment and the antithesis of human civilization; but they do not stand in opposition to God.

When Isa 43:20 spots jackals and ostriches in the wilderness, then, it does not simply pick at random two creatures that happen to be found in deserts. Rather, it names two creatures found elsewhere in Isaiah in exilic or postexilic passages that emphasize the destruction of human civilization by God and the chaotic wilderness that follows. We may wish to speak of jackals and ostriches, along with Blenkinsopp, in terms of "an Isaian topos associated with ecological degradation and the collapse of urban life."[35] However, this type of "collapse" serves as the context for

33. Gene M. Tucker, "The Peaceable Kingdom and a Covenant with the Wild Animals," in Brown and McBride, eds., *God Who Creates*, 223.

34. See, for example, the numerous references to these two chapters and the various scholarly arguments about them in Sweeney, *Isaiah 1–39*.

35. Blenkinsopp, *Isaiah 40–55*, 228.

the appearance of jackals and ostriches outside of Isaiah as well. Micah, for example, while describing the destruction of Samaria and Jerusalem, declares that he "will make a wailing like the jackals, and mourning like the ostriches" (1:8). An association of jackals and ostriches with lamentation and mourning is also implied in Job 30:29, where Job refers to himself as "a brother of jackals, and a companion of ostriches." These animals appear together yet again in Lam 4:3, where the poet bewails the fact that "even the jackals offer the breast and nurse their young, but the daughter of my people has become cruel, like the ostriches in the wilderness." This notion that ostriches were "cruel" parents, which is presupposed as well in Job 39:13–18 (albeit with different vocabulary), may have been derived from the fact that female ostriches lay eggs on the ground and allow a single mating pair to care for the eggs and offspring of several females; but it clearly sheds more light on the ancient zoological gaze than upon the natural history of ostriches. For the writer in Lam 4, however, the contrast between the assumed cruelty of ostriches and the nursing behavior of jackals underscores horrific images of Jerusalem's children, who in the wake of the city's destruction are not only starving (4:2, 4) but are being boiled and eaten by their own mothers (4:10). Once again, then, the animals symbolize chaotic conditions.

If jackals and ostriches do appear together even when, as in Lam 4:3, a contrast is drawn between them, this may indicate that they comprise a conventional word pair in poems that are concerned with desolation and wilderness. However, both animals are also seen in such contexts alone. Thus the jackal is associated with desolate circumstances in Judah in Jer 9:11 (Heb. 9:10); 10:22; and Ps 44:19 (Heb. 44:20). Hazor is described as a "lair of jackals" after it is destroyed by Babylon in Jer 49:33, while Babylon becomes a "lair of jackals" in Jer 51:37. In Jer 50:39 we find ostriches living in a destroyed Babylon, the ruin of which is compared again to God's overthrowing of Sodom and Gomorrah. The appearance of jackal or ostrich is thus associated with the destruction or absence of civilization, which produces lamentation and mourning.

Now Isa 43:16–21 is clearly informed by these ominous connotations to the appearance of jackals and ostriches. However, Deutero-Isaiah draws a rather different and somewhat unexpected picture of the animals in question. Far from lamenting or mourning, the jackals and ostriches are singled out in Isa 43 as animals who will "honor" God for providing "water in the wilderness, rivers in the desert" (43:20). Their "honoring" of God seems in fact to parallel the "praise" that comes from the people God creates in 43:21. The likelihood that this reference to jackals and ostriches "honoring" God was, in its original context, a startling image only becomes apparent after one recognizes the frequency with which these animals are associated with desolation and lament in the passages referred to above. Humans looking at jackals and ostriches apparently expect them to lament or mourn, as humans themselves would do if living in similar circumstances. Yet the prophet's gaze has fallen upon a zoological scene that provokes surprise, a scene of jackals and ostriches honoring God.

This unexpected vision of jackals and ostriches contributes to Deutero-Isaiah's project of describing developments which neither conventional wisdom nor the recent circumstances of the Israelites would lead one to anticipate. The prophet insists, after all, that God is doing "a new thing" (43:19). This announcement is made, however, to an audience whose feelings are likely represented in 49:14: "But Zion said, 'YHWH has abandoned me, my lord has forgotten me.'" The hopelessness and desolation of this sort of objection from Zion coheres well with the connotations carried by jackals and ostriches in other biblical passages. No doubt those who have experienced exile believe they have good reason to lament and wail, just as jackals and ostriches are expected to do. However, precisely in the face of such despair, Deutero-Isaiah produces an astonishing picture. If jackals wail and ostriches mourn, this is due in part to the fact that the zoological gaze finds them most often in the uncivilized chaos of wilderness, desert and ruin, where *human* values would lead to lamentation and mourning. Yet Deutero-Isaiah's evocation of a "new thing" in ch. 43 emphasizes water, rivers, and drink, necessary prerequisites for both human civilization and animal flourishing. Human values continue to shape the way in which jackals and ostriches are perceived in ch. 43, even though the reversal of context (watering instead of dryness) leads to a reversal in characterization. Exiled Yehudites may feel that they have had little reason to praise YHWH, as Deutero-Isaiah says they soon will (43:21), but the image of jackals and ostriches honoring God for "rivers in the desert" reiterates Deutero-Isaiah's contention that YHWH is about to do amazing and praiseworthy things.

Of course, this rhetorical strategy of describing astonishing animal scenes in order to predict idealized or improbable events in the human realm also occurs elsewhere in Isaiah. One such scene is found in Isa 35, which is frequently associated with Deutero-Isaiah and is similar in certain respects to Isa 43. Here the emphasis also falls on a transformation of wilderness and desert (35:1) that includes, once again, "waters in the wilderness, streams in the desert" (35:6) and a transformation of parched earth into a pool (35:7). Significantly, the latter verse also includes a reference to the dwelling place of jackals, which, though obscure, may provide a rough parallel to the changed habitation for jackals and ostriches that leads to their honoring God in ch. 43.

It may also be useful, however, to compare and contrast our passage from ch. 43 with two better-known examples of animal rhetoric, which do not include jackals or ostriches but do involve a juxtaposition of imagined transformation in the human realm with imagined transformation in the world of animals. In Isa 11:1–9, the hope for a future Davidic leader who embodies the ancient Near Eastern ideal of restoring justice and righteousness (11:1–5) is linked to a vision of peace that extends to animals:

> The wolf will dwell with the lamb,
> and the leopard will lie down with the kid,
> the calf and the young lion and fatling together,
> and a little child will lead them.
> The cow and the bear will graze,
> and their young will lie down together,
> and the lion will eat straw like an ox.
> The nursing child will play over the hole of the serpent,
> and over the viper's den the weaned child will put its hand. (11:6–8)

Although this passage appears in a chapter of Isaiah that, under older tripartite readings, would be dated to the eighth century, a number of historical critics consider 11:1–9 (or some portion thereof) to be "a later, post-exilic, expression of hope."[36] But irrespective of dating, the rhetoric of Isa 11:1–9 adopts a strategy that is, in certain respects at least, similar to the strategy found in Isa 43. In both chapters, a prediction of transformation in the world of human affairs is articulated with a vision of unexpected happenings in the zoological realm.

So, too, Isa 65 contains a description of the "new heavens and new earth" that God is going to create, when "the former things will not be remembered or come to mind" (65:17). Here again a prophet's vision falls first upon the human realm, and in particular an ideal Jerusalem, where inhabitants will live long lives with plenty to eat, few disasters, and security for their offspring. At the conclusion of this description, too, the writer's gaze turns from humans to other animals:

> The wolf and the lamb will feed together,
> the lion will eat straw like the ox;
> but the serpent will have dust for its food.
> They will not hurt or destroy on all my holy mountain,
> says YHWH. (65:25)

Although the final clause of this verse is nearly identical to the first half of 11:9, the more interesting similarities so far as my focus is concerned

---

36. R. E. Clements, *Isaiah 1–39* (NCB; Grand Rapids: Eerdmans, 1980), 122.

involve the peaceful coexistence between wolf and lamb and the vision of lions eating straw, both of which recall elements of 11:6–8. We see once again that an animal scene which most readers would consider improbable is juxtaposed to a hoped for human future, as if to underscore the startling nature of God's coming intervention.

There are certain respects, then, in which the vision of living creatures honoring God in Isa 43 stands alongside these visions in chs. 11 and 65. In all three chapters, animal images that would seem to be impossible or even "unnatural" (to use modern terminology) are used alongside images of socio-political transformation as a way of underscoring the radical nature of the changes that the prophet believes God will bring about in the future.

On the other hand, certain differences of vision also emerge from a comparison of these passages. In particular, ch. 11 and ch. 65 both represent a future of peaceful coexistence between groups of animals that are known to be antagonistic in the present. Some scholars associate this antagonism with the distinction between wild and domestic animals.[37] Interpreted in such a light, the zoological gaze of chs. 11 and 65 might be emphasizing a future in which the ability of humans to secure a living in the face of forces of chaos is guaranteed. Alternatively, one might wish to underscore the fact that the wild animals in these passages are not simply wild animals in general, but predators in particular. Inasmuch as predators are seen in numerous other biblical texts as symbols for human armies and powerful leaders, Isa 11 and 65 might be imagining a future in which the powerful no longer prey on the vulnerable.[38] In either case, it is clear that the zoological gaze that shapes these two chapters anticipates an end to some sort of conflict.

Now Franklin's discussion of the zoological gaze points out that animals are often seen through lenses shaped by human social differences. And it has long been noted that Isa 56–66 betrays evidence of having been written at a point in Judah's history later than the time of Deutero-Isaiah, when social conflicts have reemerged within Judah itself.[39] These conflicts are sometimes represented symbolically (in, e.g., 56:9–11; 59:5–6) in terms of negative animal images. It is hardly surprising, then, that "Third Isaiah" uses a scene of animal peace in ch. 65 to look ahead to a time when such conflicts are transcended, even if that time seems far removed from the poet's immediate context. Animals are viewed in

37. E.g. Tucker, "The Peaceable Kingdom," 217.
38. Cf. Walter Brueggemann, *Isaiah 1–39* (Louisville: Westminster John Knox, 1998), 103.
39. See, e.g., Berquist, *Judaism in Persia's Shadow*, 73–79.

ch. 65 through a lens shaped by the same social divisions that influenced the writing of other passages in chs. 56–66; but these animals are captured by the zoological gaze in such a way as to underscore the prophet's hope that such divisions will eventually be overcome. And if one follows the lead of those scholars who place the vision from Isa 11:1–9 in a post-exilic context as well,[40] one might go on to interpret the similar imagery found in Isa 11 in a comparable fashion.

In distinction from chs. 11 and 65, however, the zoological scene in ch. 43 does not place wild animals with domestic animals, or predators with prey. The zoological gaze of ch. 43 is not shaped by a concern to move beyond current social conflicts within Judah. It is influenced instead by Deutero-Isaiah's insistence that radically new options are available or will soon be made available to exiles who wish to return to Judah. Deutero-Isaiah's message of hope concerns return and rejoicing for desolate exiles who long for Judah, rather than reconciliation between distinct social factions inside Judah. This difference influences both the specific animals chosen for attention in Isa 43 and the ways in which those animals are characterized by the zoological gaze. For, as Franklin also notes, the zoological gaze is influenced by processes of socio-historical change.

The images of jackals and ostriches deployed in Isa 43:20 therefore need to be interpreted in relation to two rhetorical gestures. On the one hand, the verse presupposes knowledge of a conventional association of jackals and ostriches with wilderness, desolation, chaos, ruin and lament. This conventional association is found elsewhere in the Isaiah scroll, but it is found outside of Isaiah as well. On the other hand, that conventional association is not so much repeated in Isa 43 as twisted for new purposes, when jackals and ostriches are represented as honoring God rather than mourning and lamenting. Through such a representation of jackals and ostriches, Deutero-Isaiah underscores the radically new and unpredictable circumstances that God is going to bring about, and may be bringing about already, in the particular time and place that Deutero-Isaiah wishes to address.

Conclusion: Reading the Biblical Zoological Gaze
in a "Postmodern" World

If we wish to read the oracles from Isaiah that deal with animals, we do well to avoid old claims that YHWH was, in distinction from other ancient deities, a god of history rather than a god of nature. After all, Isa 43:20–21

40. E.g. Clements, *Isaiah 1–39*, 122.

uses a zoological scene, a scene from what we often call nature (though the Bible does not), to talk about a historical development. Here, as in other parts of Isaiah, a transformation in Israel's historical-political circumstances is represented in conjunction with, or in terms of, a transformation in the order of creation. The changes taking place in desert and wilderness which lead jackals and ostriches to honor God are inextricably intertwined, in Deutero-Isaiah's discourse, with the socio-historical changes undergone, or soon to be undergone, by exiles living during the time of Persian ascendance and Babylonian decline. Thus careful attention to this passage and its zoological gaze confirms the arguments of those scholars who have critiqued the ways in which oppositions between nature and history were deployed in older traditions of biblical scholarship.[41]

But if the opposition between nature and history obscures our ability to understand the ways in which biblical writers looked at animals, other oppositions do structure the biblical zoological gaze. In particular, biblical literature frequently presupposes a distinction between the chaos of uninhabited, uncultivated wilderness, and the structures of human civilization, as they existed within the agricultural-pastoral societies of Israel and other parts of the ancient Near East.[42] Non-human animals are not placed neatly by biblical writers on one side of this distinction, but rather are located differentially in relation to the distinction itself. Thus, while many biblical texts refer to Israel's domestic animals, and chs. 11 and 65 of Isaiah bring together animals from both sides of the opposition between uninhabited wilderness and human habitation, chs. 13, 34, and 43 focus upon animals that were thought to represent the realm of uninhabited waste and desolation that seemed always to threaten human well-being and survival.

It is important to recognize, however, that our context for reading biblical literature involves significant changes in perspective about such matters. It continues to be true, of course, that areas which were once inhabited by humans and have now been destroyed represent for us scenes of chaos, disaster, and desolation. For some humans, moreover,

---

41. Cf. Ronald A. Simkins, *Creator and Creation: Nature in the Worldview of Ancient Israel* (Peabody: Hendrickson, 1994); Theodore Hiebert, *The Yahwist's Landscape: Nature and Religion in Early Israel* (New York: Oxford University Press, 1996); and Fretheim, *God and World in the Old Testament*.

42. Although sharp divisions have sometimes been drawn between agricultural and pastoral societies, much recent scholarship concludes instead that "agricultural, pastoral, and trade activities...typically formed a single interdependent economic system" in Israel and the ancient Near East. McNutt, *Reconstructing the Society of Ancient Israel*, 70 et passim; and see sources cited throughout her work.

the need or desire to contend with wildness continues to be culturally significant.[43] On a global scale, however, we are no longer surrounded in the same way that the Israelites were by vast areas of wild space or uncultivated land, filled with numerous creatures that we can imagine as threats to our survival. To the contrary, it is our cultivation and spreading habitation that threatens a shrinking number of wild spaces, a growing list of threatened species, and possibly ourselves. If jackals, ostriches, or other animals mourn today, it is likely to be humans who cause them to do so.

Yet this change in context does not render irrelevant a reexamination of the biblical zoological gaze. One of the issues raised by contemporary "animal studies" is the question of definition, and, more specifically, how definitions of "the human" and "the animal" have been constructed in relation to, but also over against, one another, with ethical consequences for humans and other animals alike.[44] Although biblical literature does come up in such discussions, knowledge about biblical ways of constructing these relations is too often limited to hasty interpretations of, for example, Gen 1:26 or Ps 8 to buttress human claims of "dominion" over other animals. However, a more extensive and nuanced analysis of the various forms taken by the biblical zoological gaze may reveal a much wider range of relations constructed, not only between humans and other animals, but also between those animals and the Israelite God. Even within the Isaiah scroll, one finds several different dynamics at work in the construction of relations among humans, animals and God. These dynamics need to be studied more carefully, not only in terms of their immediate literary and original social contexts, but also in comparison with other texts in which animals play significant roles. Rather than contributing to the notion that there is a single "biblical view" (or "Jewish view" or "Christian view") of animals and their relations to humans and to God, biblical scholars may contribute to contemporary debates by encouraging recognition of the diversity of perspective and

43. Cf. Elizabeth Atwood Lawrence, *Rodeo: An Anthropologist Looks at the Wild and the Tame* (Chicago: University of Chicago Press, 1982).

44. See, e.g., Mary Midgley, *Animals and Why They Matter* (Athens: University of Georgia Press, 1983); John Llewelyn, "Am I Obsessed by Bobby? Humanism of the Other Animal," in *Re-Reading Levinas* (ed. Robert Bernasconi and Simon Critchley; Bloomington: Indiana University Press, 1991), 234–45; Jacques Derrida, "'Eating Well,' or the Calculation of the Subject," in *Points: Interviews, 1974–1994* (ed. Elisabeth Weber; Stanford: Stanford University Press, 1995), 255–87; idem, "The Animal That Therefore I Am (More to Follow)" (trans. David Wills), *Critical Inquiry* 28, no. 2 (2002): 369–418; Giorgio Agamben, *The Open: Man and Animal* (trans. Kevin Attell; Stanford: Stanford University Press, 2004).

gaze that actually exists over time and space. Awareness of such diverse perspectives may lead to greater acknowledgment of our own responsibility for the views that we accept, adopt, or promote, and to an acknowledgment of the ethical consequences of such views. At a time when our relations with other animals are becoming increasingly important for ethicists and moral philosophers,[45] greater attention to animals by biblical scholars may thus serve as a fitting way to carry on the legacy of Douglas Knight, who has long been concerned with the interface between biblical interpretation and questions about ethics and the moral life.[46]

45. Cf. Susan Armstrong and Richard Botzler, eds., *The Animal Ethics Reader* (New York: Routledge, 2003); and Cass Sunstein and Martha Nussbaum, eds., *Animal Rights: Current Debates and New Directions* (New York: Oxford University Press, 2005).

46. See, e.g., Knight's "The Ethics of Human Life in the Hebrew Bible," in *Justice and the Holy: Essays in Honor of Walter Harrelson* (ed. Douglas A. Knight and Peter Paris; Atlanta: Scholars Press, 1989), 65–88; "Cosmogony and Order in the Hebrew Tradition," in *Cosmogony and Ethical Order: New Studies in Comparative Ethics* (ed. Robin W. Lovin and Frank E. Reynolds; Chicago: University of Chicago Press, 1985), 133–57; "Moral Values and Literary Traditions: The Case of the Succession Narrative (2 Samuel 9–20; 1 Kings 1–2)," in *Biblical Hermeneutics in Jewish Moral Discourse* (ed. Peter Haas; Semeia 34; Decatur: SBL, 1985), 7–23; "Old Testament Ethics," *The Christian Century* 99, no. 2 (20): 55–59; and "Jeremiah and the Dimensions of Moral Life," in *The Divine Helmsman: Studies on God's Control of Human Events, Presented to Lou Silberman* (ed. James L. Crenshaw and Samuel Sandmel; New York: Ktav, 1980), 87–105.

Part II

TEXTS AND HISTORY

BETRAYING THE TEXT:
CREATION NARRATIVES IN THEIR AND OUR CONTEXT*

Annalisa Azzoni

The Bible appears, directly or indirectly, quite often in the news today. A sensationalistic documentary about an alleged tomb of Jesus' family, feared to shake Christianity to its core, is all over the media,[1] a Texan lawmaker dismissed the theory of evolution as a Jewish conspiracy,[2] and, more locally, here in Nashville, in the 10 o'clock news (WKRN section of Faith and Ethics) the following was reported:

> How the universe was created is one of the greatest mysteries of all time. The controversial question has many people taking sides, was it evolution or creation? The best guess from scientists so far is that the universe evolved, but now, a Kentucky college student may have shed new light on the subject. Of the 19,000 students at Western Kentucky University in Bowling Green, Kentucky, one has done something no one has ever done. Samuel J. Hunt has written an 84-page scientific proof of the Genesis record or scientific proof that God could have created the heavens and the earth just as described in the book of Genesis. Hunt said he proved that creation can be spoken into existence. He claims by the voice of God. It's based on the proven scientific phenomena called sonoluminescence, which states light is produced when sound waves pass through a liquid. In simplest terms it states, light comes from bubbles. "Now, from each

---

* This essay would never have been written if I had not encountered my colleagues and students at Vanderbilt Divinity School. It is at Vanderbilt that I have been nurtured into asking the types of questions discussed in the following pages, and where I have found meaning and relevance for my work in the present cultural and religious context. It is an honor and a pleasure to offer this to Douglas A. Knight, a pillar of biblical studies at Vanderbilt, a wonderful colleague and most encouraging friend.

1. *The Lost Tomb of Jesus*, DVD, directed by Simcha Jacobovici (The Discovery Channel, 2007).

2. Robert T. Garrett, "Memo: Stop Teaching Evolution," *Dallas Morning News*, February 14, 2007.

of these bubbles, when it expands and collapses the photons are going to
come out in all directions and together, they give off a glow," said Hunt.
"It proves God spoke everything into the universe," said Hunt.[3]

Simple enough. And reassuring. The Bible is true. Finally. The public
discourse today is polarized in such simplistic terms! True/False,
Evolution/Creation, Good Guys/Evildoers, and I could go on and on...
The example I presented here is in some way an easy target, but at the
same time it is, I think, an apt exemplar and not an aberration of such
cases in which the dominant religious discourse around the Bible
attempts to simplify what is not simple at all. If it took only 84 pages for
Samuel Hunt to prove scientifically "that God could have created heaven
and earth just as described in the Book of Genesis," one can be reassured
that one can grasp the mysteries of the universe and of human life with
one simple, straight talking, no-nonsense 84-page long read. That's good
news, isn't it? Now, I did go and check out Samuel Hunt's website, in
which you can download the paper for under 10 dollars (and receive two
free books with it, one of which is entitled "The Science of Getting
Rich"!) and I have to confess I could not bring myself to buy it. My
curiosity was not aimed at discovering the merits of sonoluminescence. I
was in fact more interested in finding out how Hunt would discuss the
physics and biology involved in the voice of God. How does God produce sound? Does God have vocal chords? And how would the bubbles
then create the rest of the world and human beings? But God's vocal
chords and the creating bubbles are really not what I want to discuss
here, and I really do not need nor want to disprove this student. It is the
fact that this piece was in the news and that it was presented as—
finally—the proof that the Bible "records" creation "as it happened" that
I have a problem with.

   It is this kind of approach that forces the Bible to be at the same time a
physics and biology treatise and a precise, if not autoptical, historical
account, which does in my mind "betray the text." We ask it to do something it cannot possibly do. We ask it to give us answers it cannot
possibly give us. In the first three chapters of Genesis we are looking for
explanations about how the universe came into being, how human beings
were created and with which sexual orientation, and even how the sanctity of marriage as an institution was established right there in the garden.
It's all there in one simple, linear story. But is it? Does it matter that
sexuality and marriage are not even mentioned in the garden story (and
may I add not even the word "sin"?) and that the creation of human

---

3. WKRN Broadcasting Transcript, February 25, 2007.

beings is presented in two different stories by different authors? If we look at Genesis, simplicity is not there at all, not even "in the beginning." Even the translation "in the beginning" is debated and debatable. What this news piece did—as many others before, I am sad to admit—is to help me realize once more how much we seem to have lost the ability to handle complexity and multiplicity.

The news is deceptively reassuring: it's all there in the text—just read it—as simple as that. Well, first of all we need to translate the text, and as we will see, the choices we make in the act of translation say as much about us as they do about the "text" we are translating. In this case, the "text" was written twenty-something centuries ago when the vision one had of the world looked less like today's typical picture of a global sphere (showing North America front and center) set among the stars of the universe and more like a stone table (or better yet, fragments of a stone tablet pieced together to make one) etched with pictorial representations of a relatively small geographical area, such as we might see in the Babylonian "Map of the World" fragments.[4]

The reality of the authors' perception of the world probably did not match ours. And furthermore, which story should we choose? The one in which God, after having ordered the cosmos and created vegetation, sea creatures, birds, beasts of every kind, and various creeping things finally decided to create human beings in God's image, "Male and female he created them" (Gen 1:27b)? Or the one in which God first created the Earthling (before the beasts and birds) and then decided to build a fitting match to help it?

Of course, these stories may be seen as complementary and smoothly flowing one from the other. I see it in that way too, as their intent, scope, and message are quite different. But if what we do is to read Gen 1–3 in a basic literal and linear sense, "as it is written," these inconsistencies should be a problem.

In this regard allow me to quote here the late James Barr, who could talk about these matters so much better than I could ever do. In discussing chronological dating of the origin of the world, he concluded: "It was a big mistake for many of the mainline religious organizations when they opposed the creationists by saying that the Bible should not be taken literally. This is not what creationists do. It is, on the contrary, what the churches and other organizations *should* do: that is, to argue that, in this respect, the Bible's figures *should* be taken literally, because it is when

---

4. For pictures, copies, and bibliographical references, see Wayne Horowitz, "The Babylonian Map of the World," *Iraq* 50 (1988): 147–65.

they are taken literally that it becomes clear that they are not historically or scientifically true."[5]

Of course, as I said, even when we read Genesis *literally* it also matters how we translate it. Many scholars today would agree that Adam, the first human being, should be translated into English as something like "earthling," on account of the etymological connection with אדמה, "earth, soil," and in order to avoid using the gendered word "man." However, although they purposefully choose a noun unmarked for gender, "earthling," rarely do they not fall into gendered language in the translation of the pronoun for which this noun constitutes the antecedent. Why would most scholars then choose *him* and *his* when referring to the earthling? The Hebrew language does not have a grammatical neuter, so in Hebrew a table is grammatically masculine, a stone is feminine, and pronouns agree with their grammatical gender. Every time we choose to use "it," "she," "he," "him," "her," or "its," in reference to nouns unmarked for gender in English we are making a choice. When we use "her" referring to Wisdom or Israel we are making an interpretive choice, just as we are making an interpretive choice when we choose to translate אישׁ as "wife" or "woman." As we say in Italian, every translator is a betrayer. All these issues of translation must and do come up when we read the text as meaningful to us today. Thus, this is the way in which I consciously choose to read Gen 1:26–27:

> And G-d said, Let us make an earthling in our image, after our likeness. They shall rule the fish of the sea, the birds of the sky, the cattle, the whole earth, and all the creeping things that creep upon earth. And G-d created the earthling in G-d's image, in the image of G-d G-d created it; male and female G-d created them.

This, I can live with. If this is a betrayal, as every translation is, it is one I can take. The first being, the earthling, does not need to be marked for gender, as clarified by what comes next, "male and female" (זקר ונקבה). Furthermore, this expression does not need to carry a meaning of polarization, the binary gender opposition which is often attributed to this text and is inherently exclusive. Why can it not mean, on the other hand, inclusion? That this primordial being contained plurality is suggested by the shift between singular and plural *and* by the expression זקר ונקבה God created them, all of them, male and female, meaning simply "all, in all their differences." The only other instances of this

---

5. James Barr, "The Pre-scientific Chronology: The Bible and the Origin of the World," *Proceedings of the American Philosophical Society* 143, no. 3 (1999): 386.

expression in the Hebrew Bible are in the flood story, where people and animals are chosen in pairs, male and female. Samples of "all" beings are taken into the ark. Again, inclusion is a possible view. Of course, the standard answer is "procreation." But does it have to be so? Please indulge me and let me exit the Hebrew Bible for a second and look somewhere else, in a linguistic context where procreation is not a possible reason for using the expression. In the Aramaic legal documents from Egypt, the records of a Jewish community in a military outpost, this same זכר ונקבה is used in most clauses in which heirs are involved, to clarify that when children are mentioned all of them are included, male and female. In that patriarchal context, male and female meant all, even the ones you don't think of. This is inclusion, not exclusion. Why can I not then choose to read inclusion in the Genesis text today, telling me that God created us, all of us, in all of our differences and beautiful uniquenesses as reflected in that primordial being?

When we move to the second story, God fashions the earthling and plants it in the garden. A little later God says in Gen 2:18, "It is not good for the earthling to be alone; I will make for it a helper as its match."

Even God was not sure what this helper should be, as God first made wild beasts and birds of the sky and brought them to the earthling to see if they would do. The matching/fitting helper is not marked for gender (and apparently not even for species) in the thought of God at this point. Or, if it is, in Hebrew this word עזר is masculine. And after all, it is only when other possibilities have been ruled out that God builds the woman, אשה, whom the earthling finally recognizes as bones of its bones and flesh of its flesh because "from man (איש) she was taken" (Gen 2:23b). Some feminist scholars would argue here that woman was created first, as she is the first gendered being, and that איש, who appears only after her creation is the leftover of אדם, but I don't. I am not interested in "firsts," as I think that establishing one's primacy over another only creates more problems. What I think is important to point out here is that sexuality is actually not explicitly addressed in the text. The text does not explain whether the earthling is sexually amorphous or androgynous. The interpreters choose to do so and they have done so for about two millennia. But when I read this story in my context today I choose not to read it as evoking binary sexuality. Instead I use this unmarked earthling and unmarked helper to ground my interpretation. The earthling, the primordial human being, needs a match, as we need a match to *help* us survive in this world today. This match is preferably human, of human flesh and bones. For Adam, it happened to be אשה, but for us today, does the match need to be marked for gender? I think not. Can this story mean for us today that as we yearn for companionship (sexual or emotional or otherwise), God somewhere in this world has made our match, of any race, sex, gender identity, and sexual orientation? I say yes.

Let me make it clear here that I do not think that this is what the authors intended (I actually bet they are turning in their graves right now), but I would argue that neither are the many interpretations which claim to own rights to the truth of the text what the authors intended. None of them can claim the objective truth of the text. I do not claim truth for my understanding, but this is the only possible interpretation I can live with in my context today. And frankly I do not think that in this sense such reading is any less justified than others.

But does what the biblical authors intended to say matter at all? I think so. We cannot ask them to teach us about sex and sexuality, as they did not even use such words, so we cannot presume to know what their thoughts were in this regard, and furthermore these texts are not about that.

What can we learn from them, then? Actually, a great deal. For example, as Jack Sasson would convincingly and eloquently argue, one may be about a brand new specific marking of time, and the other about the difficulty of coming to terms with our own mortality.[6] Others have argued otherwise. Let me instead go back to the differences in the two stories. It should come as no surprise that the authors present inconsistent accounts of how humanity came into being. As we have seen, their intent is not the same, whatever it is. What matters to me in this context right now is that they know better than to try to give us one linear historical account or a scientific treatise. Furthermore, if we look in the Hebrew Bible outside of Genesis we find references to primordial accounts which are not even mentioned in these first three chapters. All of these instances reveal a complex web of stories. The authors of which did not attempt to harmonize them at all, but then, why do we? If the biblical authors did not attempt to crystallize their stories of origins into one, fixed, one-size-fits-all account, why do we? After all, the existence of multiple and varied accounts of origin was not uncommon in the larger ancient Near Eastern milieu. Scholars have been aware for a long time that numerous other stories of origin existed in that context and that many of them show various degrees of similarity with the biblical accounts. For the most part, though, their intent is to reveal a connection of dependence. I am not proposing here that we do not find in Genesis echoes of Mesopotamian and, I would argue, Egyptian stories of beginnings. However, I

---

6. Jack Sasson, "Of Time and Immortality," *BR* 21, no. 3 (2005): 32–41, 52–54.

think that the effort to establish these dependences and to systematize ancient theogonies, cosmogonies, andro- and gynogonies into univocally dependent and ultimately coherent explanations of the universe brings us again to that loss, the loss of multiplicity and complexity. These stories speak to us in multiple ways, various languages, and different metaphors, but one of many things they teach us is that there is beauty—and truth—in this variety.

In Egypt, most references to cosmology are derived from funerary (pyramid or coffin) texts and the Book of the Dead. In a coffin text, as found in *The Context of Scripture: Canonical Compositions from the Biblical World*, the primordial matter says the following: "I am the waters, unique, without second. This is where I evolved on the great occasion of the floating that happened to me... I made my body evolve though my effectiveness... I am the one who made me. I built myself as I wished according to my heart."[7]

In other coffin texts, Atum brings into being the atmospheres above and below the earth (Shu and Tefnut) by alternatively sneezing or masturbating. Probably more appealing to our sensitivity is Shu's description of himself: "It is in the body of the great self-evolving god... that I have evolved for he created me in his heart, made me in his effectiveness, and exhaled me from his nose. I am exhale-like of form...I was not born by birth."

Papyrus Bremner-Rhind, for example, would be a nightmare for creationists: "I am the one who evolved (*ḫpr*) as evolver. When I evolved, evolution evolved, all evolution evolved after I evolved, evolutions becoming many in the emerging of my mouth, without the sky having evolved, without the earth having evolved, without the ground or snakes having being created in that place."

Other possibilities are around, though. The "Memphite Theology" calls the god Ptah, also self-evolving, "he who made the totality and caused the gods to evolve," and in a Ramesside stela Ptah is the one who builds people and begets gods.

Finally, we cannot forget about Amun, who in the New Kingdom rises to the position of supreme god: "He began speaking in the midst of stillness...he began evolution on the first occasion. Amun, who evolved in the beginning, with his emanation unknown, no god evolving prior to him, no other god with him to tell of his appearance, there being no

---

7. William W. Hallo and K. Lawson Younger, Jr., eds., *The Context of Scripture: Canonical Compositions, Monumental Inscriptions, and Archival Documents from the Biblical World* (Leiden: Brill, 2003), 1:6–7.

mother of his from whom his name was made and no father of his who ejaculated him so as to say—It is I."

Does any of this sound familiar? I am giving here only a mere selection of stories which describe the "origin of the universe" and in which multiple and not mutually exclusive accounts are given in texts of various nature. However, one must admit that in these accounts the gods are not much concerned with humankind (actually there is a text called the destruction of mankind, but as we are here more concerned with the creation of mankind this is beside the scope of the present essay).

It is in the Mesopotamian milieu that scholars have found more fertile terrain for "antecedents" of the Genesis stories and these may be more familiar to you. Most cited is *Enuma Elish*, also known by another title, bestowed upon it by scholars, "Epic of Creation," which makes a clear statement about their interpretation of it. This text, like the coffin spells or pyramid text *and* the biblical stories, is not meant to give us the historical or scientific ultimate account of how the universe came into being. It is in fact mainly concerned with the supremacy of Marduk or Aššur, depending on which version we choose. In the Babylonian version, after the primeval battle for supremacy is over, the young victorious male god splits the body of the primordial water creature and makes the universe out of it and the human being out of clay and blood. "I shall compact blood, I shall cause bones to be, I shall make stand a human being, let "Man" be its name. I shall create humankind, they shall bear the gods' burden that those may rest."[8]

Another story, Atraḫasis, begins by telling us "When the gods were man, they worked hard, their distress was much."[9] As other gods have posited themselves as ruling-class gods, these working gods are not happy with their lot. They complain and, under the advice of Enki, they devise to create a substitute to do their hard work. It is then decided that humanity should be created to "bear the yoke" and assume the "drudgery of god."[10] The mother goddess (Nintu) is then asked to mix clay with flesh and blood of a slain god and make the human being. Unfortunately, however, the expanding humanity was so noisy that the gods decided to destroy them. Sounds familiar?

I wish it were possible for me to provide other examples of stories of beginning, for there are many in which we would find echoes in the biblical creation accounts. These stories are beautiful, compelling, and they were true for someone somewhere. Did the biblical writers know at

8. Ibid., 1:400.
9. Ibid., 1:450.
10. Ibid., 1:451.

least some of them? Probably so. But whatever they may have borrowed from or shared with their neighbors, they made it their own, and they used their creative artistry to make their narratives meaningful to their own specific culture and their own specific time. In the telling and retelling of these stories the authors knew that for their audiences they must contribute something specific to their own context and use these stories as a means to convey the particular message that was in their intent. They were so sophisticated as to understand that, and if they could understand and handle such multiplicity of texts and complexity of meanings, why can't we?

JUDGES AS A PARODY OF LEADERSHIP IN THE PERSIAN PERIOD

Kristin A. Swanson

My very first class at Vanderbilt University as a Ph.D. student in Hebrew Bible was Doug Knight's "History of Ancient Israel." This was in August 1995, when the historiographic debate as to whether or not there was a United Monarchy and to what extent Jerusalem was an administrative center in the tenth century B.C.E. was in full tilt. We jumped right into this debate in the course, writing position papers on these and related issues. One of the assignments of the course was to read Herodotus' *The Histories* at the same time that we read scholarly arguments advocating a Persian-period (or later) date for the composition of the Hebrew Bible, with a "what happens when we do this" type of reading strategy. My classmates and I contributed to an online discussion board (new technology for the time!) with our observations and questions, which added to the experimental feel of the course. The class atmosphere was one of a partnership—we were all exploring new ideas together. I am grateful to Doug for modeling this approach for me, as the ideas I am exploring in this essay have grown out of my experience of reading biblical texts in an experimental kind of way with undergraduate students.[1]

* * *

In this essay I will explore the idea that the book of Judges is a satirical commentary on the leadership of Ezra and Levites as described in the books of Ezra and Nehemiah, particularly with regard to the policies towards "foreign" women. Since a comprehensive overview of the satirical elements of this book is beyond the scope of this essay, I will focus mainly on the use of parody in the book. The overarching theme of this parody is "leadership," which is seen in three main sections: Leadership

1. I would like to thank Kathleen Lunsford, Luther College '08, whose careful and cheerful work as my research assistant in the 2007–8 academic year contributed to this project; and to my colleague, Sean Burke, for his many helpful suggestions. Any errors are, of course, mine.

During the Conquest (Judg 1:1–3:6), Leadership During the Wars with Neighboring Enemies (Judg 3:7–16:31), and Absence of Leadership (Judg 17–21). I will argue that the author of Judges used biblical narratives and key characters from Genesis, Exodus, Joshua, and 1 Samuel to critique the leadership, and leadership decisions, described in Ezra 9–10 and Neh 8–10.[2]

As a model for this essay, I am using John Miles' article "Laughing at the Bible: Jonah as Parody."[3] In this piece, Miles made a distinction between satire, "...the exposure by comedy of behaviour which is standardized and, to that extent, foolish," and parody, "...that breed of satire in which the standardized behaviour to be exposed is literary."[4] In order for parody to function, the object of the satirical treatment must be easily recognizable; Miles argued that within the book of Jonah, this is the narrative of the prophetic career, and he finds elements of parody in five prophetic scenes:

- the call narrative;[5]
- the "...mockery of a biblical mockery; namely, the mockery of idolatry in Second Isaiah (cf. 44:15–17)"[6] as seen in the "polytheistic confusion" of the behavior of the sailors;[7]
- the psalm of thanksgiving;[8]
- the rejection of the prophet by the king;[9] and,
- the prophetic scene "in which the rejected prophet pours out his sorrow to Yahweh and is comforted."[10]

With his examination of Jonah as parody, Miles nuanced Millar Burrows' argument that the context for Jonah was the fifth-century B.C.E. conflict between those who remained in Judah after the fall of Jerusalem and the exiles who came from Babylonia;[11] Miles suggested that the

2. Unless otherwise noted all biblical quotations are from the NRSV.
3. John R. Miles, "Laughing at the Bible: Jonah as Parody," in *On Humour and the Comic in the Hebrew Bible* (ed. Yehuda T. Radday and Athalya Brenner; JSOTSup 92; Sheffield: Sheffield Academic, 1990), 203–15.
4. Ibid., 203.
5. Ibid., 205–7.
6. Ibid., 208.
7. Ibid., 207–8.
8. Ibid., 208–9.
9. Ibid., 210–11.
10. Ibid., 211–12.
11. Millar Burrows, "The Literary Category of the Book of Jonah," in *Translating and Understanding the Old Testament: Essays in Honor of Herbert Gordon May* (ed. Harry Thomas Frank and William L. Reed; Nashville: Abingdon, 1970), 80–107.

target of the satire was those among the Babylonian exiles "who were serious in a new, and, to some, unwelcome way about the religious writings of Israel."[12] He stated in a footnote, "My interpretation of the book of Jonah does indeed view it as a plea for greater internationalism. An attack, however comic, on the national literature is an attack on national pride."[13] He emphasized that all parties within the story are objects of the satirical commentary; that "...if Jonah is foolish in his resentment, the Ninevites, dressing their animals in sackcloth and forcing them to fast, have been foolish in their repentance."[14]

Judges, like Jonah, uses the "national literature" to critique leadership. Also like Jonah, no character comes out unscathed in the critique.

Leadership During the Conquest

Judah: The "Anti-Joshua"

The first section of the book of Judges (1:1–3:6) gives a description of the conquest of the land by the Israelite tribes under the leadership of Judah, as well as the result of the conquest. What is "easily recognizable" here as the object of parody is the conquest narrative found in the book of Joshua. The very beginning of Judges reads "After the death of Joshua...," which invites the reader to make a comparison between Judah's leadership in the book of Judges, and Joshua's leadership of the Israelites in the book of Joshua, which begins "After the death of Moses..." In Judges, the narrative begins with the Israelites inquiring of the LORD, "who shall go up first for us against the Canaanites, to fight against them?" (v. 1b). The answer: "Judah shall go up. I hereby give the land into his hand" (v. 2). Judah then allies with his brother Simeon to take each of their allotted territories. When this brief narrative is compared with Joshua's conquest of the land and defeat of enemy kings, Judah emerges as a kind of "anti-Joshua" figure; whereas Judah allies with only Simeon, Joshua's efforts are in conjunction with "all Israel" (10:29, 31, 34, 36, 38, 43). Judah sets out to take "his" allotted territory; Joshua "defeated the whole land, the hill country and the Negeb and the lowland and the slopes, and all their kings; he left no-one remaining, but utterly destroyed all that breathed, as the LORD God of Israel commanded" (10:40). This conquest was for the benefit of "all Israel."

12. Miles, "Laughing at the Bible," 204–5.
13. Ibid., 213 n. 1.
14. Ibid., 215.

Following the episode of the conquest of Kiriath-sepher (narrated in both Judg 1:12–15 and Josh 15:16–19), where Caleb offers his daughter Achsah as a prize to whoever takes the city, the remainder of Judg 1 is a recital of the lack of success of the rest of the Israelite tribes to take their allotted territories; the refrains "X did not drive out Y..." and "the Canaanites lived among them..." are repeated throughout. In the book of Joshua, what follows the Achsah narrative is a recital of the allotment of territory (taken earlier by Joshua with "all Israel") to the various tribes. Within this recital we find similar language that is used within portions of Judg 1; for example, at the end of the description of the boundaries of the territory allotted to Ephraim in Josh 16, it states as an aside "They did not, however, drive out the Canaanites who lived in Gezer; so the Canaanites have lived with Ephraim to this day but have been made to do forced labor" (v. 16). Despite the continued Canaanite presence, the conquest was still successful in that the Ephraimite territory was established. In Judg 1:29 it states, "Ephraim did not drive out the Canaanites who lived in Gezer; but the Canaanites lived among them in Gezer." Since this is the only reference to the territory of Ephraim, and is part of the description of a conquest as opposed to land allotment, the comparison with Joshua highlights the lack of a successful takeover of the land.

To summarize thus far: Judg 1, when read as a parody of Josh 10–19, portrays Judah as a type of "anti-Joshua" figure: Judah only allies with his brother Simeon (as opposed to leading "all Israel"); he is concerned only with his own territorial allotment; and, because of an "every tribe for itself" approach to the conquest of the land, the conquest is unsuccessful.[15]

It is this unsuccessful conquest that leads to the next major section within the introduction of Judges. Judges 2:11–3:6 describes the result of the Israelites' unsuccessful attempt to evict the Canaanites from the land: the Israelites abandoned the LORD and worshiped other gods, so that the LORD sold them into the hands of neighboring enemies. What follows is a synopsis of the section to come: the LORD would raise up a deliverer

---

15. This reading is contrary to Marc Zvi Brettler, "The Book of Judges: Literature as Politics," *JBL* 108, no. 3 (1989): 395–418. Brettler argued that the major theme of the introduction of Judges is the supremacy of Judah, due to the fact that Judah was successful, whereas the other tribes were unsuccessful in their attempt to dispossess the previous inhabitants of the land. Combined with what Brettler argued are pro-Judean biases in the middle and appendix sections of Judges, he suggested that the interpretation of this book articulates that the Davidic monarchy (as opposed to that of Saul) was the legitimate monarchy. See also Tammi J. Schneider, *Judges* (Berit Olam: Studies in Hebrew Narrative and Poetry; Collegeville: Liturgical, 2000).

who would save them from their enemies, but then the Israelites would relapse and worship other gods, bringing on the cycle once again. The result was the LORD's decision to "no longer drive out before them any of the nations that Joshua left when he died" (v. 21). In Judg 3:5–6 (the end of the section), these nations living in the land are specified as the Canaanites, the Hittites, the Amorites, the Perizzites, the Hivites, and the Jebusites, whose daughters the Israelites took as wives, and to whom the Israelites gave their daughters. So, as a result of the failed conquest under Judah's leadership, the Israelites followed other gods; the LORD did not drive out the previous inhabitants; and the Israelites intermarried with them.

When this section is read alongside of Josh 23–24 (the section following the allotment of land to the tribes), it once again highlights Judah's failure as a leader. In these chapters, Joshua addresses "all Israel" (23:2) and leads them in a ceremony before the LORD at Shechem. In his address, Joshua warns the Israelites not to follow other gods (23:7), and that if they intermarry, the LORD will not continue to drive out the inhabitants of the land (vv. 12–13). The people's response: "The LORD our God we will serve, and him we will obey" (24:24). Whereas in the book of Joshua, Joshua's leadership brings the people to accept the LORD, in Judges, Judah's leadership leads the people to follow other gods and intermarry.

Leadership During the Wars Against Neighboring Enemies

A full treatment of the central section of the book of Judges is beyond the scope of this essay. Here I will look at three representative narrative examples in which the subject of parody is a key biblical character: David, Moses, and Samuel.

Ehud: The "anti-David"
Nowhere in the book of Judges are satirical elements more prominent than in the episode of Ehud's battle against the Moabites (Judg 3:12–30).[16] In this narrative, Ehud, a left-handed "right-hander" (reading "Benjamin" as "son of the right") kills King Eglon, the very fat king of Moab (whose name in fact means "fatted calf") while the king is using the toilet. The king is so fat that the hilt of the sword disappears after the blade, and the contents of his bowels come out. Ehud manages to escape

---

16. For an examination of the Ehud narrative as satire, see Marc Zvi Brettler, *The Creation of History in Ancient Israel* (London: Routledge, 1995), 79–90.

and rally the Israelite troops because Eglon's courtiers think that he is taking a long time in the toilet. Within this narrative, we find wordplays, crude humor, and absurd situations, which ridicule both the Moabite king and the Israelite leader. While the fat King Eglon is killed in an undignified way, Ehud, an already marginalized character because of his left-handedness, ends up, presumably, with feces on his "bathroom hand"—hardly a dignified figure himself.

When the element of parody is introduced, the critique of leadership is further emphasized. With the central focus of this episode on Ehud's dispatch of Eglon while he is relieving himself, one is reminded of the episode in which David decides not to kill King Saul while Saul is relieving himself in a cave (1 Sam 24). Previous to this episode, Saul had been repeatedly trying to kill David; with this situation, David has the opportunity to kill Saul. Instead, he stealthily cuts off the corner of Saul's garment, and shows it to him later on in hopes of brokering a truce by showing that he had spared Saul's life.

When these two narratives are compared, Ehud appears ruthless as well as marginal and undignified. Rather than using Eglon's compromised position as a means by which to negotiate a truce (as in the example given by David), Ehud uses deceit to gain access to the king in order to kill him. In this episode in Judges, the divinely appointed deliverer is deceitful and ruthless.

Gideon: The "Anti-Moses"
Earlier I suggested that satirical elements are most prominent in the Ehud narrative; here I would suggest that the satirical elements in the narratives about Gideon are the most entertaining! In the three chapters that narrate Gideon's leadership of the Israelites against the Midianite oppression (Judg 6–8), we encounter not just examples of parody but a variety of improbable situations. Reducing the Israelite army (so that the LORD can take credit for victory) by watching his warriors drink from a river, then choosing those that lap like dogs (7:2–8); a dream of a tumbling barley cake destroying the Midianite camp (7:9–14); and an attack on the Midianite camp in which the Israelites arrive laden with trumpets and jars which they have to break in order to retrieve torches from inside the jars, which one would expect to be extinguished if they are in a closed jar (7:15–23)—when read with an eye for satire, these episodes resemble a playful spoof on Israelite warfare as opposed to a serious battle account.

There are also two clear examples of parody, in which Gideon is contrasted with the character of Moses. The first of these is Gideon's call

(6:11–24).[17] The fact that there is a call narrative alerts the reader to the potential for parody, since no other judge up to this point (or afterwards) is called to the leadership position after the manner of a prophet. Previous to the actual call narrative is a fairly lengthy description of the Midianite oppression (6:1–6), and a speech made by a prophet of the LORD (6:7–10) in which the prophet reminds the Israelites that the LORD brought them out of Egypt. Both of these give a clue that the call is a parody of Moses' call in Exod 3.

In the Judges passage, Gideon is approached by a messenger of the LORD while beating wheat in a wine press. When the messenger of the LORD first acknowledges Gideon as a leader and tells him that the LORD is with him, Gideon seems to sass him with the response, "…if the LORD is with us, why then has all of this happened to us? And where are all his wonderful deeds that our ancestors recounted to us…?" (v. 13). When the messenger responds with the specific task, Gideon, on cue for a call narrative, objects, and then demands a sign from the messenger. It is only after the sign is completed that Gideon acknowledges the messenger as an agent of the LORD, at which point he cries out to the LORD for help, fearful because he has seen the angel of the LORD face to face. After the actual call, Gideon is instructed to tear down his father's altar to Baal and Asherah, and to build an altar to the LORD. Gideon does these things, but at night, because he is fearful; and when the townspeople seek his life the next morning, it is his father who defends him, rather than Gideon defending himself.

When this call narrative is compared with Moses' call in Exod 3, Gideon, like Ehud, emerges as a flawed leader. At the beginning of Moses' call, Moses sees a burning bush and goes to investigate. Whereas Gideon is immediately depicted as fearful (beating wheat in a wine press for fear of the Midianites), Moses is not at all fearful of the strange phenomenon of a non-consumed burning bush. Gideon is sarcastic and confrontational when the messenger first approaches him; Moses, on the other hand, hides his face as soon as he realizes that the bush is a theophany. Both Gideon and Moses protest the call (Moses several times!); what is different is that Gideon requires a sign from the messenger, whereas the LORD provides Moses with signs as assurance that the LORD will be with him. Following the call, Gideon follows the LORD's

---

17. Cf. Schneider, *Judges*, 103–9; also, Gregory T. K. Wong, "Gideon: A New Moses?," in *Reflection and Refraction: Studies in Biblical Historiography in Honour of A. Graeme Auld* (ed. Robert Rezetko, Timothy H. Lim, and W. Brian Aucker; Leiden: Brill, 2007), 529–44.

instructions, but fearfully; Moses (once he survives God's attempt on his life in Exod 4) immediately assembles the Israelites, establishes himself as their leader, and confronts the Pharaoh boldly. Despite his protestations (which occur in the "appropriate" place in a call narrative!), Moses is fearless and bold when confronting the oppressor, and deferential and fearful in the LORD's presence; Gideon is fearful to the point of cowardice both before and after his actual call, and inappropriately bold and confrontational with the messenger of the LORD.

The second clear example of parody occurs near the end of the Gideon narrative, after the Midianites have been routed. Gideon requests from each of the Israelites one golden earring that they have taken as booty; once these are collected he then makes an ephod, and sets it up in his hometown of Ophrah, where "...all Israel prostituted themselves to it..." (8:27). This is a clear reference to the incident in Exod 32 when Moses' brother Aaron makes a golden calf which the Israelites worship while Moses is up on the mountain receiving the law. As a result of this, the LORD says to Moses, "Now let me alone, so that my wrath may burn hot against them and I may consume them; and of you I will make a great nation" (Exod 32:10). Moses intercedes for the Israelites, descends the mountain, destroys the calf, and, with the assistance of the sons of Levi, kills three thousand of the Israelites, leaving the LORD to punish the rest with a plague (Exod 32:11–35).

The comparison is stark—whereas Moses intervenes and intercedes for the Israelites after they have committed idolatry behind his back, Gideon is the cause of the idolatry.

Samson: The "Anti-Samuel"

Here I will focus primarily on the annunciation narrative contained within Judg 13. Very early in the episode we are introduced to the future mother of Samson, who is referred to as the wife of Manoah; the first thing we are told is that she is barren. A messenger of the LORD appears to her, and tells her that she will conceive a child, and instructs her not to drink wine or strong drink, nor to bring a razor upon the child's head, as he is to be a Nazirite to God. When she reports this visit to her husband, she states, "a man of God came to me, and his appearance was like that of an angel of God, most awe-inspiring; I did not ask him where he came from, and he did not tell me his name..." (13:6). Reading with the sexual innuendo of the verb "to come"[18] suggests that Manoah's wife is relating an incident of anonymous sex to her husband; Manoah's response is to

18. Cf. Lillian R. Klein, *The Triumph of Irony in the Book of Judges* (JSOTSup 68; Sheffield: Sheffield Academic, 1988), 114.

pray to the LORD to let the man return. In v. 9, "...the angel of God came again to the woman while she was in the field." When Manoah finally meets the messenger, he offers him food, which the messenger refuses; Manoah then offers a kid and a grain offering as a burnt offering, and the messenger ascends with the flame. Only then does Manoah realize that the man was a messenger of the LORD.

Satirical elements abound in this passage. In addition to crude humor in the form of sexual innuendo (repeated twice!), Manoah's character is dim-witted to the point of exaggeration; he neither realizes the implications of what his wife related to him about the visit in the field, nor does he recognize the messenger of the LORD until a miraculous event occurs. Parodic elements also abound. Reading with the sexual innuendo, Gen 6:1–4 immediately comes to mind, where divine creatures have intercourse with human women, thus leading to God's decision to wipe out humanity with the flood. With this reference, the reader can anticipate the havoc that Samson will wreak in the following chapters as he has vengeful rage attacks against the Philistines and chases Philistine women, resulting in his capture and humiliation by the Philistines.

This passage also calls to mind the annunciation of the birth of Isaac in Gen 18. In the case of Abraham and Sarah, two messengers of God visit Abraham (not Sarah), and make the announcement that she will bear a son. Abraham prepares a meal for the messengers, which they eat. When this is compared with Judg 13, the satirical elements described above, particularly the sexual humor, are highlighted.

The clearest parallel with Judg 13 is the narrative of the annunciation of the birth of Samuel in 1 Sam 1. In this passage, Hannah, the wife of Elkanah, is distraught because of her inability to bear a child, as well as the fact that Elkanah's other wife, Peninnah, has borne children. During their annual trip to sacrifice at Shiloh, Hannah goes to the temple and makes a vow that if she conceives and bears a son, she will dedicate him to the LORD. The priest Eli, observing her silent prayer, takes her to be drunk and scolds her, but when he hears her plight, he announces that her petition has been heard. Both the Judges and 1 Samuel passages contain the announcement of the birth of a son to a barren woman, and in both cases the announcement is made directly to the woman. In 1 Samuel, this announcement comes from Eli the priest after Hannah has prayed to the LORD at Shiloh and promised the child to the LORD's service; in the Judges passage the announcement is made after a possible sexual encounter between the woman and a messenger of God. In both narratives the child in question is dedicated to the LORD, with the obligation that no razor should touch his head; in 1 Samuel, Hannah offers this as a vow, whereas in Judges the messenger of God gives this as a command to Manoah's wife. In addition, both passages contain references to wine and strong drink—Eli initially accuses Hannah of being drunk, whereas Manoah's wife is commanded by the messenger not to partake of these beverages.

When these two biblical characters are compared, the parody becomes clear. Whereas Samuel delivers Israel from the Philistines through a burnt offering, crying out to the LORD, and setting up a memorial "helping stone" to commemorate the LORD's victory against the Philistines (1 Sam 7:5–14), Samson, the Nazirite who seems to break his vows by partying with Philistines and going near corpses by creating them at every turn, puts the Israelites at risk through his interactions with the Philistines.

Absence of Leadership

The concluding section of Judges (chs. 17–21) is marked by an absence of leaders. The cycle of apostasy, punishment, crying out, and deliverance through a leader is now over—instead, we have a series of stories in which Levites play key roles.

It is in this section of Judges that contextual clues may be found. Rather than read the repeated refrain, "There was no king in Israel" (17:6; 18:1; 19:1; 21:25), as a commentary on the Israelites' poor state of affairs because there was no monarchy (and therefore with a pro-monarchy stance), I would suggest that the refrain be read as descriptive of context, that is, as a clue to place this text and the satirical commentary it contains within a context when there was no king in Israel—the Persian period. In order to illustrate this further, I will focus primarily on the narrative of the Levite and his concubine (Judg 19) and the ensuing war between the Benjaminites and the other Israelite tribes (Judg 20–21).

The Levite: The "Anti-messenger of God"
The satire takes a dark and violent turn with the narrative of the Levite and his concubine. In this story, a "certain Levite" has a concubine, a woman from Judah, who leaves him to go to her father's house. Four months later the Levite comes after her, and her father entertains him and urges him to stay. However, he and the concubine end up leaving late in the day on the fifth day, so that it was necessary to spend the night away from home. Refusing to spend the night in a "city of foreigners, who do not belong to the people of Israel" (v. 12), they stop at Gibeah, in the territory of Benjamin, where an old man takes them in. That night the

men of the city surround the house, intending to rape the Levite; instead, the concubine is thrown out to the crowd, and gang-raped all night. In the morning, the Levite comes outside, tells her to get up, and when she does not, loads her on the donkey and takes her home. He then proceeds to chop her into pieces and sends a piece to the tribes of Israel in order to muster them to fight against the Benjaminites.

Of all the examples of parody examined in this essay, this has the most direct parallels with other biblical narratives, particularly with Gen 19:1–14. In Gen 19, two messengers of the LORD arrive in Sodom; when Lot sees them, he invites them to stay with him, but they refuse, saying that they will spend the night in the square. Lot persuades them to come into his house, but before they settle in for the night the men of Sodom surround the house with the intention of raping the messengers. Lot goes outside and offers his virgin daughters instead, but when they press against Lot, the messengers snatch Lot back inside and strike the men with blindness.

When this narrative is compared with Judg 19, the character of the Levite comes into stark contrast with the messengers. In both of these narratives, travelers are in a strange place with nowhere to stay. However, in the Genesis story, the angels are unafraid, and almost seem to prefer the option of staying in the square—it is Lot who approaches them, and has to urge them to stay with him. The Levite, on the other hand, seems to expect hospitality, and hangs around in the square until someone offers to take him in.

The next scene is strikingly similar in each narrative: the men of the city surround the house and demand that the host bring out the male traveler(s) so that they can rape him/them. In each story, the host addresses the men, calls them "my brothers," and offers a substitute—the virgin daughters in the case of Gen 19 and the host's virgin daughter and the Levite's concubine in Judg 19. What follows is the defining difference—whereas in Gen 19 the messengers rescue Lot and avoid the rape of the daughters, in Judg 19, the Levite puts his concubine outside were she is gang-raped until morning.

The following section, in which the concubine is dismembered, is a parody of 1 Sam 11:1–14, in which Saul chops up a yoke of oxen and sends the pieces to the Israelite tribes in order to muster them for battle against the Ammonites. Through this comparison the already horrifying dismemberment of the concubine is made even worse; she is treated like an animal.

Through this use of parody, the author of Judges portrays the Levite in an extremely unflattering light. In Gen 19, the messengers are brave, independent, and fast-acting in their rescue of others. By contrast, the

Levite is cowardly, selfish, and despicable in his treatment of the woman.[19]

The Conquest, Revisited

The final two chapters of Judges (a continuation of the narrative of the Levite and his concubine) mirror the opening of the book. Once the tribes are assembled at Mizpah and hear the Levite's version of the events in Gibeah, the tribes demand that the offenders be handed over. The residents of Gibeah refuse, and the Benjaminites organize an army; the rest of the tribes inquire of God, "Which of us shall go up first to battle against the Benjaminites?" The answer is parallel to Judg 1:2: "Judah shall go up first" (20:18). As the story continues, the Israelites are initially unsuccessful and suffer heavy losses against the Benjaminites. However, through a successful ambush, the Israelite tribes almost decimate their fellow tribe, then are remorseful and decide to allow them to repopulate; however, there is a problem, because the remaining tribes had taken an oath at Mizpah not to give their daughters to Benjamin (Judg 21:1). The first attempt at a solution is to wipe out the inhabitants of Jabesh-gilead (who did not turn out to fight against Benjamin) except for the virgins, who are given to the Benjaminites (21:8–14). When this proves to be insufficient, they allow the Benjaminites to raid a harvest festival at Shiloh and abduct women for themselves (21:15–24).

As with the rest of the book, satirical elements are clearly present in these final chapters. Blenkinsopp has noted parallels between Judg 21:1–14 (the annihilation of Jabesh-gilead to procure wives) and Moses' war of extermination against Midian in Num 31, as well as between Judg 20:29–48 (the ambush against the Benjaminites) and Joshua's tactics in destroying Ai in Josh 8:10–29.[20] In addition, exaggeration and absurd

---

19. See also Stuart Lasine, "Guest and Host in Judges 19: Lot's Hospitality in an Inverted World," *JSOT* 29 (1984): 37–59. Lasine argued that a comparison of Judg 19 with Gen 19 and 1 Sam 11 exposes the Levite as cowardly, callous, oblivious, and dishonest (50), in order "...to 'correct' a warped perspective toward the social category of hospitality" (46). Lasine argues that Judg 19 is not a parody of Gen 19, since a parody would use Gen 19 for "literary humor" (citing Miles); however, at other points in his study, Lasine referred to "the subtle use of irony and absurd humor" (38) on the part of the narrator of Judges, and the dismembering of the concubine as "black humor" (45).

20. J. Blenkinsopp, "Benjamin Traditions Read in the Early Persian Period," in *Judah and the Judeans in the Persian Period* (ed. Oded Lipschits and Manfred Oeming; Winona Lake: Eisenbrauns 2006), 641. Blenkinsopp suggests that Judg 19–21 may reflect Judean–Benjaminite hostilities in the early Persian period, but does not read these chapters as a satirical commentary.

situations are present in the gross numbers of casualties in the battle, the instant remorse and decision to repopulate Benjamin, and the appalling level of violence in this undertaking.

Context

As noted above, I would argue that the concluding section of Judges provides clues to read this book in a Persian-period context. First, the internal reference of Judg 20:18 to Judg 1:2 ties these sections together, and in so doing, problematizes the question of "who is the other?" In Judg 1, Judah is called to fight against the Canaanites, and at the end of the introduction we are told that the Israelites lived among the Canaanites, the Hittites, the Amorites, the Perizzites, the Hivites, and the Jebusites, intermarried with them, and worshiped their gods. In Judg 20, Judah is called to fight against the Benjaminites, to whom the rest of the Israelite tribes had pledged not to give their daughters as wives. When read together, along with the emphasis throughout the book on the Israelites' flawed leadership, the author seems to be suggesting that these categories of "foreign" and "Israelite" are very fluid, if not specious.

Second, when these two themes, the formulaic list of the inhabitants of the land, and the concern with intermarriage, are understood as a satirical commentary in Judges, they seem to ridicule the leadership decisions of Ezra (along with the Levites, at points), as described in Neh 8–10 and Ezra 9–10.

In Neh 8–10, a ceremony is described, led by Ezra (ch. 8) and the Levites (ch. 9, reading with MT). In ch. 8, the people of Israel are gathered into a square, where Ezra reads "the book of the law of Moses" to them. The Levites "…helped the people to understand the law, while the people remained in their places. So they read from the book, from the law of God, with interpretation. They gave the sense, so that the people understood the reading" (8:7–8). In ch. 9, the Levites give, in summary form, a recital of the acts of the LORD from creation onward. Near the beginning of the recital is the formulaic list of inhabitants, whose land the LORD promised to Abraham (v. 8). At the end of the recital, "…all who have separated themselves from the peoples of the lands to adhere to the law of God…" (v. 28) are called upon to make an oath to observe the LORD's commandments. The first specific commandment given is to not give their daughters to the peoples of the land or take their daughters for their sons.

These same themes appear in Ezra 9–10. At the beginning of ch. 9, Ezra is approached by an official who reports that "…the people of

Israel, the priests and the Levites, have not separated themselves from the peoples of the lands with their abominations, from the Canaanites, the Hittites, the Perizzites, the Jebusites, the Ammonites, the Moabites, the Egyptians, and the Amorites. For they have taken some of their daughters as wives for themselves, and for their sons" (9:1b–2a). Ezra has a strong reaction to the news—he rends his garment, pulls his hair out, fasts, then prays and makes a confession while weeping and throwing himself down. A crowd gathers, and one Shecaniah, son of Jehiel, suggests that they make a covenant with God to send away the wives and children. Ezra then makes the leading priests, Levites, and all Israel swear to do this. Next, Ezra assembles all the returned exiles with the threat that any who did not show up within three days would lose their property and be banned from the community. In the heavy rain, Ezra directs the assembly to separate themselves from "...the peoples of the land and from the foreign wives" (10:11b).

The author of Judges is taking three aspects of these two narratives to task. When the exiles are commanded to separate themselves from the "peoples of the land" and "foreign wives," the author of Judges, through the parallel conquest narrative of Canaanites/Benjaminites, seems to be pointing out that those so-called foreigners are, in fact, fellow Israelites. As to the pledge not to intermarry, the author seems to suggest that such pledges are ridiculous when the so-called foreigners may not even be foreign, and will likely be circumvented anyway. Was it really so honorable to abide by the pledge not to give wives to the Benjaminites, when the alternative was the annihilation of Jabesh-gilead and the abduction and rape of women at a harvest festival? Regarding the directive for men to separate themselves from their "foreign" wives, the author of Judges, through the dark and violent satire of ch. 19, seems to point out the cruel and terrifying effect that such a policy would have on the women who were sent away, without the protection of home and husband. The irony is that the Levite's concubine was, in fact, from Judah. One wonders if the author, with a nudge and a wink, left the "certain Levite" unnamed on purpose, so that we read this character as Ezra?

Conclusion

In this essay I have explored the idea that the book of Judges, as a coherent literary unit with an overarching theme of "leadership," is a satirical commentary on the leadership decisions of Ezra (and the Levites) as described in Neh 8–10 and Ezra 9–10. A key element of this satire is the parody of key biblical themes (conquest, warfare) and biblical characters (Joshua, David, Moses, and Samuel). At the heart of this critique is the identification and exclusion of so-called foreign women from the community, described particularly in Ezra 9–10. Read in this manner, Judges provides another perspective in the Persian-period debates concerning identity and community, and gives a voice to the women of Ezra 9–10.

THE PERSIAN PERIOD AND THE SHAPING OF PROPHETIC LITERATURE

Robert R. Wilson

In recent years there has been an increasing tendency to date the literature of the Old Testament to the Exilic period, the Persian period, or even later. Given this tendency, it is not surprising that scholars have begun to suggest that the prophetic literature too comes from a relatively late period. The most extreme form of this point of view is to be found among scholars who have rejected traditional claims that the oral oracles of the biblical prophets were collected during their lifetimes by the prophets' disciples and then eventually recorded in written form. Rather, these scholars claim that the picture of biblical prophecy now found in the text is a relatively late creation and that the prophetic literature itself came into existence only at a late date.

This extreme view of the composition of the prophetic literature can be traced to the work of A. Graeme Auld, who almost twenty years ago argued that the traditional biblical picture of the Israelite prophet could be seen in the process of formation in the various literary layers of the book of Jeremiah. In the earliest layers of the book, created during Jeremiah's own lifetime in the preexilic period, the title "prophet" was rarely used, and when it did appear, it carried only negative associations. Later, in the book's exhortatory prose, the title was used neutrally, while in still later prose, Jeremiah himself was called a prophet. All of this suggested to Auld that Jeremiah's prophetic oracles should simply be regarded as poetry, while prophecy as a literary form should be considered to be a relatively late phenomenon and dated to the Exilic period, the Persian period, or even later.[1]

Auld's suggestion was immediately accepted and developed by Robert P. Carroll, who also considered the biblical picture of Jeremiah's prophetic activity to be unreliable and to be a retrojection from a time much

---

1. A. Graeme Auld, "Prophets Through the Looking Glass: Between the Writings and Moses," *JSOT* 27 (1983): 3–23.

later than the prophet's own lifetime. The prophet Jeremiah was simply a poet, and the book bearing his name should therefore be studied only as literature.[2]

While Auld and Carroll reached their conclusions about the late dating of the prophetic literature on the basis of an internal analysis of the literature itself, the question of dating soon became a part of a broader discussion of the role of writing in the formation of the biblical text as it now exists. The first major step in this direction was taken by Philip R. Davies, who argued that the creation of all authoritative written religious texts in Israel was a relatively late phenomenon. Davies believes that there is little evidence of a formal educational system in Israel before the eighth century B.C.E., and that even then literacy was confined to court and temple circles. The actual production of written texts and the assembly of those texts into collections were even later, in the Persian period at the earliest. Writing was the property of scribal elites, who created texts to serve their own interests and those of the government and the temple. He is a bit vague about just what those interests might have been, but he is clear that the texts were not intended to be read by common people. In general Davies argues that the Hebrew Bible was the creation of the scribes, who worked on behalf of the ruling elites and crafted materials to keep them in power.[3]

With respect to the prophetic literature, Davies does believe that in Israel during the preexilic period there were religious figures who delivered divine messages orally to human beings and particularly to the king, although Davies avoids applying the label "prophet" to these figures. He also suggests that letters reporting these oracles might have occasionally been sent to the king and that these letters might have been filed in the royal archives under the name of the sender or under the name of the intermediary. Davies also suspects that in time oracles from a single individual might have been copied onto a single scroll for convenience in filing, although these scrolls would have in no way resembled a biblical prophetic book. In the Persian period or later, as

2. Robert P. Carroll, "Poets Not Prophets," *JSOT* 27 (1983): 25–31.

3. Philip R. Davies, *Scribes and Schools: The Canonization of the Hebrew Scriptures* (Louisville: Westminster John Knox, 1998). Throughout his discussion Davies seems to consider the role of oral tradition to be of little importance. For a more sophisticated discussion of the relationship between oral and written literary transmission in ancient Israel, see Susan Niditch, *Oral World and Written Word* (Louisville: Westminster John Knox, 1996); and James Crenshaw, "Transmitting Prophecy across Generations," in *Writings and Speech in Israelite and Ancient Near Eastern Prophecy* (ed. Ehud Ben Zvi and Michael H. Floyd; Atlanta: SBL, 2000), 31–44.

Israelites began to be more interested in creating a national history, the oracle collections were filled out with historical information to provide the oracles with a context, and at the same time some of the oracles themselves made their way into Israel's historical narratives, eventually creating the sort of prophetic stories now found in the books of Samuel and Kings.[4]

Since Davies's initial study of the role of scribes in the formation of Old Testament literature, this subject has received considerable scholarly attention. In particular, William M. Schniedewind, David M. Carr, and Karel van der Toorn have recently produced major treatments of the issue. These treatments pay much more attention to the ancient Near Eastern context of Israelite scribal activity than does Davies, and perhaps for this reason all three of these scholars provide a more nuanced and moderate view of scribal influence than the one Davies provides.

In contrast to Davies, William Schniedewind's account of text production, *How the Bible Became a Book*, is much more restrained and tries harder to engage what is known of Israel's history. However, his starting point is the same as that of Davies: writing is intimately connected with highly developed forms of government. "Nowhere did writing flourish in the ancient Near East without the auspices of the state."[5] This means that for Schniedewind historical periods marked by strong hierarchical government and a vibrant economy were also periods that saw an increase in literary production. Conversely, when the government became unstable and the economy declined, text production also declined or ceased altogether.

According to Schniedewind, the first scribes were royal scribes, and their job was to produce texts of all sorts that were needed to sustain their royal employers. The first signs of scribal activity in Israel were thus in the early monarchical period, and Schniedewind believes that text production, however rudimentary, started in the Davidic court. However, he argues that the real beginning of written biblical literature was in the time of Hezekiah, when political and economic conditions encouraged the king to expand and to strengthen the Judean state. Hezekiah's royal scribes created the first real biblical literature in order to support the king's ambitions. According to Prov 25:1, the "Men of Hezekiah" collected the proverbs of Solomon, and Schniedewind suggests that they collected other Solomonic material as well—the Song of Songs and

---

4. Philip R. Davies, "'Pen of Iron, Point of Diamond' (Jer. 17:1): Prophecy as Writing," in Ben Zvi and Floyd, eds., *Writings and Speech*, 65–81.

5. William M. Schniedewind, *How the Bible Became a Book* (Cambridge: Cambridge University Press, 2004), 35.

perhaps even Qohelet. Stories of the "golden age" of David and Solomon and the special divine favor they enjoyed may have also been shaped at this time. The scribal interest in these early kings was more than historical. There was a deliberate attempt to suggest that Hezekiah was a new David and perhaps even a new Solomon who would for the first time in years rule over a restored Davidic empire. To make the point even clearer, prophetic texts, such as Isaiah, may have been produced by Hezekiah's scribes to emphasize the pro-monarchical themes of the divine protection of Zion and divine support for the Davidic royal line. The same point was made in another way by the first edition of the book of Kings (and perhaps even more of the Deuteronomistic History), which was designed to show how Hezekiah avoided the mistakes of previous kings and ruled over a nation that was divinely protected. Other prophetic literature and the beginnings of the writing of the Torah may also have been a part of the literary explosion produced by Hezekiah's scribes.

Later, the same political use of literary materials can be seen in the time of Josiah, in whose time a book of Mosaic Law was found in the temple, presumably the first edition of Deuteronomy. This book then became the basis of Josiah's religious reform, which had both theological and political dimensions. However, with Josiah the arena of text production began to expand. No longer were texts simply the production of royal scribes. Rather, the book found in the temple was the creation of priests, or at least of scribes associated with the temple. Scribes were now using writing to advance the interests of the religious establishment, and the stage was set for future conflicts between the interests of the royal scribes and the interests of the temple scribes.

Literary production in Judah continued up to the destruction of the city by the Babylonians. However, according to Schniedewind, the literature produced by the scribes in this period had a different function. By extending earlier versions of Kings and by shaping books like Jeremiah, the scribes provided an explanation for the fall of Jerusalem and also demonstrated divine support for the exiled Judean king and the Judean community in Babylon. Because of the pro-monarchical tone of this literature, Schniedewind thinks that the exiled royal family and displaced state officials might have had a hand in preserving preexilic textual material in some sort of royal archive. However that may be, with the cessation of the monarchy literary production also ceased. It would not resume again until the period of the restoration, when the scribes would again produce literature that undergirded the embryo state. Although the scribes at first tried to produce literature that would support the reestablishment of the Davidic monarchy, they eventually turned to producing literature in the service of the emerging religious community. However, the process was slow. The nation and the economy were slow to recover, and so was literary production. At this point Schniedewind's reconstruction differs markedly from that of Davies. Whereas for Davies the Persian period was a hotbed of literary activity, for Schniedewind this period was relatively calm. When literary production finally did resume, the texts that the scribes produced had a very different form than the ones produced in the preexilic period, a fact missed entirely by Davies.[6]

Although David Carr's 2005 book, *Writing on the Tablet of the Heart: Origins of Scripture and Literature*, also stresses the centrality of scribes in the creation of biblical texts, he takes an approach that is rather different from that of Davies or Schniedewind.[7] According to his preface, Carr's interest in scribal activity grew in the first place out of his earlier work on Genesis and the formation of the Pentateuch. He is thus interested in how early material gets passed on and eventually joined to later material. In the second place, though, he is interested in the role that oral materials play in the process of text production and how texts interact in various ways with oral materials. Here he is responding to the work of Niditch and trying to incorporate her research into his reflections on the growth of the biblical text.[8] He pulls these strands together in a very complex and creative way. His analysis is too complicated and rich to be outlined easily, but the following major points need to be noted.

Carr prefaces his treatment of Israelite education and scribal activity with a thorough treatment of education and scribal training in three other ancient cultures: Mesopotamia and Egypt, where the writing systems were complex and where we know a great deal about scribal training, and Greece, where the writing system was much simpler and where again we know much about the educational process. His treatment of this comparative material is quite detailed, but he makes the following general observations. In both Mesopotamia and Egypt scribes were trained under the auspices of the state and the temple, which were the primary employers of scribes. Training in languages and writing was rigorous, and it involved a great deal of rote memorization. However, the students in the schools did not just memorize the forms of sample documents or lists of words and their equivalents, although they certainly did do that. They also wrote and memorized classic texts from earlier times. Indeed, Carr claims that students who wrote texts often did so from memory,

---

6. Ibid.
7. David M. Carr, *Writing on the Tablet of the Heart: Origins of Scripture and Literature* (Oxford: Oxford University Press, 2005).
8. Niditch, *Oral World and Written Word*.

so that the oral and the written intermingled in the process of textual creation. These earlier texts that formed the curriculum of the scribal school were the "canonical" texts of the tradition and were thus also expressions of the fundamental values of their cultures. As a result, by memorizing them, "writing them on the tablet of their hearts," the students were acculturated in their own traditions, or to put the matter more narrowly, they became part of the distinctive scribal culture. The process in Greece worked somewhat differently, but the aim of the process was the same. Education shaped good citizens of the state by conforming them to the ideals expressed in the culture's canonical texts.

When he turns to the subject of education in Israel, Carr suggests that in many ways it was analogous to what existed in Mesopotamia, Egypt, and Greece. The system was probably more informal, perhaps even without the existence of actual schools, and it probably involved only a few people. However, as in the surrounding cultures, most literate people were officials of some kind. Such people existed in Israel at an early date. The initial setting for their activity was the royal court, and when the monarchy disappeared during the exile the primary location of literary activity became the temple. In spite of the relative simplicity of the alphabetic system, few people outside of official circles could read or write to any extent. Most communication of important information took place orally, even when a written text was available.

Like Carr, Karel van der Toorn also recognizes the importance of oral literature in antiquity and even claims that the forms of oral literature influenced the shape that written literature assumed. In his *Scribal Culture and the Making of the Hebrew Bible*,[9] Van der Toorn also recognizes the difficulty of producing written literature, and, by the time that actual books began to be written, he recognizes the high cost in effort and money associated with written books. The production of books was a highly specialized business, and even though scribes in Israel would have used an alphabetic script rather than the much more complex cuneiform script of Akkadian or the hieroglyphic script of Egypt, Israelite scribes would still have to have been highly trained specialists. In this sense Israelite scribes would have been comparable to their Mesopotamian counterparts, who underwent rigorous training and who were highly rewarded both in social status and in compensation.

In Van der Toorn's opinion, then, Israelite scribes were highly trained professionals, who were in fact scholars possessing a wide range of specialized knowledge and wisdom. However, when Van der Toorn

9. Karel van der Toorn, *Scribal Culture and the Making of the Hebrew Bible* (Cambridge, Mass.: Harvard University Press, 2007).

considers the sorts of scribes who might have produced the Hebrew Bible, he differs sharply from the views of Schniedewind. Van der Toorn agrees with Schniedewind that the ancient Israelite monarchy would have needed scribes and that some scribes would have worked for the government. However, Van der Toorn does not agree that the Hebrew Bible was written primarily by scribes seeking to support political elites. Rather, Van der Toorn stresses that the scribes who wrote the Bible would have more likely been associated with the temple. There religiously oriented scribes, perhaps also priests, like the Levites, would have been responsible for producing collections of religious laws and narratives that eventually became our Pentateuch and would have also collected the prophetic oracles that eventually became our prophetic books.

In order to illustrate this process, Van der Toorn supplies two examples of scribal activity: the creation of the book of Deuteronomy, and the creation of the book of Jeremiah. In the first case, Van der Toorn rejects two common models for thinking about the editorial history of Deuteronomy: the idea that the book was created essentially as a unified text which was then copied with very little change and the idea that an original edition was created and then regularly augmented and edited. Rather, Van der Toorn suggests that the priestly scribes would have created only one or perhaps two copies of the work, both because of the amount of labor involved in making multiple copies and because the scribes did not want the text to become a public document. Rather, a new copy was made roughly once every forty years, when physical deterioration of the scroll would have required a new copy to be created. On these rare occasions, the scribes would have been able to make numerous changes and essentially to create a new work.

In the case of Jeremiah, the process was somewhat different. The initial work of collecting the oracles of the prophet was undertaken not by the temple but by the disciples of the prophet. But the writing of the book was undertaken by a scribe who may have had connections with the temple. Priests may have also been involved in the process, and the final product may have been preserved in the temple.

This quick examination of recent work on ancient Israelite text production suggests that something of a consensus is emerging on several major issues. First, there is general agreement that formal education was relatively rare in Israel and was likely to have been confined to certain elite groups. The bulk of the population could read and write only minimally or not at all. For this reason Israelite society remained primarily an oral culture until a fairly late period. Second, the people who were literate, the scribes, were the producers of our biblical text. Furthermore, because of their specialized education, they should be viewed as an elite class relative to the bulk of the population. Third, the scribes were associated either with the government or the temple. Finally, the scribes acted in the interests of their elite employers, the king and the religious establishment. Sometimes the interests of palace and temple coincided; sometimes they did not.

However, in spite of this agreement on the question of text production, some major problems remain to be resolved. Three issues in particular require further investigation. First, in spite of recent scholarly agreement that oral and written literatures existed side by side throughout much of Israel's national history, there is still no agreement about how the two types of materials interacted with each other. Carr is probably correct in suggesting that eventually all biblical texts were memorized as part of the scribal training process, but this is likely to have happened only at a very late stage of the texts' development. However, the ways in which scribal text creation operated in the Exilic period and the Persian period remain unclear. How and under what conditions did scribes modify received material and add to it? Did they simply amplify written texts on the basis of their own ideas and perceptions, or were they guided by other written texts or oral traditions? If the latter, then where did the new material come from? Was it generated by the government or the temple? In the end, how much control did scribes have over what they wrote? Was the process the same with all types of material, or were Pentateuchal texts and traditions treated differently from prophetic and wisdom texts? Much additional research must be done before these questions can be answered.

A second complex of issues that requires further investigation concerns the location of scribal activity, particularly during the Exilic and Persian periods. If the emerging consensus is to be accepted, then it is necessary to conclude that much scribal activity took place during these periods. However, this conclusion is difficult to harmonize with the claim that scribes worked primarily under the auspices of either the palace or the temple. During the Exilic period Israel was not in control of its own governance, and during the Persian period local political control of the postexilic community in Israel remained ultimately in the hands of the Persians. In neither case is it likely that the state would have employed scribes to create biblical literature supporting state interests. Similar problems are raised by the suggestion that scribes operated under the auspices of the temple. Such a situation is unlikely to have been possible during the Babylonian Exile, although it is possible that literary activity could have taken place among the people left in the Land during this period. In the Persian period, the temple was rebuilt, although the texts thought to have been produced in this period show a great deal of variety in religious content, and this fact raises questions about how much scribal activity might have taken place in the context of the restored temple. Taken together, these observations suggest that the notion that Exilic- and Persian-period scribal activity was palace or temple related is unduly narrow. Other possibilities need to be explored.

Insight into the social setting of Israelite scribal activity might be enriched by comparing the contexts in which Mesopotamian scribes conducted their business. To be sure, in Mesopotamia there is ample evidence that scribes worked for the temples and for the government, but it is clear that they worked outside those contexts as well. One of the most detailed pieces of evidence on this point comes from Assyriologists who are engaged in studying Old Babylonian texts from Sippar, where a number of archival collections have been preserved.[10] The texts in question usually have colophons that mention scribal names and the dates on which the tablets were written. This fact allows analysis of the work of individual scribes and permits a reconstruction of the volume of scribal activity taking place in the city during the Old Babylonian period. To be sure, the data are certainly incomplete, but by the standards used by Assyriologists the site provides a fair amount of evidence, and certain trends do emerge.

At Sippar in the Old Babylonian period, twenty scribes are referred to more than ten times in the existing corpus, and five of those scribes are referred to more than twenty times. So far the best attested scribal name is that of Šumum-lisi, who appears in a number of tablets. In one archive alone, one coming from the house of the Chief Singer of Temple Dirges—Inanna-mansum and his son Ur-Utu—Šumum-lisi's name appears 151 times. Altogether there are 174 textual references to him over a career in Sippar that lasted for eighteen years. He seems to have been the preferred scribe of the Chief Singer, who hired him more than any other scribe attested in the corpus. However, Šumum-lisi also worked for other people in Sippar, and the Chief Singer also used other scribes. By studying the dates on the tablets, it can be determined that on a particular day Šumum-lisi wrote one or two tablets for the Chief Singer and that on the same day another scribe also wrote a tablet. This would suggest that Šumum-lisi worked for the Chief Singer part of the day and then left, presumably because he had work elsewhere. When he was not available, the Chief Singer used another scribe. Archaeological

---

10. The following discussion of scribal activity from Sippar is based on Michel Tanret, "The Works and the Days... On Scribal Activity in Old Babylonian Sippar-Amnānum," *RA* 98 (2004): 33–62.

excavations of the house of the Chief Singer have shown that scribal materials, including fine clay, were present in the house, so presumably the scribes did their work in the home of their employer. Exercise tablets were also found in the house, evidence that someone there was being given scribal training, probably Ur-Utu the Chief Singer's son. It has been calculated that Šumum-lisi may have written as many as one text every two-and-a-half days for the Chief Singer. Although we do not know how much the scribe was paid, the calculated workload explains why he needed to take on work from other clients. Of these other clients, he did a significant amount of work for Iddin-Ea and Ipqu-Annunītum, two brothers who were both judges and whose family was involved in the palace wool trade.

Although the Chief Singer was a temple official and the two brothers worked for the state, they did not hire scribes to work on temple or state business. Rather, scribes were engaged to create economic texts and letters relating to private businesses. Thus there are records of barley loans, receipts, field leases, contracts, and deposits. These were private archives, and they remained in the possession of the employers who commissioned them.

An examination of the titles used by Šumum-lisi over the years provides another interesting piece of information. Early in his career he most frequently used the title DUB.SAR, scribe, but as his career progressed he began to use more frequently the title DUMU.É.DUB.BA.A, literally "son of the tablet house." The latter term is often taken to be synonymous with DUB.SAR and to be simply another way of designating a scribe, but it is possible that DUMU.É.DUB.BA.A is an honorific title that identifies a master scribe or perhaps a teacher. If so, then teaching was perhaps another source of income for Šumum-lisi as his skill and reputation increased.

This quick survey of scribal activity at Sippar suggests some hypotheses about the daily work of scribes that might be kept in mind when we think about scribal activity in Israel, particularly during the Exilic and Persian periods. First, although governmental and religious activities at Sippar undoubtedly required the services of scribes, even in this hierarchically organized and economically developed city, scribes were also used by individuals conducting private business. This would suggest that although state formation and economic development may be necessary conditions for a dependence on writing to emerge, it does not therefore follow that scribes worked only for the government or the temple. Basically, scribes worked for whoever needed their services and could afford to pay them. This fact would in turn suggest that we should exercise caution in claiming that all scribal activity was state related, as Schniedewind argues, or that the scribes who wrote the Bible were priests or were at least employed by the temple, as Van der Toorn claims. Rather, scribes were also necessary to support private businesses and were needed to draw up personal and business contracts of all sorts. This sort of activity clearly went on during Israel's exile in Babylon as well as after the exiles' return to their land.

Second, even in an economically vibrant city such as Sippar there was not a strong demand for scribes, so there were probably relatively few of them at any given time in a particular location. Numbers were limited by demand.

Third, outside of the few scribes who may have worked full-time for the palace or the temple, scribes worked for private clients and did whatever their employers wanted done. This situation may well be the one reflected in the most famous biblical text about the creation of a literary work, Jer 36, where the prophet dictates oracles to Baruch the scribe. There is no reason to suppose that Baruch was Jeremiah's full-time employee. More likely he was a scribe for hire, who was paid for individual services. Jeremiah uses him again in Jer 32 to draw up documents relating to the purchase of a field. How the scribe was paid is not made clear in the story, but it is worth noting that Jeremiah seems to have had friends in the royal court. In short, in the exchange between scribe and client, the scribe does what the client wants, and the client provides the content for the writing that the scribe produces. The scribe does not generate the content, although the scribe may provide the appropriate form. In theory it would also be possible for a group rather than an individual to engage the services of a scribe, although at least in the biblical text there are no good examples of this practice. This is not to say, however, that scribes were not capable of producing texts on their own, without acting on the orders of a client. Rather, text production could have been initiated for a number of different reasons. All of this, and particularly the entrepreneurial character of scribal activity, could be relevant to the question of how biblical texts could have been written in the Exile in the absence of a Judean government or temple.

Fourth, once a text is created, it remains with the person or group that commissioned and paid for it. In the examples from Sippar, the tablets remained with the client and became part of a private archive. In the Jeremiah example, the prophet, who was the client, had the right to dispose of the text. In the case of the documents relating to the field, he ordered them to be put in a private archive; in the case of the scroll, the prophet ordered the scribe to communicate the text by reading it aloud to various people and groups. In short, texts were not created only for temple or state archives. They were in private hands as well. This is an important point to remember when thinking about the creation of biblical texts. Many texts from Mesopotamia seem to have been the property of the scribes themselves. They are said to be personal copies, even when they are found in public spaces such as the temple or the palace. This suggests that scribes might have maintained personal libraries and created or copied texts primarily for this purpose.

Finally, the Sippar texts suggest that even in highly structured cities education could take place on a small scale, in this case in the home of the client rather than in the home of the scribal instructor. Teaching reading and writing could be simply another aspect of a skilled scribe's activities, although this is not to suggest that there could not have been other venues for education as well.

To be sure, by the Neo-Assyrian and Neo-Babylonian periods the government seems to have tried to exercise greater control over Mesopotamian scribes, and this might have created a more restricted picture of scribal activity than the one found in Old Babylonian Sippar. However, the scribes' roles in general economic activities, their teaching activities, and their work for private clients very likely continued. For this reason further study of Mesopotamian scribal activity in the later periods could shed new light on Israelite scribal practices in the Exilic and Persian periods.

A final issue raised by recent research into scribal activity in Israel is the claim that the scribes who wrote the Bible represented the views of political and religious elites and produced literature designed to keep those elites in power. While some exilic and postexilic literature may be open to this interpretation, it is not clear that this claim can be supported in all cases. This is so because of the variety of positions maintained in the literature from these periods. If all of the literature represented the views of the palace or the temple, more unanimity might be expected.

The variety of theological and political positions held by the scribes can easily be illustrated by looking briefly at three prophetic books thought to have been written or edited during the Exilic or Persian periods: Ezekiel, Jeremiah, and Second Isaiah.

In the case of Ezekiel, most of the book seems to have been produced during the Babylonian Exile, and the oracles in the book are dated between July 593 and April 571 B.C.E. From the perspective of the author, the true Israel is the community exiled to Babylon in 598, and other Israelite communities are not considered part of that group. The exiles from the first deportation will eventually return to the land, but the restored community will be a form of theocracy, with the restored Davidic monarch having only a small role in governance (Ezek 40–48). In religious terms, the perspective of the book is that of the Zadokite priesthood, although the prophet has also been influenced to a certain extent by Deuteronomistic thought.

The situation in Jeremiah is rather different. Here the perspective is Deuteronomistic throughout, and the Davidic monarchy receives very little attention. The book envisions a return to the land after the exile, although the shape of that future government is unclear. Subtle political support for a particular group of Babylonian exiles may be present in the so-called biographical narratives in Jer 26–45, however. The stories in this section often mention specific individuals by name or at least indicate the groups to which they belong. The stories generally focus on public opposition to Jeremiah's message and are often quite clear about the identity of the prophet's supporters and opponents. The supporters hear the prophet's message of disaster and try to take action to prevent the judgment, while the opponents threaten Jeremiah, although they never succeed in killing him. The stories thus imply that the reaction of this latter group is responsible for the final destruction of Jerusalem and for the exile itself. Although these stories are sometimes read simply as inspiring accounts about how the prophet suffered for the sake of the divine word, such a reading ignores the political edge that the stories may have. By placing direct blame for the exile on particular individuals and groups in the preexilic period, the scribal authors may be attempting to exclude those individuals and groups from positions of power in the Exilic and Persian periods. In short, the biographical texts may be trying to shape Persian-period governance in the restored community.

The situation that exists in Second Isaiah is different still, both with respect to the book's political views and with respect to its religious perspectives. In the case of the book's political perspective, although Isaiah as a whole seems to accept the notion of the eternal election of the Davidic dynasty (Isa 7–12), Isa 40–55 has only a few references to the possible restoration of a Davidic monarch after the exile. Rather, Second Isaiah advocates giving sole political control of postexilic Judah to the Persian king Cyrus, who is described as God's Messiah and said to be the agent of Judah's redemption (Isa 45). This view seems to have triggered major opposition within the exilic community, a fact which prompts the scribes to mount strong arguments against the opponents (Isa 45:9–13). With respect to religious views, the book advocates a return to Zion and a restoration of religious life there. However, the book seems to address its call to return to a small group rather than to the whole community. This group is said to be experiencing opposition to its plans, presumably from other Israelites in exile (Isa 51:7–8, 12–16), but in spite of this opposition the group will play a major role in the reinhabited Zion (Isa 52:11–12).[11]

In short, even a cursory examination of prophetic material from the Exilic and Persian periods suggests that the scribes responsible for these texts did not all share the same political and religious views. It is therefore unlikely that they were advocating the views of a single political or religious elite. Rather, the diversity of views in this material suggests that scribes in this period advocated a number of different political and religious positions, either because they held these positions themselves or because they represented the diverse positions of the people who employed them. In either case, the scribal contribution to the formation of the prophetic writings appears to be more complex than recent scholarly discussion of the topic has suggested.

11. For a recent discussion of the community being addressed in Second Isaiah, see Stephen L. Cook, *Conversations with Scripture: 2 Isaiah* (Harrisburg, N.Y.: Morehouse, 2008), 15–16.

"DIGGING IN THE CLAWS":
DANIEL 4 AND THE PREDATORY NATURE OF EMPIRE

Deborah Appler

Claudius Aelianus, a Roman rhetorician, writing around 200 C.E., recounts the miraculous rescue of baby Gilgamesh by an eagle and recalls that Gilgamesh was not the only great leader with a close encounter with an eagle.[1] He writes, "I have also heard that Achaemenes the Persian, from whom the Persian nobility descend, was cared for by an eagle."[2] Indeed, the eagle plays an important role in the history and legends of the Persian Empire. Pierre Briant remarks that this animal is linked to royal Persian power.[3] Before marching to war Cyrus awaits an eagle to signal the gods' approval and to provide assurance of a successful battle.[4] As the Persians militarily expand their empire, they conquer nations bearing the royal standard that proudly displays this bird. The ancient historian Xenophon describes this standard as "a kind of golden eagle, with wings extended, perched on a bar of wood and raised upon a lance."[5] This raptor that leads the Persians into battle

---

1. King Senechorus of Babylon, believing the prophecy that his grandson will usurp his throne, imprisons his daughter to prevent her from conceiving. Surreptitiously, the young woman becomes pregnant and her guards, wishing to evade the king's anger, throw the child down from the acropolis to his certain death. However, an eagle's keen eye and swift speed intercept the child's fall and land Gilgamesh safely to the ground. Gilgamesh goes on to become one of the great kings of Babylon.

2. Claudius Aelianus (12.21), *Historia animalium* (*Animal Stories*) quoted from Otto Rank, *The Myth of the Birth of a Hero: A Psychological Exploration of Myth* (trans. G. Richter, and E. J. Lieberman; Baltimore: The Johns Hopkins University Press, 2004), 20. Pierre Briant (*From Cyrus to Alexander: A History of the Persian Empire* [Winona Lake: Eisenbrauns, 2002], 158) states that by Darius' time this myth was important.

3. Briant, *From Cyrus to Alexander*, 111.

4. Ibid., 242, referencing Xenophon in his *Cyropaedia* (II.1.1).

5. Xenophon, *Anabasis* I.1, quoted from in *The Works of Xenophon* (trans. H. G. Dakyns; London: Macmillan, 1897), 114

represents an empire that, like the eagle, stalks its prey with keen eyes, swiftly swoops in, and digs its claws into the resources and livelihood of the people it colonizes. It is this nature of national sovereignty or empire to which Dan 4 responds.

Daniel 4, one of the folkloric tales (Dan 1–6) that likely reflects the hardships imposed on Jews in the Diaspora by their Persian overlords, provides words of hope and resistance to the colonized as well as reproach to those in power, hoping to motivate them to rescind their oppressive policies. Both of these audiences, colonized and colonizer, are addressed on some level by the story. On the one hand, Dan 4 speaks to a well-educated and elite audience, those in Yehud responsible for preserving the text and who were also policy makers and who, like Daniel, had some influence over the empire. So, in many ways Dan 4 as a text is aimed at those better situated to impact socio-economic change in Yehud. On the other hand, the oppressed in the land, to whom written texts might have been less accessible, were likely empowered by the story of a character named Daniel, a political activist, who was willing to transcend his role as dream interpreter to confront the emperor with this ruler's injustice, and, perhaps, rally the oppressed to action. Daniel himself is a bridge between the elite and the colonized. He was afforded an excellent education by the empire and became the chief of the magicians in the emperor's court, presumably living quite comfortably. Yet he experienced oppression at the hand of Nebuchadnezzar who changed his name to Belteshazzar, educated him in Babylonian ways, and worked to take away Daniel's identity. Daniel 4 provides both the text and the movement necessary to bring down the violent structures of empire. Because this liberating strategy is as true today as it was in Daniel's time, I will bring in a modern example of a similar strategy of both liberation texts and personal activism in the form of Vandana Shiva,[6] an Indian activist. Her texts, *Earth Democracy* and *Biopiracy*, are written in English to reach policy makers, but her activism is in her country, in her language, and with her people, just like Daniel. To show the power that these strategies can have, I will read the rhetoric of Nebuchadnezzar's dream (4:10–12) and punishment (4:32–33) within the socio-political and economic context of the Persian Period, focusing on the ways Persians acquired wealth from the colonized in subtle and not so subtle ways. To help unpack the complexities of empire, I will draw

6. Vandana Shiva, *Biopiracy: The Plunder of Nature and Knowledge* (Boston: South End, 1997), *Earth Democracy: Justice, Sustainability and Peace* (Boston: South End, 2005).

on the biblical economics analysis set forth by theological economist Ulrich Duchrow.[7] To lay a groundwork for my reading, a few words should be said about dating Dan 4. This task is admittedly difficult and controversial. Though the text is set in the Babylonian exile, there are few who believe that it was written during this period. In addition, the situation of the king in Dan 4, identified as Nebuchadnezzar, better suits Nabonides, the Babylonian king who neglects the Marduk cult and forgoes the important Akitu Festival as he sojourns for many years in Tiema, an oasis village.[8] Daniel 4 easily reflects life in Persia under an empire that can be both benevolent—certainly Cyrus is heralded by Deutero-Isaiah for calling the exiles home (45:13), and predatory, as I will soon argue. John Berquist and Daniel Smith-Christopher are among those willing to place the origin of Dan 4 in a Persian setting, Berquist because it models the popular Persian short story,[9] and Smith-Christopher because these stories reflect a Persian occupation and could easily have been assembled from many separate sources under Persian rule.[10] While I will locate Dan 4 in a Persian socio-political context, the realities of an empire that oppresses these ancient people exist for us today as we battle an often oppressive global economy.

The Great Nebuchadnezzar, who boasts that he has "mighty power," and "glorious majesty" (v. 30), and who, in his dream, is represented as a tree reaching into the heavens that provides fruit, shade, housing, and

7. Especially Ulrich Duchrow, *Alternatives to Global Capitalism: Drawn from Biblical History, Designed for Political Action* (2d ed.; Utrecht: International Books, 1998).

8. This event is corroborated in the "Prayer of Nabonidus" discovered at Qumran. The scholarly consensus is that the first six chapters of Daniel are earlier than the last six since they suggest a greater Jewish tolerance toward their colonial overlords than do the latter six that likely reflect intense suffering under Antiochus IV Epiphanes (215–164 B.C.E.).

9. See Jon L. Berquist, *Judaism in Persia's Shadow: A Social and Historical Approach* (Minneapolis: Fortress, 1995), 222. Berquist also suggests that since reading scripture does not appear to be one of Daniel's acts of piety so essential in later Judaism, a Persian setting seems appropriate (227).

10. Daniel Smith-Christopher, "Daniel the Book of," in *NIB* (ed. L. Keck; Nashville: Abingdon, 1996), 7:17–152. Others who suggest at least a Persian oral tradition are Rainer Albertz ("The Setting of the Aramaic and Hebrew Book of Daniel," in *The Book of Daniel: Composition and Reception* [ed. J. Collins and P. Flint; Leiden: Brill, 2001], 1:182); Lawrence Wills (*The Jew in the Court of the Foreign King: Ancient Jewish Court Legends* [Minneapolis: Fortress, 1990], 194). For more discussion on the composition of Daniel see the remaining articles in *The Book of Daniel: Composition and Reception*, vol. 1.

food for all living beings" (vv. 10–12) will be cut down to size (v. 23). Nebuchadnezzar self-identifies as a great benefactor, though his Jewish subjects see him quite differently. In reality, Nebuchadnezzar's wealth is not of his own making but a result of his ability to pirate the fruits of the colonized—the land, food production, and human power. Nebuchadnezzar rules his empire as an eagle searching for goods on which to grasp in order to fill his insatiable appetite for power. This is revealed in Daniel's rhetoric. As the king receives his punishment and transforms from human to a carrion bird,[11] he becomes in the animal kingdom his role in the human kingdom (vv. 32–33). This imagery underscores the predatory nature of Persian domination and colonization in general.

The language of colonization and resistance to Persia's sovereignty runs through the fourth chapter of Daniel. The scene opens with a reminder of how vast is the size of the empire as the king offers a doxology to "all peoples, nations, and languages that live throughout the earth" (v. 1)—presumably those he controls. In its heyday the borders of Persia would have run from Northern Africa to the west and to the border of India on the East. Many languages would have been spoken throughout the empire. To illustrate, the Behistun Inscription, a tribute to Darius' great rise to power, was carved on a limestone cliff along the busy road between two capital cities, Babylon and Ecbatana, and was written in Elamite, Old Persian, and Babylonian so a greater number of subjects could read it.[12]

In Dan 4:1–3 the king appears to be basking in his new-found faith after witnessing the God of the Jews save Shadrach, Meshach, and Abednego from the fiery furnace (ch. 3). While the king is quick to proclaim God's sovereignty, he promptly regresses to his previous comfortable position of wealth and power, "I, Nebuchadnezzar, was living at ease (שלה) in my home and prospering (ורענן) in my palace" (v. 4). Both of these Hebrew words signal excess, gluttony, and a disregard for the well-being of other people.[13] They also sum up the predatory policies of the Persian Empire, an empire where the king and his loyal servants lived in ease and prospered, while the commoner suffered.

---

11. "His hair grew as long as eagle's feather and his nails/claws like birds claws" (Aramaic, נשר, "eagle" or "vulture," Dan 4:33).

12. See Smith-Christopher, *NIB*, 7:72.

13. This is indicted in the prophets and Psalms. Ezekiel reminds Judah that the guilt of Israel was "pride, excess of food, and prosperous ease" and Israel did not aid the poor and needy (16:49). The psalmist reminds us that "Such are the wicked; always at ease, they increase in riches" (73:12).

Ulrich Duchrow's discussion of the socio-economic and political-ideologies undergirding biblical traditions identifies three characteristics of kingship systems, city-states, and empires. These are: the accumulation of land, accumulation of labor as a means of production and imposed duties and taxes.[14] The profits from these sources have the potential to be used to defend the nation and care for the poor, or to build power for the local elites,[15] the choice taken by Nebuchadnezzar. Duchrow continues:

> Externally city-states and empires began to *behave as conquerors*. In economic terms this behavior was characterized by three main things: direct oppression of *looting campaigns*; forced labour, or *slavery*; and institutionalized oppression through the imposition of duties, or *tribute*.[16]

These colonizing policies created an increase in the gap between the rich and the poor and an environment that allowed the king and his elites to live lives of ease and prosperity while subjects struggled to survive. This is the socio-economic setting Daniel was living in.

Jon Berquist notes the mostly non-militaristic approach instituted by Darius I (522–486 B.C.E.) to strengthen his empire and accumulate further wealth and power. Berquist writes: "Through the creation of a formalized bureaucratic structure, Darius was able to control production and trade, and thus imperial income, with sources besides conquest."[17] Yet, the violence inflicted on those colonized in Yehud through its colonizing bureaucracy was often as painful and physically destructive as being continually assaulted by military force. The ancient world changed radically with Darius I's new economic system, which included a redistribution of power through the division of the kingdom into twenty provinces (satrapies), with Persian born and trained governors appointed to collect tributes and enforce Persian policy.[18] But Darius' most

14. Duchrow, *Alternatives to Global Capitalism*, 129.
15. Ibid.
16. Ibid.
17. Berquist, *Judaism in Persia's Shadow*, 61.
18. Ezra reflects the presence of laws imposed by Persia on the inhabitants of Yehud: "All who will not obey the law of your God and the law of the king, let judgment be strictly executed on them, whether for death or for banishment or for confiscation of their goods or for imprisonment" (7:26). Ramat Rahel, located immediately outside of Jerusalem, might have served as a Persian administration center for the collection of taxes and tribute. Many seals and 85% of all of the Yehud stamps found in Judah have been discovered on this site, suggesting its importance. See Lester Grabbe, *A History of the Jews and Judaism in the Second Temple Period*. Vol. 1, *Yehud, the Persian Province of Judah* (LSTS 47; New York: T&T Clark International, 2004); Oded Lipschits and David Vanderhooft, "Yehud Stamp Impressions of the Fourth Century BCE: A Time of Administrative Consolidation?,"

innovative and influential achievement was the promotion of a universal monetary system centered on minted coins.

The rise of state-backed Persian coinage rapidly transformed the empire into an export economy that traded more efficiently with the international community.[19] Duchrow, applying ethicist Ton Veerkamp, argues that money served multiple functions in Persia: "as means of exchange, as a means of accumulation, as a means of maintaining worth, as a mobiliser of resources, as a means of exploitation, as God."[20] Money was a commodity easy to hoard! According to Ephraim Stern, local leaders were empowered by the empire to mint silver coins, albeit under the guarded eyes of Persian officials. Persians alone, however, were allowed to mint gold coins in order to control the local economies of the colonies.[21] Appropriately, a few silver coins found in Yehud are inscribed in Aramaic with יהד and stamped with the picture of an Egyptian eagle (a carrion bird), the symbol of this economy's predatory nature.[22] The birth of a monetary system imposed hardships on Yehud whose economy was agrarian or, as Lester Grabbe suggests, based on an Asiatic mode of production.[23] This mode of production is a subsistence economy where the community produces resources that stay local, with the exception of the excess yield that goes to the crown to pay taxes. It is not generally an export economy, but this changed when Darius demanded tribute in coinage and metals instead of yields from crops. The social and economic structure in the colonies began to break down as locals scrambled to convert their goods into money or precious metals or face the wrath of the empire at the hands of its military forces.

Bas-reliefs found in the Adapana, the great hall at Persepolis commissioned by Darius the Great (549–486 B.C.E.), depict tribute

in *Judah and the Judeans in the 4th Century BCE* (ed. Oded Lipschits, Gary N. Knoppers, and Rainer Albertz; Winona Lake: Eisenbrauns, 2007), 75–94.

19. Ephraim Stern, "Between Persia and Greece: Trade, Administration and Warfare in the Persian and Hellenistic Periods (539–63 BCE)," in *The Archaeology of Society in the Holy Land* (ed. Thomas Levy; 2d ed.; London: Leicester University Press, 1998), 435; Duchrow, *Alternatives to Global Capitalism*, 134.

20. Duchrow, *Alternatives to Global Capitalism*, 134. Berquist credits Darius' coins with devaluing the Babylonian economic system (*Judaism in Persia's Shadow*, 90).

21. Stern, "Between Persia and Greece," 435. Stern notes that many coins have been unearthed with few duplications. Many Persian-period silver coins with the inscription יהד (Yehud) have been found in the region.

22. See Grabbe, *A History of the Jews and Judaism*, 65.

23. Lester Grabbe, *Judaism from Cyrus to Hadrian*. Vol. 1, *The Persian and Greek Periods* (Minneapolis: Fortress, 1992), 21.

bearers presenting their gold and silver to the Persians who escort them.[24] Tributes were often given in precious metals, which were then amassed in the Persian treasury instead of minted for the economy.[25] The Persian economy, claims Smith-Christopher, is a system of hoarding precious metals. Even the great Hellenistic conqueror Alexander found the amount of precious metals stored at Susa, Ecbatana, and Persepolis astonishing.[26] The Persian Empire imposed a plethora of tributes and taxes on its subjects. Yehud paid taxes at the harbor, the market place, tolls for the new roads that were built, and even taxes on animals.[27] These were on top of gifts that were required by the Persian king and the enormous quantities of supplies each province had to provide to the king's armies as they came through town. The impact of tribute and taxes on the local economy cannot be ignored. Grain, an important subsistence crop, was uprooted for "cash" or "high yield crops"—crops like olives and grapes that were sold at market price, prices set by the empire and out of Yehud's control.[28] Grabbe points out that because crops were sold for cash instead of used for food, the local economy was severely impacted by hunger.[29] Consequently the poor had little choice but to sell their land (or endure its seizure), take out loans, and sell anything that could be transformed into coinage. Nehemiah 5:1–5 captures well the plight of many commoners in Yehud under the Persians. The people in Yehud complain of land loss, lack of grain, indebtedness, and being forced to sell their children into slavery, perhaps to build the new palace at Susa or the new capital at Persepolis. Artaxerxes I's (465–423 B.C.E.) policy of not taxing Persian citizens for his military escapades led to a greater tax burden for non-Persian subjects.[30] As land became confiscated by the empire, the people of Yehud lost control of their natural resources—their land, their crops, their human power, and their economic right to earn a living. Persia's predatory economic structure is

---

24. Brent Strawn, "A World Under Control," in *Approaching Yehud: New Approaches to the Study of the Persian Period* (ed. Jon L. Berquist; Atlanta: SBL, 2008), 85–116.

25. Grabbe, *Judaism from Cyrus to Hadrian*, 116.

26. Smith-Christopher, "Prayers and Dreams: Power and Diaspora Identities in the Social Setting of the Daniel Tales," in *The Book of Daniel: Composition and Reception* (Leiden: Brill, 2001), 278.

27. Smith-Christopher drawing on Richard Frye ("Prayers and Dreams," 279).

28. Duchrow, *Alternatives to Global Capitalism*, 134.

29. Grabbe, *Judaism from Cyrus to Hadrian*, 121. See also Berquist, *Judaism in Persia's Shadow*, 62.

30. Berquist, *Judaism in Persia's Shadow*, 106.

anything but benevolent, a portrait of this empire that many scholars have painted throughout the years.

While Cyrus' edict inviting the Judean exiles to return to their homeland and rebuild their Temple appears compassionate, Smith-Christopher raises doubts that such benevolence is a reality for those living under military and economic occupation.[31] He draws on the work of Ken Hoglund who claims Nehemiah's task "was more military than spiritual"[32] and offered on behalf of Persian interests. Facing a growing Greek threat, Artaxerxes I required that Yehud fortify its walls.[33] In reality the Temple served the purposes of the empire as an economic center for taxes and tariffs; a place for communal exchange.[34] That this is the Temple's roll becomes more plausible when Darius, impatient with the slow progress made by those commissioned to build it, puts pressure on Yehud to have it immediately completed.[35] Those sent to oversee the restoration of Jerusalem, as well as all returnees from Babylon, were in many ways potential agents of the empire or, what John Kessler calls "Persian charter groups."[36] It is therefore of little surprise that the king in Daniel is represented as a tree that is situated at the center of the earth and as tall as the heavens and visible "to the ends of the earth" (4:11). Nebuchadnezzar, like an eagle, sits high above the world, and has a clear view of his prey either through his own eyes or the eyes of his royal "watchers." According to Smith-Christopher, a group called "the king's eyes" served as the "Persian Secret Service."[37] Their job was to ensure that the king's agenda was maintained by his subjects. The king was always watching. There was no one living under this colonial ruler who did not see or feel the colonial impact. Even Ezra, who was in good stead with Artaxerxes II and sent to revive Jerusalem, laments Yehud's bondage (Ezra 9:9): "For we are slaves; yet our God has not forsaken us in our slavery." The empire could be quite harsh. Archaeological

31. Smith-Christopher, *NIB*, 7:27.
32. Ibid, 7:29.
33. Berquist, *Judaism in Persia's Shadow*, 108; Smith-Christopher, *NIB*, 7:23.
34. Duchrow, *Alternatives to Global Capitalism*, 134.
35. Berquist, *Judaism in Persia's Shadow*, 63.
36. John Kessler labels the returnees as "geographically transplanted elite" or a charter group sent by the Persians to help Persia control the social, political, and economic institutions (John Kessler, "Diaspora and Homeland in the Early Achaemenid Period: Community, Geography, and Demography in Zechariah 1–8," in Berquist, ed., *Approaching Yehud*, 142. While the Murašu documents found in Nippur suggest a thriving banking business for this Jewish family in Babylon, this was the exception and not the rule. The Persian policies were far from benevolent.
37. Smith-Christopher, *NIB*, 7:73.

evidence suggests that Artaxerxes II quelled an uprising of Jews in Jericho, and Samarian refugees fled to wadi ed-Daliyeh for safety.[38] Nebuchadnezzar is an emperor who claims to have mighty power (תקף חסן) and glorious majesty (יקרחדר) and uses it (Dan 4:30). The height of the tree representing Nebuchadnezzar suggests, not only his huge presence in the colonies, but also his great hubris.

Nebuchadnezzar's vision emphasizes that this tree or empire is wealthy, so much so that everyone can be fed (v. 12). However the Persian economic system is breaking the backs of the people forced to serve the emperor. The people suffer as a result of the structural violence of colonialism that exists in the shape of the Persian global economic system. Yet, the economic plight of Daniel and the colonized in Yehud is not so different from the struggle of those suffering under today's Global economic market system, particularly those living in the two-thirds world. It is not so far-fetched to compare ancient empires with today's global capitalism, even if nations organize differently in these different chronological periods. Duchrow turns to Immanuel Wallerstein who justifies such comparison: "There is one feature common to the political economy of empires and the capitalist global economy: they both are forms of surplus acquisition by those in control of the means of production, at the expense of the majority."[39] The farm movement in India supported by Vandana Shiva and others provides an excellent case study of the continued violence of empire through neo-Colonialism.[40] The claws of empire still dig in deep.

Raj Patel recounts the following: Kistaiah, a farmer from Andhra Pradesh in India, despondent from the mounting debt he continued to incur from his unproductive rice fields, was forced to borrow from a bank and local money lender to drill for water. Earning $.75 per day at the peak of his farm's productivity and seeing no end in sight, Kistaiah waited for his family to turn in for the night. He took down his organophosphate, dissolved it in water, drank it, and calmly died.[41] Kistaiah is

---

38.   There is evidence of Jewish revolts found in papyri discovered at both wadi ed-Daliyeh (outside of Jericho) and at Ketef Jericho dated to the rules of Artaxerxes II and III (Ephraim Stern, *Archaeology of the Land of the Bible*, vol. 2 [New York: Doubleday, 2001], 362, 438).

39.   Duchrow, quoting Immanuel Wallerstein in *The Modern World-System* (New York: Academic, 1994), 16, quoted in *Alternatives to Global Capitalism*, 214.

40.   Neo-colonialism is applied by post-colonial critics to identify the continued colonization of developing nations, now through economic methods.

41.   Raj Patel, *Stuffed and Starved: The Hidden Battle for the World Food System* (Brooklyn: Melville House, 2007), 24.

one of roughly 17,000 Indian farmers who committed suicide that year.[42] Lee Kyung Hae, a Korean farmer and activist, fed up with the injustice heaped on farmers by the global market through groups like the World Trade Organization (WTO) and Multi-national corporations, climbed on a barricade at the WTO meeting in Cancun on September 10, 2003, shouted "the WTO kills farmers" and killed himself.[43] Vandana Shiva recounts that, while India has not had a famine since 1942, a 1991 study of 8000 deaths of children by starvation found "that before trade liberalization and globalization no child in the zero to six age group had died as a result of lack of food."[44] By 2002, 47% of children's deaths were a direct cause of hunger despite 65 tons of food rotting in storage because people cannot pay its price.[45]

While nations today rarely use military force to acquire land and colonize peoples, a strategy used by the Persian Empire, the global economic system has led to a new type of colonization that creates pain, injustice, and insecurity by controlling who is allowed to grow food and to make a living off nature. Due to liberalizing international trade, first through GATT (General Agreement on Tariffs and Trade) established in 1947 to boost economic recovery after World War II, and then through its replacement, the WTO in 1995, multi-national corporations like Cargill are empowered to build up monopolies. Shiva claims that policies such as WTO's Agreement on Agriculture, penned by former Cargill Vice President, move beyond trade—they determine "how food is produced, and who controls food production."[46] The move from more productive local small-scale farming to less sustainable agribusiness not only puts millions of subsistence farmers out of business and into poverty, it places food production in the hands of a few and the world at the mercy of the mighty.[47] Under the auspices of the "Green Revolution," which pledged to improve the world through environmentally friendly genetically modified crops, local economies throughout the world have

42. Vandana Shiva, *Earth Democracy*, 120. Shiva recounts that the suicide rate for Indian farmers committing suicide averaged 17,000 a year between 2002 and 2006.

43. Ibid., 76.

44. Ibid., 34.

45. Ibid.

46. Ibid., 35.

47. For example, Cargill, Archer Daniel Midlands (ADM), and Bunge have majority control over the global grain trading. For a useful discussion of the food crisis, see Canadian Catholic Organization for Development and Peace, "Hunger and the Pursuit of Profit: Food System in Crisis," June 2008, online: http://www.devp.org/devpme/eng/advocacy/doc/DPFood.pdf.

been undermined as land is confiscated and market prices for goods driven down for farmers by corporate predators. Shiva writes:

> Instead of a culture of abundance, profit-driven globalization creates cultures of exclusion, dispossession, and scarcity. In fact, globalization's transformation of all beings and resources into commodities robs diverse species and people of their rightful share of ecological, cultural, economic, and political space. The "ownership" of the rich is based on the "dispossession" of the poor—it is the common, public resources of the poor which are privatized, and the poor who are disowned economically, politically and culturally.[48]

As in the Persian economy, many local people in India are unable to feed themselves.

Another strategy of the new multi-national colonizer is to patent or "enclose" that which grows naturally, like seeds. Monsanto, a United States-based company who owns the largest number of seed lines of the ten companies that control over 55% of the world's seed supply,[49] justifies its ownership of much of the world's seed patents on the need to protect and improve technology on these life forms.[50] Shiva argues that these patents have more to do with territorialism than innovation; the colonization of life processes, called "biopiracy," has a serious impact on Third World agriculture.[51] Seeds that Indian farmers have developed over the years or that are indigenous to Indian culture often become the intellectual property of corporations and move beyond the legal control of indigenous peoples. Farmers are required to sign agreements that seeds may not be saved to be replanted without legal retribution. This places heavy financial burdens on already poor farmers who now have to buy seed each year and discard perfectly usable seeds from previous seasons or risk patent violations and litigation.

Neem, a tree indigenous to India that has been used for centuries as a source of medicine and as a natural pesticide, was patented by W. R. Grace and others, giving these companies exclusive research and

---

48. Shiva, *Earth Democracy*, 2–3.

49. John Seabrook, "Sowing for Apocalypse: The Quest for a Global Seed Bank," *The New Yorker* (August 27, 2007): 69, as cited in Ellen Davis, *Scripture, Culture, and Agriculture: An Agrarian Reading of the Bible* (Cambridge: Cambridge University Press, 2009), 52 n. 190.

50. See the Monsanto website for their rationale behind patenting every seed they can possibly grab: "Should Crucial Technology Be Patentable?," online: http://www.monsanto.com/monsanto_today/for_the_record/biotech_patents.asp (accessed November 18, 2009).

51. Shiva, *Biopiracy*, 53.

economic rights to India's natural resources.[52] Since India failed to patent the plant, Grace and others considered Neem to be up for grabs. Under Grace's patent it was no longer legal for Indians to profit from their own natural resource or their intellectual property; Grace drew on traditional knowledge of the plant to manufacture a more ecology friendly pesticide. Once again, the economic and societal benefits of natural resources revert to the multinational corporations.

These are only a few examples out of many that illustrate the predatory economic control that global markets have over the resources of the two-thirds world. Yet neither Daniel nor Vandana Shiva, and the Indian Farmer's Movement that Shiva champions, are content to remain colonized. Both offer words of resistance to those in power as these texts challenge the nature of sovereignty imposed on them. Shiva's resistance texts that I have drawn from are written to the powerful and not necessarily to the masses in India. They are intentionally written in English and aimed at policy makers and those who might be able to influence power structures. The text of Daniel also functions this way. It is framed in language that those in power understand with the intent to enable political change. Duchrow argues that the Bible protests the unjust economic systems in the ancient Near East—that these texts illustrate how these social systems function while simultaneously offering alternatives.[53] This plays out as Daniel proclaims his opposition to the empire that Nebuchadnezzar represents when he interprets his dream.

Danna Fewell and Philip Chia are among those who recognize Daniel's focus on God' sovereignty (שִׁלְטָן) that was contrasted with Nebuchadnezzar's.[54] Fewell aptly states, "Nebuchadnezzar thinks that he is the sovereign of the world, but he is not even the sovereign of his own story."[55] Chia notices in Dan 1 that the narrator reverses the power structure in the story by directing the mouth of the king to proclaim God's supreme power over the colonizer![56] This also plays out in Dan 4, where God's sovereignty is proclaimed by the restored king: "I blessed the Most High, and praised and honor the one who lives forever. For his

---

52. Ibid., 69–72. India chose not to patent Neem under the Insecticide Act of 1968 because its benefits had been known and used for thousands of years

53. Duchrow, *Alternatives to Global Capitalism*, 135. Duchrow places Daniel, however, completely in the Hellenistic period.

54. Danna Nolan Fewell, *Circle of Sovereignty: Plotting Politics in the Book of Daniel* (Nashville: Abingdon, 1991); Philip Chia, "On Naming the Subject: Postcolonial Reading of Daniel 1," in *The Post Colonial Biblical Reader* (ed. R. S. Sugirtharajah; Malden, Mass.: Blackwell, 2006), 171–85.

55. Fewell, *Circle of Sovereignty*, 72–73.

56. Chia, "On Naming the Subject," 180.

sovereignty is an everlasting sovereignty, and his kingdom endures from generation to generation" (v. 34). Before Nebuchadnezzar gets to this point, he gets his comeuppance in the reversal of images that appear in the text.

King Nebuchadnezzar dreams a frightening dream. His response is in line with the actions of a despot; he issues a decree (טעם, v. 6) to get what he wants (v. 6). Daniel, one of the colonized Jews who is chief of the magicians (v. 8), responds to the edict and interprets this dream. The issuance of a decree appears two other times in ch. 4 (vv. 17, 24), only these times it is not Nebuchadnezzar with the authority to make such proclamations. These decrees are given first by the watcher as he renders to Nebuchadnezzar his punishment for arrogance and injustice (v. 17) and then by the Most High to assert the possibility of Nebuchadnezzar's restoration when he declares God to be sovereign (v. 24). The act of decree, usually the means employed by the empire to control the colonized, is now used to indict it. Likewise, the watcher provides a sense of catharsis for those who are always watched by their Persian overlords; God, the true sovereign, has eyes continually focused on them too.[57] The watcher brings news from God to Nebuchadnezzar that the tall and mighty tree that represents his earthly sovereignty will be leveled to a stump (v. 23). The truth is, such wealth and power cannot be sustained. Artaxerxes I discovered this when his massive military campaigns emptied the treasury of coins and many of his provinces were stripped clean of metals and other natural resources. The watcher also foretells that, should Nebuchadnezzar not proclaim God's sovereignty, he will be driven away from society for seven years to live among the wild animals, where he will have an animal's "mind" (לבב). Perhaps the "band of iron and bronze" that the dream conveys lies in the field next to the stump (v. 15) symbolizes the imperial policy of hoarding metal. Instead of providing comfort and power to Nebuchadnezzar, these iron and bronze fetters will be used to oppress him as he has oppressed his people. The Aramaic term ענין translated "oppressed" in the NRSV (v. 27) relates to the Hebrew עני and carries the sense of inflicting violence. The system that the Persian Empire has built is structurally and often physically violent. Daniel takes on this oppressive structure and becomes a political activist as he boldly confronts the king. Daniel entreats Nebuchadnezzar to turn from acts of oppression (ענין, v. 27) when he moves from being dream interpreter (vv. 19–26) to truth teller (v. 27).

Unlike Joseph and other dream interpreters, Daniel takes a bold move and confronts the emperor directly with his injustice. To bring such harsh

57. Smith-Christopher, *NIB*, 7:73.

words is dangerous. Daniel, presumably, knows that he is risking death at the hands of a king who thought little of throwing Daniel's friends in the fiery furnace for not acknowledging royal sovereignty (ch. 3). Regardless, Daniel counsels the king, "break off your sins with righteousness, and your iniquities with mercy to the oppressed, so that your prosperity may be prolonged" (v. 27). For those in Yehud who wanted the chance to confront the cause of their misery, Daniel provides hope and encouragement. He also opens possibilities for the king to change his ways. Clearly the king is not immediately affected by Daniel's advice. For twelve months it is assumed that he continued his predatory policies.[58] Nevertheless, the day of reckoning finally comes.

While standing high above the city on the roof of his palace (v. 28) Nebuchadnezzar brags about Babylon, the beautiful capital that he built. While he is gloating, a voice from the heaven speaks and the punishment is executed. Curiously, instead of receiving the mind of an animal as foretold in the dream (v. 16), Nebuchadnezzar is described as becoming or, at the very least, resembling an eagle. His hair is as long as eagle's feathers (שערה כנשרין) and claws like birds (וטפרוהי כצפרין, v. 30). Fewell suggests that "a man who thinks like a god must become an animal to become human."[59] There is truth to this. The once great eagle that perches on a high tree searching for prey to sink its claws into is now brought low to eat grass like an ox (v. 33). This eagle, this great predator, has lost its power. The symbol of Persian hegemony now appears comical and powerless.

Daniel's willingness to speak truth to the powerful likely brought hope and sustenance to those under Persian domination. Even for the poorest of the poor in Persia, there is a possibility for justice and a reason to keep living and challenging the empire. This same hope continues in the Indian narrative as the farmers take on the multinationals.

Mahatma Gandhi declares that "the earth provides enough resources for everyone's need, but not for some people's greed."[60] It is this greed that Shiva confronts as she organizes farmers in India to continue fighting MAHYCO Hybrid Company, a subsidiary of Monsanto, who wants to introduce genetically modified crops into India's soil.[61] Thus far they have succeeded in keeping Monsanto at bay. Shiva and the Indian

---

58. "At the end of twelve months he was walking on the roof of the royal palace of Babylon" (v. 29).

59. Fewell, *Circle of Sovereignty*, 72.

60. Quoted in Shiva, *Earth Democracy*, 13.

61. Arpan Mukherjee, "India Mulls GM Food Crops Despite Stiff Resistance," *Wall Street Journal* (28 October 2009).

Farmers' Movement hope to challenge these self-indulging multi-nationals and have incorporated Gandhi's strategy of *satyagraha* ("struggle for the truth"), a non-violent approach to justice.[62] When a treaty is unjust and opens doors to monopolies and colonization of indigenous resources, there will be resistance. Farmers, demanding access to their intellectual property, vow to break the treaties and ignore patents placed on their intellectual property. They insist on being able to continue their own indigenous seed lines without interference and control by companies like W. R. Grace and Monsanto. The farmers want to protect bio-diversity and create sustainability for the local community so that there is ample food and so that the food chain is not endangered.[63] They are also fighting for their right to practice traditional medicine and to make a living by working the land that they claim as their birthright. It took ten years of legal struggle against W. R. Grace and the US Department of agriculture, but on March 8, 2005 the European Patent Office revoked the patent on Neem.[64] The Farmers' Movement was able to overturn many of RiceTec patent claims to Basmati rice, rice that has been grown for centuries in India and covers 10–15% of India's rice fields.[65] Fights over water rights with Coca-Cola are presently in process in India.

There is hope that there can be a merciful global economy some day as Daniel's audience dreams of a benevolent Persia. The mighty king obtained the mind of an animal, perhaps even before transforming into an eagle. The text implies that only an animal could be so insensitive to the violence he inflicts on his subjects. When Nebuchadnezzar regains his senses after his ordeal, however, he proclaims God's sovereignty over everything in the world: "Now I, Nebuchadnezzar, praise and extol and honor the King of heaven, for all his works are truth, and his ways are justice; and he is able to bring low those who walk in pride" (v. 37). This king is now able to recognize that he needs to build a just world and that his arrogance, if not checked, will once again cause the real Sovereign, the God Most High (v. 34) to cut him down to size. Unfortunately, Nebuchadnezzar has demonstrated in the past a short attention span. After the power of the experience faded, he most likely returned to his predatory nature—it is human nature. But there is always

---

62. Shiva, *Biopiracy*, 98, and *Earth Democracy*, 92–93.

63. Shiva recounts that in Zambia in 1974 the fields were planted with hybrid maize. Twenty percent of the hybrids were infested with mold and destroyed while the indigenous varieties remained virtually untouched (ibid., 100).

64. Ibid, 145–46.

65. Ibid, 147–48.

hope. Walter Brueggemann, speaking about Dan 4, reminds us "the empire is understood by the narrative as a potential place for mercy; Nebuchadnezzar is presented as a ruler who is capable of mercy to the oppressed."[66] Empires can be brought to a potential place of mercy when brought under God's sovereignty.

66. Walter Brueggemann, "At the Mercy of Babylon: A Subversive Rereading of the Empire," *JBL* 110 (1991): 14.

RUTH AND ESTHER AS MODELS FOR THE FORMATION OF GOD'S PEOPLE: ENGAGING LIBERATIONIST CRITIQUES*

Cheryl B. Anderson

Introduction

It is safe to say that the biblical narratives of Ruth and Esther are known in most, if not all, Christian faith communities. The stories about these two female characters are presented early, in children's Sunday School classes, and they are presented regularly in sermons and Christian education classes for adults. The books of the Bible that bear their names are readily recognized as part of the Christian canon and, as such, they offer guidance for our faith and serve as "a measuring stick" to evaluate believers' lives in accordance with that faith.[1] We know Ruth and Esther to be exemplary models of loyalty, faithfulness, and commitment to the people of God, and we are told to act likewise.

However, we tend not to know (or, if we know, we tend not to consider) the critiques of that dominant portrayal of Ruth and Esther offered by feminist/womanist, queer, and postcolonial readings, referred to here collectively as "liberationist critiques." The goals of the present study are to engage these critiques by presenting the challenges they pose to conventional readings of these texts, and, after discussing these critiques, to identify themes yet within these texts that avoid the problematic implications. Finally, an interpretive approach will be proposed that allows Ruth and Esther to be read as models of Christian formation that are inclusive and mutually enriching.

In general, the books of Ruth and Esther have much in common. Not only are they both found in the Writings of the Hebrew Bible, they are in

---

* A slightly modified version of the present study appeared as a chapter in Cheryl B. Anderson, *Ancient Laws and Contemporary Controversies: The Need for Inclusive Biblical Interpretation* (New York: Oxford University Press, 2009). I am grateful to Oxford University Press for granting permission for the material to be reproduced here.
1. Daniel J. Harrington, "Introduction to the Canon," in *NIB*, 1:7.

the *megillot*, or five scrolls, and, as such, they are each associated with a specific Jewish festival: Ruth (Pentecost) and Esther (Purim).[2] More specifically, though, the female character after whom each book is named acts within a foreign environment. Ruth is a Moabite in Judah and Esther is a Jewish woman in Persia. Their respective narrative contexts express a concern with the formation of Jewish identity in the Second Temple period (538 B.C.E. to 70 C.E.).[3] The underlying questions are the following: Should we include foreigners in our Jewish community (Ruth)? And, correspondingly, when we are in the midst of foreigners, how can we maintain our Jewish identity (Esther)? Even though these questions about community identity and its preservation were posed in another time and place, they remain of critical importance for people of faith today—both Jewish and Christian. The easy answers to these questions would be to exclude all who are different or simply assimilate by adopting the dominant religious and cultural identity, but the books of Ruth and Esther resist such easy answers. Nevertheless, such answers have been given to or have been adopted by certain marginalized groups. It is therefore as a form of resistance that liberationist readings have developed and their critiques are considered in the following sections of the present study.

Ruth: A Woman, a Daughter-in-Law, and a Moabite

Feminist/Womanist Critiques: Empowering the Marginalized
The story of Ruth can be a positive one for women. For example, the black South African biblical scholar Madipoane Masenya reads the book in the context of post-apartheid South Africa, with its legacy of white superiority that severely damaged African self-identity.[4] In that context, she argues that the story of Ruth the Moabite is one that reminds "all of us, particularly the powerful, that God is not partial to any person." Therefore, Masenya continues, God does not define us on the basis of race or gender, but on the basis of our availability "as agents of God's transforming *ḥesed* in the lives of our neighbors," where the Hebrew word *ḥesed* means "kindness, lovingkindness, faithfulness, or loyalty."[5] Similarly, for the Taiwanese biblical scholar, Julie Chu, Ruth is the story

---

2. Bruce C. Birch et al., *A Theological Introduction to the Old Testament* (2d ed.; Nashville: Abingdon, 2005), 449.
3. Ibid., 429.
4. Madipoane Masenya (ngwana' Mphahlele), "Ruth," in *Global Bible Commentary* (ed. Daniel Patte; Nashville: Abingdon, 2004), 86.
5. Ibid., 89.

of a woman whom a man, Boaz, describes as "worthy"—hence she is an equal partner to some extent (3:11) who is valued "more than seven sons" (4:15).[6] Furthermore, she finds in Ruth a demonstration that a mother and her daughter-in-law can cooperate rather than compete, as is sometimes the case in her cultural context.[7] For women of color, who are in contexts where issues of race as well as gender are constantly before them, Ruth's story is one of "a subversive character in that she subverts gender and ethnic boundaries in her actions."[8] In her South African Indian womanist reading of Ruth, Sarojini Nadar articulates the power of Ruth's story in the following way:

> At the beginning, Ruth is portrayed as oppressed in every sphere. She is a woman, a foreigner, a widow, and childless. By the end, we see that Ruth, through dexterity and intelligent action, has managed to cast aside all oppressive roles assigned to her.[9]

In contrast, some feminist scholars in the United States find certain aspects of the Ruth narrative to be deeply problematic. Summarizing the work of biblical scholars Katherine Sakenfeld, Amy-Jill Levine, and others, the theologian Kwok Pui Lan writes that it "does not challenge patriarchal and heterosexual familial structures."[10] More specifically,

> ...a widow can only find economic security through remarriage; marrying a man with some means (no matter the age difference) guarantees financial gains; giving birth to a son is the greatest responsibility of women; a male child is more valuable than a female child; and the authority of the mother-in-law is over the daughter-in-law.[11]

6. Julie L. C. Chu, "Returning Home: The Inspiration of the Role Dedifferentiation in the Book of Ruth for Taiwanese Women," *Semeia* 78 (1997): 50–51.

7. Ibid. In contrast, Amy-Jill Levine finds ambivalence in the relationship between Ruth and Naomi and a lack of appreciation on Naomi's part for her daughter-in-law's efforts. See Levine, "Ruth," in *Women's Bible Commentary* (ed. Carol A. Newsom and Sharon H. Ringe; exp. ed.; Louisville: Westminster John Knox, 1998), 84–90. See also Ellen Van Wolde, "Texts in Dialogue with Texts: Intertextuality in the Ruth and Tamar Narratives," *BibInt* 5 (1997): 1–28.

8. Sarojini Nadar, "A South African Indian Womanist Reading of the Character of Ruth," in *Other Ways of Reading: African Women and the Bible* (ed. Musa W. Dube; Atlanta: SBL, 2001), 171.

9. Ibid.

10. Kwok Pui Lan, "Finding a Home for Ruth: Gender, Sexuality, and the Politics of Otherness," in *New Paradigms for Bible Study: The Bible in the Third Millennium* (ed. Robert M. Fowler, Edith Blumhofer, and Fernando F. Segovia; New York: T&T Clark International, 2004), 141.

11. Ibid. See also Danna N. Fewell and David M. Gunn, *Compromising Redemption: Relating Characters in the Book of Ruth* (Louisville: Westminster John Knox, 1990).

Similarly, Masenya, who otherwise sees Ruth as a positive text for women, acknowledges that the suggestion of a sexual encounter between Ruth and Boaz on the threshing floor (3:6–15) implies in a patriarchal society (both Israelite and African) "that women would even risk to avail their bodies for male abuse as a coping strategy."[12] She notes, furthermore, that "in a world where women are not expected to have control over their bodies, it is common place to find women availing their bodies, whether willingly or not, as a coping mechanism to survive through marriage."[13] Likewise, Anna May Say Pa, in her Asian (Burmese) woman's reading of Ruth 3:1–5, sees the text as reinforcing cultural notions of submission, self-sacrifice, and obedience that often work to the detriment of Asian women.[14]

Just the same, Kwok acknowledges that "feminist scholars want to retrieve liberating moments in the story, since it is rare to find women with such major roles in a book in the Bible."[15] As Masenya identified, one of those "liberating moments" is that, in spite of the constraints of patriarchal hierarchies and ethnic boundaries, Ruth is not defeated by her circumstances but takes action to change her dire situation and, as such, she is a model for impoverished and marginalized women in southern Africa—and elsewhere.[16]

Queer Critiques: Challenging the Exclusive Focus on Males

Another of the "liberating moments" offered in the book of Ruth is that, contrary to earlier notions of Ruth as a woman committed to her deceased husband, she can be seen as "a woman-identified woman who is forced into the patriarchal institution of levirate marriage in order to survive."[17] From this perspective, other elements of "a woman-identified" world are evident. Naomi tells her daughters-in-law to return to "your mother's house," rather than the usual reference to the father's house (1:8); and both Naomi and Boaz recommend that Ruth stay among the women in

---

12. Madipoane Masenya, "Struggling with Poverty/Emptiness: Rereading the Naomi–Ruth Story in African-South Africa," *JTSA* 120 (2004): 58.

13. Ibid.

14. Anna May Say Pa, "Reading Ruth 3:1–15 from an Asian Woman's Perspective," in *Engaging the Bible in a Gendered World: An Introduction to Feminist Biblical Interpretation in Honor of Katharine Doob Sakenfeld* (ed. Linda Day and Carolyn Pressler; Louisville: Westminster John Knox, 2006), 47–59.

15. Kwok, "Finding a Home," 141.

16. Masenya, "Struggling with Poverty/Emptiness."

17. Laura E. Donaldson, "The Sign of Orpah: Reading Ruth Through Native Eyes," in *Ruth and Esther, A Feminist Companion to the Bible* (ed. Athalya Brenner; 2d series; Sheffield: Sheffield Academic, 1999), 132.

the fields (2:8, 22–23), indicating that "it is in the company of women that Ruth, like Naomi, will find safety."[18] Finally, when Ruth's son is born, the women of the neighborhood name him and he is referred to as Naomi's son, rather than that of her deceased husband or sons (4:17).

The clearest statement by Ruth as "a woman-identified woman," of course, is found in the first chapter. Ruth 1:16–17 reads:

> Do not press me to leave you
>   or to turn back from following you!
> Where you go, I will go;
>   where you lodge, I will lodge;
> your people shall be my people,
>   and your God my God.
> Where you die, I will die—
>   there will I be buried.
> May the Lord do thus and so to me,
>   and more as well,
> if even death parts me from you.

As Rebecca Alpert writes in her lesbian (or queer) reading of the text, if the speakers here were of opposite sexes, such a statement would certainly be read as "a poetic statement of (sexual) love" and its affirmation of and commitment to a woman results in its widespread use in lesbian ceremonies—both Jewish and Christian.[19] Alpert rightly contends that "without romantic love and sexuality, the story of Ruth and Naomi loses much of its power as a model for Jewish lesbian relationships," and that to add such elements is a form of midrash, "reading between the lines," is supported by "literary, historical, and logical possibilities."[20] For example, a literary possibility is based on the statement in 1:12 that Ruth "clung" to Naomi because the Hebrew verb there (*dabaq*) is the same used in Gen 2:24 to describe the model heterosexual relationship: "Therefore a man leaves his father and his mother and *clings* to his wife, and they become one flesh."[21]

---

18. Levine, "Ruth," 86.

19. Rebecca Alpert, "Finding Our Past: A Lesbian Interpretation of the Book of Ruth," in *Reading Ruth: Contemporary Women Reclaim a Sacred Story* (ed. Judith A. Kates and Gail Twersky Reimer; New York: Ballantine, 1994), 91–96.

20. Ibid., 95.

21. For a bisexual reading that challenges reading Ruth as a story about *either* a heterosexual relationship (Ruth and Boaz) *or* a homosexual one (Ruth and Naomi), see Celena M. Duncan, "The Book of Ruth: On Boundaries, Love, and Truth," in *Take Back The Word: A Queer Reading of the Bible* (ed. Robert E. Goss and Mona West; Cleveland: Pilgrim, 2000), 92–102.

Alternatively, the story of Ruth and Naomi portrays a non-sexual affirmation of women as friends—in other words, female bonding—that develops across various differences. As expressed by the womanist biblical scholar Renita Weems, "Ruth and Naomi's legacy is that of a seasoned friendship between two women that survives the test of time despite the odds against women as individuals, as friends, as women living without men."[22] Weems then suggests that, from this narrative, we should "take seriously the quality of our relationships with the women and men in our lives" and "refuse to be forced to choose between two good relationships—a romantic partnership with a man and a sustaining friendship with a woman."[23]

Postcolonial Critiques: Struggling against the Colonial Empire
Ruth is a Moabite, a tribe descended from an incestuous relationship between Lot and his daughters (Gen 19:30–38) and barred from membership in the ancient Israelite community by law (Deut 23:3–6). In the narrative, Ruth ignores the possibility of exclusion and goes to Judah with Naomi; in so doing, however, she loses her land, her people, and her own gods. In other words, the price of inclusion is relinquishing who she is and all that she has known. Some scholars from groups that have experienced forms of Western colonialism notice the striking similarity between their stories and that of Ruth. Indeed, their encounter with a colonial or the global empire has meant the loss of land and of indigenous traditions, and specific comparisons can be made to the African American and Native American historical contexts.

First, as the African American biblical scholar Randall Bailey has written, the same association of deviant sexuality with the Moabites and Ammonites has been made with African Americans in order to justify their social oppression and their devaluation as a people.[24] In the very same way, Andrea Smith (Cherokee) notes that the early colonizers in the United States marked Native Americans as a sexually perverse group to justify their actions.[25] Moreover, the pattern is to associate deviant practices particularly with the women in the targeted community, whether

22. Renita J. Weems, *Just a Sister Away* (rev. and updated ed.; West Bloomfield: Warner, 2005), 27.
23. Ibid., 36.
24. Randall Bailey, "They're Nothing But Incestuous Bastards: The Polemical Use of Sex and Sexuality in Hebrew Canon Narratives," in *Reading from This Place: Social Location and Biblical Interpretation in the United States* (ed. Fernando F. Segovia and Mary Ann Tolbert; Minneapolis: Fortress, 1995), 121–38.
25. Andrea Smith, *Conquest: Sexual Violence and American Indian Genocide* (Cambridge: South End, 2005), 7–33.

it is "the wanton Jezebel" of the black community or "the exotic hooker Suzie Wong"[26] of the Asian community, to give just two examples. From this perspective, Ruth the Moabite's behavior with Boaz on the threshing floor (Ruth 3) illustrates such associations of "foreign" women with deviant sexuality. Consequently, Ruth's brazen actions may only be acceptable in the narrative because she is a foreigner. In that case, Levine argues, "it is the reader's task to determine whether the book affirms Ruth or ultimately erases her, whether she serves as a moral exemplar or as a warning against sexually forward Gentile women."[27]

Second, Ruth's apparent assimilation into the Israelite community marks her erasure as a Moabite—a form of cultural erasure that is comparable with the treatment of Native Americans by colonial settlers. By the end of ch. 4 in the biblical narrative, Ruth's voice is not heard at all and the emphasis shifts to the genealogy of the Davidic line. Ruth has been absorbed into the community, even if not fully accepted as a member. By all appearances, the same strategy of assimilation helped colonizing powers conquer indigenous populations in the Americas. As Laura Donaldson points out, Thomas Jefferson's solution to "the Indian problem" was intermingling between whites and certain Indian groups, and severe disruption of cultural patterns, land loss, and the elimination of leadership roles for Native women resulted.[28] In this context, postcolonial readings of Ruth have been proposed which seek to counter the cultural erasure that comes about from assimilation. Correspondingly, Orpah, the other Moabite daughter-in-law in the narrative, the one who does return to her mother's house, as Naomi suggests (1:6–14), becomes more important as a model for colonized populations. Because Orpah, unlike Ruth, symbolizes the preservation of indigenous cultures, Donaldson feels that, for Native women, Orpah becomes "the story's central character."[29] She states:

> To Cherokee women, for example, Orpah connotes hope rather than perversity, because she is the one who does not reject her traditions or her sacred ancestors. Like Cherokee women have done for hundreds if not thousands of years, Orpah chooses the house of her clan and spiritual mother over the desire for another culture.[30]

26.   Gale A. Yee, *Poor Banished Children of Eve: Woman as Evil in the Hebrew Bible* (Minneapolis: Fortress, 2003), 159.
27.   Levine, "Ruth," 85.
28.   Donaldson, "The Sign of Orpah," 137–38.
29.   Ibid., 142.
30.   Ibid., 143. See also Judith E. McKinlay, *Reframing Her: Biblical Women in Postcolonial Focus* (Sheffield: Sheffield Phoenix, 2004), 37–56.

From this perspective, one postcolonial reading of the book of Ruth is to emphasize Orpah as a biblical character. Another postcolonial reading, done by Musa Dube, is to imagine that Ruth never forgot her heritage and that, after returning home, Orpah became the regent queen and a priestess.[31] Then, according to Dube, in the last of a series of "unpublished letters from Orpah to Ruth," Orpah, asks that Ruth instill in her children a respect for her native people (and theirs), the Moabites. In this imagined correspondence, Orpah writes to Ruth that she should tell her children the stories of the Moabites: "of their origins, of their kindness, of their hospitality, and of their struggles for survival."[32] In other words, the harmful effects of cultural absorption can be reduced if those in the midst of a colonial power remember who they are and inform those in power of the humanity and dignity of their people. The positive but usually limited view of Ruth's acceptance as an individual must be expanded to mean that a deeper understanding and respect results for her group—and other traditionally excluded and despised groups.

Dube, in a more recent article, sees in Ruth and Naomi's relationship the same unequal relationship that exists between nations in today's international setting.[33] Specifically, Dube determines that the relationship between Ruth and Naomi is an unequal one since Ruth pledges herself to Naomi but Naomi does not reciprocate. Consequently, "Ruth's pledge to Naomi has the tones of a slave-to-master relationship rather than an expression of mutual love between women or two friends" and this human relationship "connotes the relationship between Judah and Moab."[34] In the narrative, she argues, Moab, the subordinate nation, is associated with death (most notably, Elimelech and both sons die there) but the resources of Moab (Ruth's fertility) can be used for the benefit of Judah, the dominant one. Consequently, for Dube, Ruth's story is "unusable as a model of liberating interdependence between nations," yet creating and maintaining mutually beneficial relationships is "indispensable" to healing our world today.[35]

The preceding discussion shows that interpretations of Ruth vary widely, even within liberationist circles. Such lack of uniformity, of course, is related to the variety of social contexts in which the text is

31. Musa Dube, "The Unpublished Letters of Orpah to Ruth," in Brenner, ed., *Ruth and Esther*, 145–50.

32. Ibid., 150.

33. Musa Dube, "Divining Ruth for International Relations," in Dube, ed., *Other Ways of Reading*, 179–95.

34. Ibid., 192.

35. Ibid., 194.

interpreted. At the same time, though, some of the diversity is due to the text itself. In Carolyn Pressler's opinion, the range of readings is attributable, to some degree, to the storyteller and the artful way in which various themes are woven into the book: "Ruth is about economic survival *and* about loyalty *and* about accepting foreigners *and* about the loyalty of one woman to another." Pressler is aware that "the storyteller has put a number of ideas in conversation with one another" and, therefore, "the conversation continues through centuries of interpretation."[36] Clearly those conversations continue in our own day and time. As we will see in the next section, such a range of interpretations also exists for the book of Esther.

Esther: A Woman, a Queen, and a Minority

Feminist/Womanist Critiques: Who Really Wins?
At first glance, Esther is a biblical character who has three strikes against her: she is female, an orphan, and, as a Jew in the Persian Empire, a member of a marginalized group. In spite of the odds against her, she marries the king, making her the queen, and she uses her influence with the king to save her people when their lives are threatened. All of this should make her the obvious hero/ine of the story, but her role has not always been given its due. As Sidnie Ann White Crawford tells us, "the tendency among scholars was to exalt Mordecai as the true hero of the tale and to downplay or even vilify the role of Esther."[37] For example, one commentator wrote that "Between Mordecai and Esther the greater hero is Mordecai, who supplied the brains while Esther simply followed his directions,"[38] and another questioned her sexual ethics, accusing her of having sought to join the king's harem "for the chance of winning wealth and power."[39] An early stage of feminist critique, then, was to simply acknowledge Esther's efforts in the unfolding of the story.[40]

36. Carolyn Pressler, *Joshua, Judges, and Ruth* (Louisville: Westminster John Knox, 2002), 264 (italics in original).

37. Sidnie Ann White Crawford, "Esther," in Newsom and Ringe, eds., *Women's Bible Commentary*, 133.

38. Carey A. Moore, *Esther* (AB 7B; Garden City: Doubleday, 1971), lii; Crawford, "Esther," 133.

39. Lewis Bayles Paton, *A Critical and Exegetical Commentary on the Book of Esther* (ICC; Edinburgh: T. & T. Clark, 1908), 96; Crawford, "Esther," 133.

40. See, e.g., Katheryn Pfisterer Darr, *Far More Precious than Jewels: Perspectives on Biblical Women* (Louisville: Westminster John Knox, 1991), 164–93; and Jon L. Berquist, *Reclaiming Her Story: The Witness of Women in the Old Testament* (St. Louis: Chalice, 1992), 154–66.

It did not take long, though, before questions were raised about Esther's appropriateness as a feminist model. Essentially, the concern was that "the book of Esther is about the status quo, maintenance of it, and finding a proper place within it."[41] Addressing the gender messages in the story, Susan Niditch shows that

> Its heroine is a woman who offers a particular model for success, one with which oppressors would be especially comfortable. Opposition is to be subtle, behind the scenes, and ultimately strengthening for the power structure.[42]

According to the South African biblical scholar Itumeleng Mosala, patriarchal gender roles are not challenged in the text: "Esther struggles, but Mordecai reaps the fruit of the struggle."[43] Not only is Mordecai the one who ends up with the deceased Haman's house and royal position (8:1–2), but the text clearly indicates that gender struggles are less important than the struggle for national survival.[44] In an immediate crisis, it might be true that national survival is the most pressing issue, but all too often marginalized groups are *always* in a struggle for survival and so the issue of gender equality is infinitely deferred. Instead, gender equality must be seen as an integral part of national survival here and now. Nevertheless, the status quo is not maintained uniformly in the text because a reversal does take place in the book of Esther—a threat against the Jews becomes a threat against the Persians. Yet, as Nicole Duran surmises, "what has not reversed is the relative positions of men and women" because Esther accomplishes what she does "by using the gender role assigned to her, not by opposing it."[45] So who really wins in the narrative? Not Esther!

At this point the female character in the book that takes on new importance is Vashti, the first queen mentioned in the book, whom King Ahaseurus deposes. While he was enjoying a banquet, attended by all of his top (male) officials, he commanded that Queen Vashti be brought before him "wearing the royal crown, in order to show the peoples and

41. Susan Niditch, "Esther: Folklore, Wisdom, Feminism, and Authority," in *A Feminist Companion to Esther, Judith, and Susanna* (ed. Athalya Brenner; A Feminist Companion to the Bible 7; Sheffield: Sheffield Academic, 1995), 33.
42. Ibid.
43. Itumeleng J. Mosala, "The Implications of the Text of Esther for African Women's Struggle for Liberation in South Africa," *Semeia* 59 (1992): 136.
44. Ibid.
45. Nicole Duran, "Who Wants to Marry a Persian King? Gender Games and Wars and the Book of Esther," in *Pregnant Passion: Gender, Sex, and Violence in the Bible* (ed. Cheryl A. Kirk-Duggan; Semeia 44; Atlanta: SBL, 2003), 81.

the officials her beauty; for she was fair to behold," but she refuses to go (1:11–12). As could be expected, the king is furious and his advisors warn him that word of Vashti's actions will spread to all women, and that when that happens, the women will "look with contempt on their husbands" (1:13–17). To head off that crisis, Vashti is sent away, a new queen is to take her place, and a royal decree is sent out that "every man should be master in his own house" so that "all women will give honor to their husbands, high and low alike" (1:17–22). After this incident, any doubt about the patriarchal nature of the culture described here is eliminated. As Linda Day observes, "men are the acting subjects, gaining their power by means of the objectification of women"; "the degree of their worthiness is the degree to which women are able to, or choose to, please men"; and "female worth is measured by male assessment, adjudicated in the eyes of a man."[46]

In such a context, Vashti's refusal is truly a massive act of disobedience, and her banishment functions as a warning to other women who might consider acting in this way. Vashti's apparent strength and willingness to speak her mind when the odds are against her make her an attractive role model for feminists. Often, though, too strong a contrast is made between a supposedly independent and rebellious Vashti and a relatively passive and obedient Esther. It must be pointed out that both women are "guilty of disobedience in terms of approaching the king, hence of taking control over her relationship with her husband."[47] Vashti refuses to appear before the king when invited, but Esther appears before the king without being invited, an act that was punishable by death (4:9–17). Moreover, Esther may have owed Vashti a debt of gratitude:

> King Ahasuerus might not have been so predisposed to forgive Queen Esther her brazen disobedience had not his first wife taught him that, like it or not, some women make their own decisions. At least with Esther, the king was willing to hear her out.[48]

Even if this book offers somewhat positive images of women in Vashti and Esther, there is still a problem with the sexual exploitation of young girls in the text. In ch. 2, the king chooses his next queen by having "all of the beautiful young virgins" from all of the provinces brought to him and "the girl who pleases the king [will] be queen instead of Vashti" (2:1–4). Each girl is brought to the king for a night. The

46. Linda M. Day, *Esther* (Abingdon Old Testament Commentaries; Nashville: Abingdon, 2005), 42.
47. Mieke Bal, "Lots of Writing," in Brenner, ed., *Ruth and Esther*, 227 n. 27.
48. Weems, *Just a Sister Away*, 118.

obvious implication is that the king had intercourse with each of these females (probably teenage girls), because they were returned to a different harem, the harem of the concubines, the next morning (2:12–14).[49] For the females who are forced to participate in this competition, there are dramatic consequences "in a society where virginity is a girl's only ticket to respectable adulthood."[50] The selection scheme described is an abuse of power that denotes "an all-powerful monarch, whose every need, including sexual ones, had to be taken care of, irrespective of the women he violated in the process."[51]

Given the plot's development, Sarojini Nadar contends, little attention is paid to King Ahasuerus's selection process—the narrative quickly shifts from Vashti to Esther—and the result is to "erase" from our awareness the sexual violence against females that occurs.[52] The problem is that when such texts are read today in contexts with a high incidence of rape, whether South Africa or, I would add, the United States, they tend to desensitize us to that ongoing violence as well, similarly erasing it from our awareness. To reverse that tendency, if we become more aware of the inherent violence of such biblical texts and start to contest it, we will be better able, as people of faith, to confront and contest sexual violence today.[53] Going beyond the hyperbole and humor in the book of Esther, Nicole Duran is left with two key questions: "what *really* happens to a woman who disobeys her husband, in a society that gives the husband complete authority over his wife?" and "what *really* happens to the girls whom the man in power considers unworthy?"[54] So who really wins in the narrative? Not females.

Queer Critiques: To "Pass" or Not to "Pass" Is the Question
When Esther is presented to the king she does not divulge that she is Jewish (2:10). Interestingly, Mordecai had told her not to tell, even though Mordecai had identified himself as a Jew (3:4). His warning Esther not to inform anyone of "her people or her kindred" means that

49.   Sidnie Ann White Crawford, "Esther," in *NIB*, 3:889.
50.   Nicole Duran, "Who Wants to Marry a Persian King?," 73.
51.   Sarojini Nadar, "'Texts of Terror': The Conspiracy of Rape in the Bible, Church, and Society: The Case of Esther 2:1–18," in *African Women, Religion, and Health* (ed. Isabel Apawo Phiri and Sarojini Nadar; Maryknoll: Orbis, 2006), 88.
52.   Ibid., 88–89.
53.   Ibid., 89–90. See also Cheryl B. Anderson, *Women, Ideology, and Violence: Critical Theory and the Construction of Gender in the Book of the Covenant and the Deuteronomic Law* (JSOTSup 394; London: T&T Clark International, 2004), 101–17.
54.   Duran, "Who Wants to Marry a Persian King?," 84 (italics in original).

Mordecai either sensed or knew from experience that being non-Jewish brings about privileges and opportunities that being Jewish in the Persian court forecloses. In the same way, African Americans have known that to be non-African American in a racist society would confer advantages. As a survival strategy, some light-skinned people of African descent would "pass" for white, that is, they would not divulge that they were African American, thereby enabling them to have access to education, housing, and employment that would be denied otherwise. In our post-civil rights era, the need for "passing" to avoid lawful restrictions by race is less likely to occur.[55] Nevertheless, the need to "pass" due to sexual orientation continues. A homophobic environment means that if gays and lesbians divulge who they truly are, they confront the general population's prejudices and discrimination by law. Before, heterosexual African Americans were discriminated against solely due to their race, while some other racial/ethnic groups were exempt. Now, negative impacts are experienced by gays and lesbians, whether they are African American or members of other racial/ethnic groups. To avoid that effect, some gays and lesbians "pass" as heterosexual and do not divulge their full identity.[56] Under these circumstances, Esther's lack of candor feels very familiar and her strategy comes across as a viable model of survival.

On the one hand, therefore, a queer critique recognizes that Esther's way of dealing with prejudice, by "passing," may be needed. On the other hand, there is the recognition that Vashti's defiance is instructive and necessary. As Gary Comstock writes in his book, *Gay Theology Without Apology*, "Vashti's refusal, not Esther's behind-the-scenes manipulations," can be encouraging and empowering.[57] Although recognizing that her story was meant to intimidate women (and others) by demonstrating the cost of refusal and resistance, Comstock argues that "we can turn that story around." In so doing, we can change her story from one of unacceptable behavior as usually thought into one which shows "that Vashti's actions were righteous and her punishment was unjust."[58]

---

55. There is no assumption here that racism no longer exists. For a discussion of contemporary forms of racism, see Patricia Hill Collins, *Black Sexual Politics: African Americans, Gender, and the New Racism* (New York: Routledge, 2005).

56. For a full discussion of "passing" and African American gays and lesbians, see Horace L. Griffin, *Their Own Receive them Not: African American Lesbians and Gays in Black Churches* (Cleveland: Pilgrim, 2006).

57. Gary David Comstock, *Gay Theology Without Apology* (Cleveland: Pilgrim, 1993), 56.

58. Ibid.

Referring to the significance of Vashti in liberationist theologies, both feminist and queer (referring specifically to Comstock's work), Linda Day elaborates on the continuing message of Vashti's story for any group that has been marginalized and silenced.[59] Pragmatism may point to Esther's model as the better one, she agrees, but sometimes personal integrity requires following in Vashti's footsteps:

> Yet in certain situations persons need to stand up against what they perceive to be immoral or unjust, to speak for righteousness without regard for the consequences. Freedom can prove to be expensive. But there are moments in life when enduring enslavement, in whatever guise it presents itself, is no longer an option, and one becomes willing to pay that price. At such turning points, one can only maintain personal integrity by standing up and taking the risk.[60]

In summary, a queer critique of Esther utilizes both Esther and Vashti as viable models. The message is clear: sometimes you have to "go along to get along"; at other times you have to "act up." To pass or not to pass is the question.

Postcolonial Critiques: Imperial/Colonial Powers, Marginalization, and Violence

Whether it was actually written during the Persian or the Hellenistic period, the book of Esther is set in a time when a foreign imperial power ruled Judea. In that context, Jews were a marginalized community and relatively powerless. Sidnie Ann White Crawford has argued consistently that, for these reasons, Esther becomes the model of success for Jews. Her argument is that, because Esther is basically powerless as a woman (and an orphan), her situation is comparable to that of diasporan Jews who are also powerless with respect to the imperial dominance:

> Because she was successful in attaining power within the structure of society, she served as a role model of diaspora Jews seeking to attain a comfortable and successful life in a foreign society.[61]

59. Day, *Esther*, 43.
60. Ibid.
61. Crawford, "Esther," 133. To the contrary, Randall Bailey finds in his reading of the text a condemnation of the king and Haman as well as of those Jews, Esther and Mordecai, who collaborate with the imperial regime. See Bailey's "That's Why They Didn't Call the Book Hadassah! Intersec(ct)/(x)ionality of Race/Ethnicity, Gender, and Sexuality in the Book of Esther," in *They Were All Together in One Place? Toward Minority Biblical Criticism* (ed. Randall C. Bailey, Tat-siong Benny Liew, and Fernando F. Segovia; Semeia 58; Atlanta: SBL, 2009), 227–50. I would like to thank Professor Bailey for making a pre-publication copy of his study available to me.

In today's context, a postcolonial critique examines how groups or nations survive their marginalization, whether that marginalization occurs politically, militarily or economically, and how the Bible has been used to support such marginalization.[62] From this postcolonial perspective, the book of Esther is problematic.

In Esther, a royal decree has gone out, at Haman's urging, that all Jews are to be destroyed (ch. 3). Esther, however, prevents the decrees implementation and thousands who were "enemies of the Jews" (non-Jews), in addition to the ten sons of Haman, are killed instead (ch. 9). In the narrative, Esther is a 'trickster' because "she ultimately succeeds in reversing the evil that was supposed to befall her own people by "tricking" the king to join her side."[63] Using a postcolonial critique, this does indeed demonstrate one of the survival strategies of the powerless, as Masenya contends.[64] Unfortunately, though, groups that are forced to survive as tricksters in this way are also forced to support the maintenance of the oppressive system since they dare not challenge that system itself.

Another problematic aspect of the narrative is the obvious retaliatory violence involved. In the past, anti-Jewish Christian interpreters have interpreted the text in ways that condemned Judaism by "treating the story's violence as normative and essential to Judaism rather than as a defensive response to mortal danger."[65] Given the reality of the Shoah (the more appropriate term for the "Holocaust"), where the annihilation of Jews was attempted and partially successful, Christians must reconsider such interpretations.[66] More specifically, Christians should reflect on the damaging ways in which Christianity has been constructed unfairly in opposition to Judaism and negatively influenced the interpretation of biblical texts such as Esther.[67]

62.   See, e.g., R. S. Sugirtharajah, *The Postcolonial Bible* (Sheffield: Sheffield Academic, 1998), and Musa W. Dube, *Postcolonial Feminist Interpretation of the Bible* (St. Louis: Chalice, 2000). For a survey of recent postcolonial feminist writings, see Susanne Scholz, *Introducing the Women's Hebrew Bible* (Introductions in Feminist Theology 13; London: T&T Clark International, 2007). I am grateful to Professor Scholz for giving me access to a pre-publication copy of her manuscript.

63.   Masenya, "Esther and Northern Sotho Stories: An African-South African Woman's Commentary," in Dube, ed., *Other Ways of Reading*, 47.

64.   Ibid.

65.   Day, *Esther*, 21.

66.   Ibid.

67.   Timothy K. Beal, *The Book of Hiding: Gender, Ethnicity, Annihilation, and Esther* (London: Routledge, 1997), 12.

Rather than being laudatory, however, the violence in the book of Esther shows the harm caused by volatile mixtures of colonialism and racial/ethnic/religious differences:

> Esther reminds modern readers of the ties between colonialism and violence and of how tension and hostility, when built up among different peoples brought together by imperialist powers, result in cycles of reciprocal revenge and persecution.[68]

Referring to the tragedy of September 11, 2001 and the subsequent global "war on terror" declared by the United States government, Wong Wai Ching Angela writes that it shows the massive damage caused when, in a "spirit of revenge" there is "a sweeping resolve from all sides to use violence for violence."[69] The book of Esther, therefore, glorifies a national identity that "promotes the establishment of an exclusive community by a victory over ethnic rivals gained through revenge and destruction."[70] Wong, disheartened by the interreligious/racial/ethnic struggles around the world today, must conclude that the book of Esther does not model ways for different groups to respect and accept one another. Instead, Wong contends that Esther must invite us to work towards creating a multicultural sense of community that includes "many ethnicities, languages, religions, and cultures."[71] I could not agree with her more.

Conclusions

In traditional interpretations of their narratives, Ruth and Esther are unquestionable paragons of virtue and exemplary models for the life of faith. Yet the preceding discussion has shown the range of challenges to those interpretations offered by feminist, queer, and postcolonial readings. Having considered these challenges, we can no longer ignore them. We have to ask ourselves: How can we now use these texts as models for the formation of God's people, but avoid the negative consequences that the liberationist critiques have identified? An answer to this question requires a reading strategy that opens up these texts in new ways. For example, new questions must be allowed for the book of Ruth—concerning Orpah after she returned home and Ruth after her baby was born—and for the book of Esther—concerning the fate of Vashti and the

68. Wong Wai Ching Angela, "Esther," in *Global Bible Commentary* (ed. Daniel Patte; Nashville: Abingdon, 2004), 137.
69. Ibid., 139.
70. Ibid., 137.
71. Ibid., 140.

slaughtered "Other." Such a reading strategy cannot be simplistic, literal, or one that reads biblical passages in isolation. To the contrary, the reading strategy proposed here is a process that looks at texts thematically, intertextually, and contextually.

Thematically, there is a strong continuity between Ruth and Esther because they both engage in the work of redemption. Johanna Bos defines redemption as "the responsibility people have for one another"; therefore, "redeemers are people who are appointed to take care of people who cannot take care of themselves."[72] Accordingly, Ruth is a redeemer because she makes herself responsible for Naomi's wellbeing and provides her with a son.[73] Similarly, Esther is a redeemer because she makes herself responsible for her people's wellbeing and removes the threat against their continued existence. Although there are specific biblical laws that refer to the responsibilities of a redeemer, those responsibilities can be thought of more expansively.[74] Following Bos's lead, the role of the redeemer is to carry out acts that maintain the overall welfare of the community (Esther) and reintegrate into the community those that would otherwise be separated from it (Naomi and Ruth).

Furthermore, the contours of the redeemed community itself are discernable in Ruth 4. Sakenfeld suggests that, although it is different from the more commonly accepted eschatological texts, Ruth 4 provides a vision of hope, "an extended metaphor for God's New Creation that we must find ways to re-express in language appropriate to God's continuing work in our midst."[75] In her analysis, she identifies the following features of this vision:

> a community that is characterized by reciprocal movement from margin to center and from center to margin, by racial/ethnic inclusiveness, and by adequate physical sustenance for all; a community of upright individuals together creating and affirming justice and mercy; a community in which weeping turns to joy and tears are wiped away; a community in which children are valued and old people are well cared for; a community in which a daughter is greatly valued.[76]

72.	Johanna Bos, *Ruth and Esther: Women in Alien Lands* (New York: General Board of Global Ministries of The United Methodist Church, 1988), 2, 4.
73.	Ibid., 4.
74.	Lev 25–27; Num 18, as well as the law of levirate marriage found in Deut 25:5–10 and alluded to in Ruth.
75.	Katharine Doob Sakenfeld, "Ruth 4: An Image of Eschatological Hope: Journeying with a Text," in *Liberating Eschatology: Essays in Honor of Letty M. Russell* (ed. Margaret A. Farley and Serene Jones; Louisville: Westminster John Knox, 1999), 63.
76.	Ibid.

Sakenfeld admits that it is this vision that must be culled from the text rather than the expressions of the ancient Israelite culture identified there or the questionable means of achieving the vision in the narrative.[77] In other words, perceiving the story of Ruth as the story of a new vision of community towards which we should all work does not mean that the cultural biases of an ancient time and place have to carry over into our own contexts. Plus, reading Ruth 4 as an eschatological text emphasizes the role that human beings must play in bringing about that vision. Sakenfeld notes that more conventional eschatological texts, such as Jer 31 and Ezek 47, offer divine promises and indicate that human actions are not needed because "all is in God's hands."[78] In contrast, neither the book of Ruth nor that of Esther includes a report of direct intervention by God; and in Esther, there is no mention of God at all.[79]

Next, reading these texts intertextually means that Ruth and Esther are read in conjunction with at least one other biblical text. Notably, Bos has observed, as have others, that there are similarities between Esther and the Exodus story.[80] She thinks of these books as two poles of the Exodus experience where Esther represents the pole of oppression and the Exodus story represents liberation. An intertextual reading of Ruth and Esther, therefore, indicates that redemption is associated with liberation and that to redeem (or liberate from oppression) is the work of the people of God. The relative absence of God in both books indicates that human beings are called to act and not rely solely on divine intervention. As described by Fewell and Gunn, in spite of appearances to the contrary, God is in the book of Ruth because "God can be found somewhere in the mixed motives, somewhere in the complicated relationships, somewhere in the struggle for survival, anywhere there is redemption, however compromised."[81] Correspondingly, to do acts of redemption is to do God's work in the world.

Furthermore, in her work on Ruth, Jacqueline Lapsley identifies a pattern of blessing, where Boaz invokes a divine blessing on Ruth (2:12), Naomi on Boaz (2:19 and 2:20) and Boaz on Ruth (3:10), and the women bless YHWH for not leaving Naomi without kin (4:14).[82] Lapsley finds that "the centrality of their relationship to God empowers them to

---

77.   Ibid.

78.   Ibid., 56.

79.   Johanna Bos, *Ruth, Esther, Jonah* (Atlanta: John Knox, 1986), 3.

80.   Ibid., 41.

81.   Fewell and Gunn, *Compromising Redemption*, 105.

82.   Jacqueline Lapsley, *Whispering the Word: Hearing Women's Stories in the Old Testament* (Louisville: Westminster John Knox, 2005), 105.

seek blessings for others, and to act out blessings for others through their own acts of *ḥesed*.[83] A liberationist reading of Ruth and Esther, consequently, demands that the people of God create a new kind of community, one that blesses, and we are to do that by redeeming/liberating/freeing those who are usually excluded because of marginalization, exploitation, or other types of oppression.

Any community must confront the various differences that exist among human beings (and other communities) based on gender, class, race/ethnicity, sexual orientation, religion, and national origin. All too often, though, a determination that a group is different based on one or more of these criteria means that group becomes "less than" or unacceptable to some degree and it then becomes acceptable to mistreat that other group. The contemporary notion of "liberating interdependence" accepts these differences and affirms the interconnections between (and within) cultures, sexes, races, religions, and nations while it seeks connections that are not oppressive and exploitative.[84] In other words, liberating interdependence "defines the interconnectedness of relationships that recognize and affirm the dignity of all things and people involved."[85]

Such considerations are crucial because, all too often, the freedom of one group has occurred at the expense of another. Historically, those who have experienced oppression have gone on to become perpetrators of oppression.[86] Hopefully, a commitment to liberating interdependence may help to break the cycle of violence. Conventional readings of Ruth and Esther describe the creation of a community, but that community continues to be marked by exclusion, exploitation, and violence, as the feminist/womanist, queer, and postcolonial critiques contend. However, the vision of community offered in Ruth 4, as Sakenfeld suggests, is inclusive, sustaining, and affirming. As people of faith, we are called not just to create a community, but to create a certain kind of community, one of liberating interdependence—a redeemed community in which the negative consequences of exclusion and exploitation have disappeared.

Finally, the strategy presented here requires contextual readings. As stated earlier, feminist/womanist, queer, and postcolonial readings of Ruth and Esther tell us that conventional barriers to community membership and participation must be removed. For that to happen, though,

83. Ibid.
84. Dube, *Postcolonial Feminist Interpretation*, 185.
85. Ibid., 186.
86. Scott M. Langston, *Exodus Through the Centuries* (Blackwell Bible Commentaries; Malden, Mass.: Blackwell, 2006), 4–8.

marginalized groups have to be aware that they are excluded and "to cry out on account of their taskmasters" (Exod 3:7). To develop this awareness, they must read biblical texts contextually—that is, the group must consider their own historical memories and their cultural/political/economic circumstances to determine if their experience is closer to that of Ruth or Orpah or to Esther or Vashti, and so forth. In other words, today's groups must resist the tendency to identify immediately with the privileged "chosen" group in these narratives, when their realities more closely resemble those of the excluded groups. Such resistance is difficult to muster because these same marginalized groups are usually told that the traditional reading, the reading of "the chosen people," is the only valid one. Yet, as mentioned before, if they ignore the marginalization occurring in the text, they are more likely to ignore the marginalization occurring in their own lives. Developing such an awareness is a complex task, though, because within any one group are individuals with differing relative privileges. Consequently, some in the group may experience privileges based on race or class, but others within the same group may experience disadvantages based on sexual orientation or gender. Allowances for diverse experiences must be made, therefore, within groups and between groups.

Basically, the objective of a liberationist reading is to re-consider each of these categories that are traditionally used to exclude—such as gender, sexual orientation, and national/cultural identity—and then ask new questions. Since the responsibility as a person of faith is to redeem, those with privileges according to these criteria must ask themselves: How have I/we excluded some groups and how should I/we act to incorporate them fully in the community? Correspondingly, those who are currently excluded or denied full participation based on these criteria must ask themselves: How can my/our voices be heard and what kind of redemption/inclusion do I/we seek? Given these elements, a liberationist reading of Ruth and Esther, or any other biblical text for that matter, is thematic, intertextual, and contextual. Finally, it is a dynamic process that requires the critical reflection and participation of all alike, incorporating the dominant and the subordinate characters in the text and the current winners and past victims in our world today.

Ruth and Esther were marginalized women who were disadvantaged in three different ways in their contexts as female, widow, and foreigner (Ruth), and female, orphan, and foreigner (Esther). They are remarkable figures in a cultural setting and a biblical canon in which women are most often unnamed and are acted upon rather than able to act in their own right. From this perspective, Ruth and Esther serve as models of hope and inspiration for marginalized groups today. They also serve, though, as a reminder that marginalized groups, those who experience the trauma of exclusion and violence, must speak out. Simultaneously, Ruth and Esther prod the privileged into doing acts of redemption that serve the wellbeing of the full community, and redemption can be achieved only by including those once excluded. God calls us to form redeemed communities, but we can only do that if we heed the voices we usually prefer to ignore. The choice is up to us.

READING PERSIAN DOMINION IN NEHEMIAH: MULTIVALENT LANGUAGE, CO-OPTION, RESISTANCE, AND CULTURAL SURVIVAL

Herbert R. Marbury

Nehemiah 10 and 13 admonish against intermarriage between the *golah*, or the Jerusalem community, and the *ʿam haʾarets*, or the people of the land. The rhetoric is separatist and immediately disconcerting. Imagine the mass divorces—the putting away of wives and the wholesale disintegration of families. For those of us who are heirs to the socially liberal ideologies of the civil rights and other movements of the 1960s and '70s, it offends even the most stalwart of our moral sensibilities. Why would one want to study such a phenomena? Perhaps such rhetoric holds more than is readily apparent. For the purposes of this discussion, rhetoric is language that intends to induce the cooperation of the hearer and is inextricably embedded in the social world.[1] It simultaneously subverts and directs power. Such rhetoric is political; it takes sides. Because hearers as much as speakers participate in the hermeneutical circuit, rhetoric can mean differently to different hearers. Construed this way, rhetoric possesses multiple significations. The same rhetoric can appeal to opposing sides of a singular conflict while strategically promoting various interests in unexpected ways. I argue that this is the case with the separatist rhetoric of the Jerusalem community.

Three significations have shaped much of scholarship on the rhetoric, namely, theological, cultural, and imperial. First, studies concerned with the rhetoric's theological signification generally focus on the restoration of the cult, the significance of the "holy seed," and take Ezra and

---

1. Bernard L. Brock, Robert L. Scott, and James W. Chesebro, "An Introduction to Rhetorical Criticism," in *Methods of Rhetorical Criticism: A Twentieth-Century Perspective* (ed. Bernard L. Brock, Robert L. Scott, and James W. Chesebro; Detroit: Wayne State University Press, 1990), 9–23. Edward W. Said, *The World, the Text, and the Critic* (Cambridge, Mass.: Harvard University Press, 1983), 4–6.

Nehemiah's religious devotion as the impetus for the rhetoric's production.[2] This approach risks discounting Persia's interest in the separatist rhetoric and attributes far more autonomy to Yehud than was enjoyed by other regions under Persian domination. It assumes that the Persian king allowed a radical restructuring of the social world of the most important city of the province simply to appease a small minority. It also assumes that the Persian-funded temple in Yehud was a symbol of the king's devotion to or at least patronage of the local cult rather than a part of the regular bureaucratic apparatus operative in provinces throughout the empire. In effect, this view makes the Persian imperial authorities beholden to the Jerusalem cult and its community, a reversal of the relationship of imperial domination. Second, studies guided by anthropological approaches and concerned with the rhetoric's cultural significations

2. Such an approach begins with the assumption that Ezra and Nehemiah returned to Jerusalem because the cult was in disarray, the returnees had neglected the temple, the wall of the city was in ruins, and most importantly, the "holy seed" had defiled itself by mixing with the "people of the land." Devotion to their faith compelled the two reformers to seek Persia's permission to work in Jerusalem. Adherents to this view argue that Ezra and Nehemiah intend to restructure the community according to the dictates of the Pentateuch, particularly Deut 6. These studies generally hold one of three positions to describe Persia's cooperation with the reformers' plans to carry out such radical social restructuring. First, Ezra's and Nehemiah's plans only incidentally coincided with Persian interests for internal organization in the provinces. Second, the Persians were simply benevolent kings, supportive of religious freedom in the provinces, and tolerant of the religious desires of local cults. Third, the Persians gave the province some special dispensation as a reward for remaining loyal to the crown during the revolt of 485 B.C.E. For example, Noth argues that Ezra's mission was an attempt to give the religious community in Judah "a new and binding organization since the old tribal federation and its organizations had dissolved..." Martin Noth, *The History of Israel* (New York: Harper & Brothers, 1958), 331–32. Koch sees Ezra's mission as a means of establishing religious law. For him, the separatist rhetoric functioned to make a distinction among the people between the sacred and the profane. Klaus Koch, "Ezra and the Origins of Judaism," *JSS* 19 (1974): 173–97. Miller and Hayes argue that the separatism signified a religious purity; see J. Maxwell Miller and John H. Hayes, *A History of Ancient Israel and Judah* (Philadelphia: Westminster, 1986), 472. Birch appeals to Daniel Smith's argument that the separation signified a concern for ritual purity and an attempt to protect the community from pollution; see Bruce C. Birch, *Let Justice Roll Down: The Old Testament, Ethics, and Christian Life* (Louisville: Westminster John Knox, 1991), 307–9. See also Smith, *The Religion of the Landless: A Social Context of the Babylonian Exile* (Bloomington: Meyer-Stone, 1989), 139–51. Grabbe argues from literary and historical perspectives that the rhetoric indicated a concern for piety and is based on Mosaic Law; see Lester L. Grabbe, *Ezra–Nehemiah* (New York: Routledge, 1998), 143–50.

generally focus on interethnic struggles in Yehud. They emphasize the threat of Persian or "outsider" cultural hegemony perceived by members of the Jerusalem community invested in ethnic identity maintenance.[3] Third, studies that focus on the imperial signification see the Persian Empire as key to understanding the rhetoric. They argue that the interests of the Persian Empire lie at the very heart of the rhetoric production.[4] Most of these studies understand the rhetoric as possessing a univocal dominant signification that stems from either the province's internal impulses or external dynamics. However, each of the three significations is not only plausible, but also probably inhered simultaneously within the social matrix of Yehud. Internal and external concerns drove Yehud's fortunes. As a part of the imperial system that included Ebr-Nahara and Egypt, the province experienced daily the exigencies of imperial rule. Particularly, its temple faced fiscal pressures similar to those of its counterparts in Babylon, Egypt, and throughout the imperial system. Internally, various groups vied for status, power, and security. Both internal and external concerns intersect in the economic dimensions of the Jerusalem temple. If so, then an interpretation that foregrounds these economic concerns can reveal the interplay between the theological, cultural, and imperial significations of the rhetoric. I argue that the separatist rhetoric in Neh 10 and 13, constructed by the postexilic Jerusalem priesthood, served as a powerful response to imperial fiscal pressure. It was oriented in two directions. It was directed, first, toward meeting the Jerusalem temple's fiscal burdens under imperial policies of depletion, and second, toward maintaining the Jerusalem community's economic stability and cultural cohesion.

---

3. For example, see Joseph Blenkinsopp, *Ezra–Nehemiah* (OTL; Philadelphia: Westminster, 1988), 173–77, 363–64, and Smith, *The Religion of the Landless*. Both argue that the rhetoric promoted religious and ethnic identity maintenance.

4. For example, see studies by Jon Berquist and Kenneth Hoglund. Both take further Peter Frei's hypothesis that the Persian Empire exercised extensive control over Yehud. For these studies, the Persian Empire and the exigencies of imperial rule influenced more significantly the social organization of the small province than previous studies admit. See Jon L. Berquist, *Judaism Under Persia's Shadow* (Minneapolis: Fortress, 1995), 110–19; Kenneth Hoglund, *Achaemenid Administration in Syria-Palestine and the Missions of Ezra and Nehemiah* (SBLDS 125; Atlanta: Scholars Press, 1992), 201–40; see also Peter Frei and Klaus Koch, *Reichsidee Und Reichorganisation im Perserreich* (2d ed.; OBO 55; Fribourg: Universitätverlag, 1996).

Persian Dominion: A View from Babylon and Egypt

Between 539 B.C.E. and 525 B.C.E., Persian conquests of Babylon and Egypt ruptured the cultural continuity of native rule and brought radical shifts in state policies toward temples and priesthoods. Temples were the central, organizing, and unifying institution in ancient Near Eastern societies.[5] Because local temples and their respective priesthoods mediated the power of the local deity, managing them was an important component of successfully administering a satrapy. The Persians understood local priesthoods' ability to bestow divine legitimacy upon the ruler, particularly one who was now foreign. Achaemenid Persian kings shared administrative goals with both the Babylonian kings and Egyptian pharaohs, namely, to exercise control over a temple's power, popular influence, and property without alienating the support of their influential priesthoods. As had their predecessors, the Persian kings deployed an effective combination of persuasive propaganda and intimidating military power to control temple systems and appropriate their economic surpluses. In Persian inspired literature, Cyrus II the great appears as the restorer of religious traditions. Similarly, in the biblical literature, Cyrus is the one who restores Jerusalem by allowing the captives to return to their homeland, to rebuild the temple, and to serve Yahweh.

In Isa 45:1 Cyrus is even proclaimed "messiah," the only non-Israelite so honored. However, these portrayals mask Cyrus's role in orchestrating the cooperation of local temples toward imperial ends. Far from liberating the former Babylonian subjects in order to restore them to their native communities, Cyrus was a conqueror. At least two imperial interests in local priesthoods motivated his activities. First, the crown needed native priesthoods to depict the rule of the new Persian king as legitimate to the local populations. To this end they exploited local priesthoods' familiarity with local customs and religious traditions. Second, the imperial system depended upon temple surpluses. To fulfill these interests, Cyrus deployed a sophisticated set of tactics at the intersection of religious hermeneutics and political expediency. With religious and royal propaganda he elicited or coerced to support Persian rule. He developed alliances with local priesthoods by granting them increased wealth and elevated social statuses (but no real political power), if they cooperated,

---

5. John M. Lundquist, "What Is a Temple? A Preliminary Typology," in *The Quest for the Kingdom of God: Studies in Honor of George E. Mendenhall* (ed. H. B. Huffmon, F. A. Spina, and A. R. W. Green; Winona Lake: Eisenbrauns, 1983), 205–19.

or threatening to seize their wealth and diminish their social statuses, if they did not.[6]

The empire first deployed this strategy in Babylonia. In the city of Babylon, Nabonidus, the last of the Neo-Babylonian kings, had so mismanaged his relationship with the priesthood of the national deity Marduk that his reign faced a crisis of legitimation. Taking advantage of Nabonidus' predicament, Cyrus forged relationships with local priesthoods. While his army fought the ground war, Cyrus, with the assistance of Babylonian priesthoods, claimed a bloodless victory. Using Babylonian religious traditions, he portrayed himself as a devotee of the god Marduk, a patron of the neglected Marduk priesthood, and redeemer of the city of Babylon. According to the literature, Cyrus comes to reestablish the proper traditions of Babylon neglected by Nabonidus. Cyrus even co-opts Marduk, claiming that the deity forsook Nabonidus and delivered him into Cyrus's hands. At every turn, Cyrus was more hermeneutically sophisticated at deploying a foreign (Babylonian) religious tradition than Nabonidus was at using his native religious tradition to legitimate his own reign. Presumably, Babylonian priestly elites, well versed in the stories and symbols of local religious traditions, but disenfranchised by Nabonidus' policies, composed the literature to ingratiate themselves to the new ruler. In Babylon, the priesthood portrayed Cyrus and his successors as the legitimate rulers. By the end of Cyrus' campaign, he so commanded the loyalty of the priesthood that even when Nabonidus attempted to rescue the gods from Cyrus's advance by transporting statues from local shrines to the capital city of Babylon, his own priesthood turned against him. His desperate act of cultic devotion became fodder for the rewritten traditions of cultic elites now loyal to Persia. They reported that Nabonidus absconded with the gods against their will:

> From […], Ashur and Susa, Agade, Eshnunna, Zamban, Meturnu, Der, as
> far as the region of Gutium, the cities on the other side of the Tigris,
> whose dwelling-places had [of o]ld fallen into ruin—the gods who dwelt
> there I returned to their home and let them move into an eternal dwelling.
> All their people I collected and brought them back to their homes. And
> the gods of Sumer and Akkad, which Nabonidus to the fury of the lord of

---

6. Briant thinks that even Udjahorresne, who was the architect of Cambyses' and Darius' royal ideologies in Egypt, did not receive a single position of political power and influence. He believes that the Medes were the only non-Persians trusted with politically influential positions; see Pierre Briant, *From Cyrus to Alexander: A History of the Persian Empire* (trans. Peter T. Daniels; Winona Lake: Eisenbrauns, 2002), 81.

the gods had brought into Babylon, at the order of Marduk, the great lord, in well-being I caused them to move into a dwelling-place pleasing to their hearts in their sanctuaries. May all the gods, whom I have brought into their cities, as before Bel and Nabu for the lengthening of my life, say words in my favor and speak to Marduk, my lord: "For Cyrus, the king, who honors you, and Cambyses, his son…"[7]

The priesthood claimed that Cyrus, in turn, restored these deities to their local shrines:

I settled all the lands in peaceful abodes. Furthermore, I resettled upon the command of Marduk, the great lord, all the gods of Sumer and Akkad whom Nabonidus has brought into Babylon to the anger of the lord of the gods, unharmed, in their (former) chapels, the places which make them happy.[8]

In return, the Persian conqueror received the gratitude and the loyalty (or at least the fealty) of the local priesthoods and other elites.

Just as Cyrus made use of the priesthoods in Babylonia,[9] his successors, Cambyses and Darius I, employed the Egyptian priesthoods of the sanctuary of Neith at Sais to represent Persians as legitimately descendant from the Saite kings of the XXVIth Dynasty. In Egypt, the network of exchanges is more apparent than in Babylon. Cambyses and Darius I made overt alliances with temples and with cultic elites. Udjahorresne, an Egyptian priest, reported that both Cambyses and Darius I instructed him to create for the two Persian rulers grand pharonic titles such as those used by the previous Saite kings and to mold their images to fit that of a native Egyptian pharaoh. The Statue of Udjahorresne reads:[10]

I asked the majesty of the King of Upper and Lower Egypt Cambyses on account of all the foreigners who had set themselves down in the temple of Neith should be expelled there from in order to cause that the temple of Neith should be once more in all its splendor as it had been earlier. Then his majesty commanded to expel all the foreigners who dwelt in the temple of Neith, to tear down their houses and their entire refuse which was in the temple. His majesty commanded to purify the temple of Neith

---

7. Amélie Kuhrt, *The Persian Empire: A Corpus of Sources from the Achaemenid Period* (New York: Routledge, 2007), 1:72–73.

8. *ANET* 3:315–16.

9. See M. Cogan, *Imperialism and Religion: Assyria, Judah and Israel in the Eighth and Seventh Centuries B.C.E.* (SBLMS 19; Missoula, Mont.: Scholars Press, 1974), 33–34.

10. Udjahorresne calls him "The Great King of all foreign lands. His majesty handed over to me the office of chief physician. He caused me to be beside him as a 'friend' and 'controller of the palace', while I made his royal titulary in his name of the King of Upper and Lower Egypt Mesuti-re."

and to restore to it all its people [...] and the hourly-priest of the temple. His majesty commanded that offerings should be given to Neith, the Great One, the Mother of God, and to the great gods who are in Sais as it was earlier in it... The King of Upper and Lower Egypt came to Sais.[11]

In return for Udjahorresne's work, Cambyses rid the temple of foreigners, ordered its purification, restored land to the goddess of Neith and established libations for Osirus. Later, Darius elevated Udjahorresne to the status of Chief Physician of the House of Life, a highly respected position but one that carried little political authority. Darius continued Cambyses' patronage of the temple at Sais, completed the construction of the temple at El-Kharga and the restoration of the House of Life, the fourth-century medical school at Neith.[12]

Clearly, Persian imperial rule employed temples in both Egypt and Babylon to bestow the local deity's legitimation upon its rule. However, beyond creating a religious ideology that legitimated Persian rule, was there any other benefit to the Persian administration of temple systems? Yes. Not simply the center for the local cult, temples controlled wealth. Temple economies were major economic producers in Babylon and in Egypt. Often they dominated the economies in their locales. Larger temples with more powerful and influential priesthoods held tenure to *latifundia* and counted hundreds of slaves among their inventories.[13] As a routine practice, kings placed land and slaves under a temple's administration. With these human and natural resources, temples produced huge agricultural surpluses, and increased the value of the land and slaves to the crown.

Early on, Persian kings employed an extensive imperial bureaucracy to exploit this vast economic resource. Satraps, Persian governors, and other lesser officials closely monitored the agricultural production of temples. They protected the interests of the king by ensuring that the portions of temple surpluses requested were sent to royal residences

11. See Kuhrt, *The Persian Empire*, 118. See also "Statue Inscription of Udjahorresne" in Miriam Lichtheim, *Ancient Egyptian Literature* (Berkeley: University of California Press, 1980), 38.

12. Herbert Eustis Winlock, ed., *The Temple of Hibis in El Khargeh Oasis* (New York: Arno, 1941), 7–9. While the temple's construction began under the last of the Saïte kings, the bulk of the work has been dated to the reign of Darius. There, he is called the son of Re and ray of Amon-Ra. See also J. Yoyotte, "Les inscriptions hiéroglyphique: Darius et l'Égypt," *Journal Asiatique* 260, no. 3–4 (1972): 253–56.

13. M. A. Dandamaev, "The Culture of Babylonia: Neo-Babylonian Society and Economy," in *The Assyrian and Babylonian Empires and Other States of the Near East, from the Eighth to the Sixth Centuries B.C.* (ed. John Boardman et al.; CAH; New York: Cambridge University Press, 1991), 270.

throughout the empire.[14] In Babylon, the Persian satraps and other imperial officials sent orders for goods and services produced by the temple as revenue for the crown. These orders generally included the phrase, "If not he will incur the punishment of Gubaru."[15] Gubaru, the satrap of Babylonia and Ebr-Nahara was given enough administrative latitude to govern very closely temple affairs, including receiving notification about the number of dead and runaway slaves. Since Egyptian temples owned huge tracts of land, taxes from those lands made excellent sources of income. Persian officials enforced the punishment of persons who stole temple property and temple shepherds who had failed to provide their requirement of sheep and cattle to the empire. At the same time, they increased fiscal pressure on the temples by not tithing, as had their Babylonian predecessors. Instead, in return for imperial protection, temples were required to pay taxes in cash, namely, silver. If they could not produce cash, then they were forced to supply all manner of in-kind tributes, including sheep, goats, cattle, barley, sesame, dates, wine, beer, spices, oil, butter, milk, wool, and provisions for state officials. Moreover, temples were required to provide slaves and skilled labor, such as farmers, herdsman, gardeners, and carpenters for service on royal estates.[16] Often these taxes levied against temple surpluses placed severe hardship on temple economies. Briant cites an example where the Persian authority required the Eanna of Babylon to deliver spices to the royal estate at Abanu. In order to fulfill the request, the temple went into debt for large amounts of silver.[17]

In Egypt, the evidence of Persian dominion shows an increasing hold on temple affairs. A demotic papyrus reports a decree by Cambyses that ordered the severe reduction of the funding of all local temples except for three.[18] Despite his favorable treatment in the Greek sources, Darius was more consistent and severe. There is no evidence that he lifted any of the harsh monetary policies of his predecessor, Cambyses. If anything, his

---

14. Amelie Kuhrt, *The Ancient Near East: C. 3000–330 BC* (Routledge History of the Ancient World 1; New York: Routledge, 1995), 689.

15. Briant, *From Cyrus to Alexander*, 73.

16. M. A. Dandamaev, "Achaemenid Babylonia," in *Ancient Mesopotamia, Socio-economic History: A Collection of Studies by Soviet Scholars* (ed. I. M. Diakonoff; Moscow: Nauka, 1969), 309–10.

17. Briant, *From Cyrus to Alexander*, 73.

18. Two reasons that Cambyses may have spared the temple at Memphis from the fiscal hardship were its strategic importance since it was the only Persian stronghold in the Delta Marshes and its status as the seat of the Persian satrap. See W. Spiegelberg, *Die sogenannte demotische Chronik des Pap. 215 der Bibliothèque Nationale zu Paris* (Leipzig: J.C. Hinrichs, 1914), column C, 6–16.

policy of bureaucratic intensification, taxing the provinces in a more consistent and organized manner, and his role as a legislator, gave him *more* control than Cambyses. Darius instructed his satrap to compose a legal compendium in both Aramaic and Demotic to standardize temple laws and to give Persian officials juridical authority in temple affairs,[19] even power in choosing temple officials.

The well-managed Persian bureaucratic machine was formidable, but it was not the only mode by which the Persians regulated temples. The empire's programmatic response to resistance—violence—was even more intimidating. While disputed, there are reports that in Babylonia, Xerxes destroyed temples that fomented rebellion.[20] In Egypt, an Aramaic papyrus from the colony at Elephantine reported Cambyses' use of force against temples.[21] Herodotus reported a public display of brutal force used against Egyptian priests and the public slaughter of 2000 young Egyptian males.[22] The threat of military force looming over the Egyptian priesthoods buttressed Cambyses' power to regulate local temples.

Ultimately, the Persians understood well the power and influence that temples held; they allowed their forces to occupy and destroy some temples but protected others.[23] The kings diminished and increased temple funding at will. They supported larger, more influential temples such as the one in Memphis, as a public display of generosity. Other temples throughout Egypt and Babylon, they raided and taxed. Taken in

---

19. W. Spiegelberg, "Drei demmotische Schreiben aus der Korrespondenz des Pheredates des Satrapen Darius I, mit den Chnumpriestern von Elephantine," *SPAW* 64 (1928): 604–22.

20. With regard to the veracity of the account and anti-Persian bias in the Greek sources, see Amélie Kuhrt and Susan Sherwin-White, "Xerxes' Destruction of Babylonian Temples," in *Achaemenid History*. Vol. 2, *The Greek Sources* (ed. Heleen Sancisi-Weerdenburg and Amélie Khurt; Leiden: Nederlands Instituut Voor Het Nabije Oosten, 1987), 70. The historicity of this specific account is less important than the imperial power to which it attests.

21. M. A. Dandamaev, *Slavery in Babylonia from Nabopolassar to Alexander the Great (626–331 B.C.)* (DeKalb: Northern Illinois University Press, 1984), 260–61; Spiegelberg, "Drei Demmotische Schreiben."

22. Herodotus, *The History* III.14 (LCL).

23. Briant, *From Cyrus to Alexander*, 58. Briant cites Udjahorreset's testimony that Cambyses ended the Persian occupation of the temple at Saïs at his request, which implies previous Persian occupation. See also Cowley, *Aramaic Papyri of the Fifth Century B.C.*, no 30. The papyrus from the mercenary colony at Elephantine attests, "Already in the days of the kings of Egypt our fathers had built that temple in the fortress of Yeb, and when Cambyses came into Egypt he found that temple built, and the temples of the gods of Egypt all of them they overthrew, but no one did any harm to that temple."

total, their behavior amounted to a carefully considered method of propagandistic persuasion and military coercion that closely regulated imperial temple systems, directed their ideologies, and appropriated their surpluses, all with a view toward control.

A Turn to Judah: Was Persian Administration Similar?

The nature of Persian dominion in Judah is central to a study of the separatist rhetoric. Was the Jerusalem temple given any special dispensation as the province inhabited by Yahweh's people? Why would the Persians administer Jerusalem's temple any differently than others? Would Darius go to great expense to fund the construction of a temple there unless its economic function was similar to that of other temples throughout the empire? Would the king exempt Jerusalem's temple and its priesthood from fiscal pressures imposed upon the rest of the empire? More importantly, how could its priesthood, with little material resources, respond to policies of imperial temple administration. There is no evidence that the temple in Jerusalem would not have been taxed by the Persians. It would have been required to meet certain taxation targets set for it no differently than those set for any other Persian temple. That burden would have increased significantly, as later kings desperately needed revenue to fund a far-flung and protracted war against the Greeks. Charles Carter has argued, based on archaeological surveys, that Yehud was a small, poor province.[24] Its economic resources were few. Operating under a foreign tributary economy, much of what little surplus it produced would have been siphoned off to fill imperial coffers. This factor affected the temple in Yehud more significantly than it impacted larger temples with more vast agricultural and human resources, such as the Eanna in Babylonia and Neith in Egypt. While those temples also struggled under burdensome Persian policies of economic depletion, the temple in Yehud, center of a small, poor province, struggled to a greater extent.

Beyond economic struggles, Yehud faced additional challenges. This small province was rife with ethnic diversity. As it was with much of the rest of the satrapy of Ebr-Nahara and the satrapy of Egypt, groups of varying ethnicities and social statuses competed for resources and power and not everyone in Yehud was an adherent of the Jerusalem temple. The minority Jerusalem community found itself pitted against several groups—some wealthier and more established. However, the *golah* arrived with imperial patronage. Niels Peter Lemche describes this

---

24. Charles E. Carter, *The Emergence of Yehud in the Persian Period: A Social and Demographic Study* (JSOTSup 294; Sheffield: Sheffield Academic, 1999).

relationship well, "By allowing elite groups of the Jewish society to return to their homeland, ...the king [of Persia] created a bond of personal loyalty between his regime and this new Jewish group, whom he could count on to help him govern his far-flung empire."[25] Just as the Persians allied themselves with priesthoods in Babylon and Egypt and instituted policies that facilitated state control enabling them to extract funds from those provinces, the Persians replicated the same model by forging a relationship with the returnees. Darius's funding for the Second Temple cemented Persia's bond with its priesthood. It gave them status and internal power, but also constantly reminded them of their imperial obligations. To this end, Persia appointed individuals loyal to the empire to serve as local officials in the province.[26] Cultic elites of the newly constituted *golah*, no different from their counterparts in Babylon and Egypt, must accept similar financial obligations to Persia. In other words, at one level, these "returnees" became *de facto* agents of the imperial system, and facilitated its hold on Yehud. In this relationship, the political interests of the empire worked in tandem with those who returned. The empire sought to expand and to maintain order, leaving the "returnee-elite" no choice but to control a "homeland" in order to stay in power. So, not only did the Persians want the immigrants to attain and maintain power in this western province of the empire, but the "returnees" themselves saw this as an opportunity to gain a measure of power and affluence that they may not have enjoyed in Babylon.[27]

One of the groups with whom the *golah* competed for power was a landed gentry class called the ʿ*am haʾarets*.[28] In Neh 13, the writer signifies upon[29] this group with the names of the traditional enemies of Israel (Deut 6 and Deut 23). Since the *golah* contended with this gentry

25. Niels Peter Lemche, *Ancient Israel: A New History of Israelite Society* (Biblical Seminar 5; Sheffield: Sheffield Academic, 1995), 180.

26. In Neh 5:14 we read that Nehemiah was the governor in the land of Judah. Neh 5:1–14 demonstrates his authority over priests, nobles, and other officials in the land.

27. Lemche argues that many of the exiles in Babylon were unable to maintain their former social and economic standing for lack of education or because of the Babylonians' suspicions of their loyalties. Consequently, many were reduced to the status of peasant farmers. See Lemche, *Ancient Israel*, 180.

28. Ernst Würthwein, "Amos-Studien," *ZAW* 62, nos. 1–2 (1950): 10–52.

29. By the phrase "signifying upon" I have in mind rhetoric's work of "troping" a trope. For a fuller discussion, see H. L. Gates, *The Signifying Monkey: A Theory of African-American Literary Criticism* (New York: Oxford University Press, 1988), 44–61. Gates defines signifying as "a trope that subsumes other rhetorical tropes, including metaphor, metonymy, synecdoche, and irony (the 'master' tropes), and also hyperbole, litotes, and metalepsis."

class for land and power from the position of a local minority, they were forced to engage the people of the land as a group. Only as a tightly cohesive collective could they compete with wealthy classes that evolved in Judah during the period of Babylonian domination. The struggle between these competing groups became a battle for the control of land. Tenure to arable land gave the former exiles the communal foundation from which to create wealth in the agrarian economy. Wealth in the hands of its devotees assured the temple that its community would be able to contribute the funds it needed to meet the imperial tax burden. The temple now only needed to construct the ideological basis for maintaining the *golah* community's land tenure, while affirming imperial rule. Such an ideology appears encoded in the separatist rhetoric.

One plausible context for the separatist rhetoric is the first half of the reign of Artaxerxes I. Artaxerxes I inherited an empire in severe economic decline. Two decades of Xerxes' policies of depletion would have left the Jerusalem temple unfunded, as it was under Darius' administration.[30] Burdensome fiscal requirements placed upon it and other temples throughout the empire as Persia funded campaigns against the Greeks and defended itself against yet another Egyptian revolt would force priestly activity to rely even more on its only source of funding, the tithe. The resulting economic scarcity in Judah would make legislating to preserve wealth an imperative. In such a predicament, any priesthood would encourage, even legislate the practice of tithing. But such legislation is only fruitful if the temple community possessed tenure to arable land.

So why legislate against intermarriage? In this context, intermarriage's most significant effect on the *golah* is its ability to transfer property, and thus wealth and status, from one group to another. Admonitions against intermarriage served to maintain land tenure within the group. We can assume that the men of the golah were not giving their daughters to less wealthy members of the *ʿam haʾarets*, but instead saw the marriage as an opportunity to gain in wealth and status.[31] In other words, not many parents willingly allow their daughters and sons to "marry down" the socio-economic ladder, but rather, they "marry up." In terms of sons marrying into the *ʿam haʾarets*, we can assume that there was some potential social benefit realized by an alliance between the two families.

30. Berquist, *Judaism Under Persia's Shadow*, 89–90.
31. For a fine study focusing specifically on intermarriage in Ezra 9–10, see Willa Mathis Johnson, "The Holy Seed Has Been Defiled: The Interethnic Marriage Dilemma in Ezra 9–10" (Ph.D. diss., The Graduate School, Vanderbilt University, 1999).

However, this benefit would not be realized immediately, as in the case of a *golah* daughter marrying an ʿ*am haʾarets* in exchange for a bride price. Of concern to the Jerusalem temple was the potential exogamy had to alienate land from *golah* families. Losing land to families who were not a part of the temple community or to those who were not adherents of the religion of Yahweh would shift the balance of wealth and power between social groups and would leave the *golah* further impoverished. In the instance of a *golah–ʿam haʾarets* marriage, there was no guarantee that the progeny would remain adherents of the temple or follow laws governing the tithe. In this regard, the separatist rhetoric of Neh 10 and 13 reflects struggles for control of material resources in the economic realm of Yehud. Nehemiah 10 ties together two central themes that are reaffirmed in Neh 13:4–31, namely, the crises of exogamy and the importance "house of God." In *this* connection, is a clear statement of the burdensome nature of Persian economic policy and the priesthood's response, the separatist rhetoric.

The Separatist Rhetoric in Context

Nehemiah 10 is cast as a response to the concerns raised in Neh 9. In Neh 9, the priesthood frames the problem of Persian dominion in a recitation of the pivotal events in Israelite history, namely: the creation in 9:6, the promise of Abraham (9:7–8), the Exodus, the call of Moses, the giving of the Law at Sinai (9:9–15), the wilderness wandering (9:19–21), and the conquest of the land. Interspersed between the recollection of Yahweh's saving acts is a lament for the wickedness (הרשענו) of their ancestors, and an affirmation of Yahweh's faithfulness despite the dis-obedience of Israel. The chapter culminates with a critique of their current social reality of imperial dominion, stating in vv. 35–37,

> Here we are slaves to this day—slaves in the land that you gave to our ancestors, to enjoy its fruit and its good gifts. Its rich yield goes to the kings whom you have set over us because of our sins; they have power also over our bodies, and over our livestock at their pleasure, and we are in great distress.

This final statement, in 9:37 (Eng.), makes the problem, the great distress, ובצרה גדלה, clear; it is Persian control over *golah* wealth—even the very bodies of the golah themselves. Signaled by the phrase "and because of all of this" (ובכל זאת, Neh 9:38 [Eng.])[32] the chapter opens by taking up same concern and offers the Priestly response to this "great

---

32. See Blenkinsopp, *Ezra–Nehemiah*, 311.

distress." The swearing of an oath opening Neh 10 calls the people to confront the crisis. Listing Nehemiah first, the document gives the names of the priests, the Levites, leaders, gatekeepers, singers, temple slaves, and all who have separated themselves from the people of the land. The listing goes even further by including their wives, daughters, and sons.[33] Usually these subordinate members of the family unit would not be named explicitly, but in this instance they are precisely the subject of this legislation. Immediately after listing the participants, the oath becomes more emphatic and binding, calling the people to join in a curse (ובשבועה), invoking the oath's enforcement by a cultural system of shame and honor. As if this were not enough to ensure compliance, the oath is framed as the law of God as given through Moses.[34] In so doing, the rhetoric vests the priesthood with the legitimacy of the ancient liberator, and his stature as the law-giver in the historical consciousness of the people. The rhetoric leaves no questions about either the seriousness with which the priesthood perceives the problem or the urgency with which they call the people to respond.

Finally, we read the first provision of the oath. How does the rhetoric intend the *golah* to respond to this "great distress?" Immediately following the signatories and the preamble communicating the oath's binding nature, v. 30 gives the provisions of the communal oath. Its first provision reads, "We will not give our daughters to the people of the land, nor will we take their daughters for our sons." By juxtaposing it to legislation concerning tithing in the following provision in v. 33, the rhetoric connects the preservation of group wealth and the support of the monetary needs of the temple.

After a brief mention of the violation of the sabbath, the text lists the forms in which the *tithe* is to be brought to the temple. On its face, this מצות, "commandment/obligation," in v. 33 is intended to fund temple functionaries and temple rituals. This list of tithes recalls some of the "Priestly" traditions of the tithe found in the Pentateuch. For the audience, it may connect support of this temple with support of the Solomonic temple. This association represents the act of paying the *tithe* as a continuation of an ancient ancestral tradition. At the top of the list is silver— one-third of a shekel שלישית השקל to be given annually from each household. This obligatory one-third shekel recalls the older tax of

33. Ibid., 314.
· 34. Neh 10:29 reads, "to join with their kin, their nobles, and enter into a curse and an oath to walk in God's Law, which was given by Moses the servant of God, and to observe and do all the commandments of the LORD our Lord and his ordinances and his statutes."

one-half shekel instituted by Moses for support of the sanctuary, and as a ransom preventing the onset of any plague (Exod 30:11–16). The former tax, situated in the wake of the Exodus, acted as a preventative against the recurrence of the devastating plagues sent upon Egypt. Looming behind this present tax is the devastation of the Babylonian exile and the mandate to obey the priesthood so as to prevent any future tragedy. Carter maintains that silver coinage in Yehud was very rare, and that a full-monied economy would not come about until the Hellenistic period. If this is so, then the placement of silver at the top of the list emphasizes all the more the urgency of the needs of the distressed temple.[35] The remainder of the list, the rows of bread, the regular grain, offering the sin offering, and the first fruits, collected by the Levites, all represent the agricultural surpluses that served simultaneously as *tithe* and as imperial tribute. Nehemiah 10:37 gives a list of grain, wine, and oil, which the Levites must bring to the storehouses of the temple. The commodities mentioned here are exactly those required to be sent by the Babylonian temples to royal estates and to imperial officials at the order of the satrap of Ebr-Nahara.[36] All of these signify the fiscal needs of the temple.

Since the text states the problem, the "great distress," as the people's complaint against Persian control of their economic surplus, one would expect that this oath, the priesthood's rhetorical response, to address exactly that. Yet the response, separation from the ʿ*am ha* ʾ*arets*, Sabbath observance, and tithing, focuses instead on the temple, its rituals, and its needs. Instead of serving to replenish that which Persia has taken from the *golah*, the response depletes the people's resources even further. This time, however, instead of wealth seized from the people for the empire, wealth is persuaded from the people for the temple. At the very least, there is a rhetorical disconnect, or maybe even a sleight of hand, where the *people's* distress is voiced in 9:36–37, but the remedy in ch. 10 satisfies the *temple's* needs. As if to clarify this disconnect, the oath concludes in 10:39 with the simple affirmation, "We will not neglect the house of our God." There is no confusion in the intentionality of the rhetoric. It is meant to support the "house of our God" against the "great distress," that is, Persian taxation of the economic surpluses of the temple.

---

35. See Carter, *The Emergence of Yehud*, and Matthew W. Stolper, *Entrepreneurs and Empire: The Murasu Archive, the Murasu Firm, and Persian Rule in Babylonia*, Publications de l'Institut et archéologique néerlandais de Stamboul (Leiden: Nederlands Instituut Voor Het Nabije Oosten, 1985).

36. See M. A. Dandamaev, *Iranians in Achaemenid Babylonia* (Columbia Lectures on Iranian Studies 6; New York: Mazda, 1992).

The separatist rhetoric of ch. 13 is a more emphatic presentation of the same rhetoric in ch. 10. The three provisions of the oath of ch. 10 are present. In ch. 13 they are violations of the Law committed by the people of Judah. Eliashib has neglected the temple by allowing Tobiah to reside in one of the storerooms (13:4–5), Judahites are transacting with foreign merchants on the Sabbath (13:15–22), and once again intermarriage has polluted the holy seed (13:22–31). Reiterating of the concern over intermarriage emphasizes the problems' urgency. In 13:23, Nehemiah is disturbed that because of the intermarriages in Yehud, half of the children no longer speak the language of Judah but speak instead, the foreign language of their mothers. If Wurthwein is correct, then these children may have been captivated by the allure of the wealth of this landed gentry class, and so have chosen the languages and cultures of their more affluent maternal families. Could the Jerusalem temple rely upon these sons, who would inherit their fathers' land, to adhere to the dictates of Mosaic law, by supporting the temple as had their fathers? If not, the temple community faced even further economic hardship. No wonder we read in v. 25 a rapid succession of verbs portraying Nehemiah's active engagement with the exogamists. Nehemiah contends with them ואריב, then beats them ואכה and pulls out their hair ואמרטם. His work here is no longer legislative, as in ch. 10—it is "hands on," so to speak. It is no longer resigned to using ancient traditions to persuade the *golah* to comply; instead, it is active. In this statement, the rhetoric resorts to the only means of physical enforcement at the priesthood's disposal, it conjures an image of power in the form of violence, directed against the transgressors by the real authority of the province, a Persian governor.

Why did intermarriage function in this manner? In a context where a smaller cultural group exists in the midst of a larger, wealthier, more dominant group, the balance of the network of cultural exchanges flows toward the larger group, so that the smaller group trades its cultural markers in favor of those of the wealthier, more dominant group. Ultimately, the smaller group is no longer distinguishable from the larger. This scenario describes the dynamic between Wurthwein's *'am ha'aretz* and the *golah*. The net effect of intermarriage in Yehud diminished the wealth of the *golah* collective, and the number of adherents to the temple. With each instance of intermarriage, the Yehudite priesthood saw the collective's land base and likewise its own potential revenue and ability to meet the imperial tax levy erode.

Provisional Conclusions

In the end, however, the Jerusalem priesthood found itself in a precarious position. On one hand, the priesthood was pressed by the empire to meet the fiscal burden placed on the temple in order to satisfy imperial authorities. On the other hand, it had no choice but to work within an already established cultic tradition in order to enjoy legitimation by Mosaic Law. In the small, poor province, the priesthood had little in the way of material resources to appropriate in the service of cultic maintenance or even to meet the burdens of imperial rule. They were not, however, content to stand idly by and watch as their revenue, power, and community diminished as a result. Instead, they resorted to ideological resources of which they made good use. Using collective memory as a signifying resource, the priesthood grounded the rhetoric in the symbols already operative in the collective historical consciousness of the *golah*. The *ʿam haʾarets* became associated with the specters of Ammon and Moab, and typified as the enemies of this new Israel. The rhetoric signified upon the authority of Mosaic Law and the mythical power of the exodus and conquest foundation stories. Moreover, it raised the issue of separatism in the form of Moses's instructions as to who must be excluded from the *qhl yhwh*. The contemporaneous social context reinscribed these instructions of old with the new realities of ethnic competition, imperial domination, and strict adherence to the dictates of the cult.

In the rhetoric, lines distinguishing tithe to the temple and tribute to the empire become blurred when they intersect at the maintenance of the temple. The temple itself held multiple significations. It was simultaneously the imperial bureaucratic and financial center of the province and the "house of our God." Constructed at the behest of Darius, whose predecessor, Cyrus, had already been given the blessing of Yahweh in Deutero-Isaiah, the temple held the dual significations of royal and religious ideologies. The separatist rhetoric reflected both, allowing the empire and the community to construct different meanings within the same rhetoric. For the empire, it assured the maintenance of a loyal cult and the flow of resources to the imperial center. For the Jerusalem community, it was patently theological. It framed the creation of a Yahwistic collective constructed according to the dictates of Mosaic Law. It called upon their ancient traditions, laws, and personalities, now long relegated to their collective historical consciousness and reinscribed them with the contemporary realities of life for the *golah* under Persian domination. It invoked ancient covenants, reinterpreted their meanings and called the people to adhere to them. In the wake of the Babylonian devastation of

587 B.C.E., adherence to the dictates of the priesthood assured them that Yahweh would protect them from a recurrence of such calamity. As long as the temple retained the financial and popular support of the community, then imperial authorities remained satisfied, the priesthood retained imperial impremateur, and the cultic and ethnic identity of the *golah* community remained intact. In the end, the priestly rhetoric carved out a social space of cultural existence that allowed the Jerusalem collective to survive imperial domination and ultimately outlast the empire itself.

Might the Rhetoric Still Speak?

This study, grounded in history, not only raises questions for academic readings of the Ezra–Nehemiah corpus, but perhaps offers some perspective on contemporary realities of Church and State engagement. The Jerusalem priesthood's work helped the community make sense out of a social world in utter disarray. In as much as they were successful, the Jerusalem priesthood maintained the cohesiveness of the collective and constructed an ethnic identity durable enough to meet the challenges of life under Persian domination. Nonetheless, was the rhetoric also pernicious? Absolutely. Certainly, our reading of the text must raise questions about the vicious destruction of families, the collusion with imperial oppression that called the people to accept rather than resist imperial domination, and to become invested in the power of an imperially allied cult. These priestly-imperial transactions raise poignant questions for contemporary U.S. congregations. In a society where the state increasingly relies upon so-called faith based organizations to provide public services and simultaneously appropriates financial resources to coerce ideologies that support its public policy, U.S. clergy find themselves in a precarious position similar to that of the Jerusalem priesthood. Over the last decade, many churches have accepted tens of millions of dollars from recent administrations' faith-based funding program. These funds, similar to the strategic influxes of funding that Persia gave Jerusalem, have built churches and community centers, provided opportunities for job training and more. In so doing, "faith-based funding" revitalized neighborhoods and infused desperately needed capital into economically depleted areas. As did the priesthoods in Judah, Babylon, and Egypt, modern-day pastors eagerly construct ideologies to comport themselves to the political orientations of the current administration. Much in the same manner that the Jerusalem priesthood's collusion with imperial interests promised the immediate survival of the community, contemporary instances of public funding promise an apparent liberation from the social forces that threaten the existence of many economically deprived groups. Yet, this "faith-based" liberation also comes with a concomitant repression. The separatist rhetoric promoted a dynamic of exclusion that purported the destruction of families and silenced the voices of those who would protest Persian activity. Similarly, contemporary collusion between the state and religious communities silences voices of opposition in those same faith communities. Further, Persia's attempt to co-opt the religion of the Jerusalem temple led to a separatist ideology in Judah that connected ethnic identity to political loyalty, and forced any authentic expressions of Yahwism to be defined in opposition to the ʿam haʾarets. Similarly, state collusion with contemporary religious communities continues to create its own formations of separatism in our world. These Church–State exchanges force so-called authentic expressions of Christianity, Judaism, and Islam to define themselves in opposition to those who dissent from current government policies. In recent years, those who believe that governments should distribute resources to support people who live on the margins of life, that it is an obligation of conscience to question current war policies, that the right to reproductive choice is a private matter, or that stark domestic and global income disparities threaten human society have often found themselves in opposition not only to their government but their own religious communities as well.

Such a reading finds the voice of God at that place of hermeneutical understanding (*Verstehen*), where the social world of the ancient priesthood encounters our own. There, as we investigate the priestly rhetoric and its effects, the text presses us to raise questions about the rhetoric that we construct, rhetoric that we use in our pulpits, in our Bible studies, and in our faith communities. Whose voice does it silence? Whose voice does it privilege? For those of us who struggle to attend to the survival of our own communities, and attempt to construct the ideologies that speak to their various identities, the activity of the post-exilic priesthood challenges us to consider our own resistance to or collusion with repression. We also must ask, "At what benefit and at what cost?" Such an encounter with the text calls us to raise more self-critical questions in our own communities and to seek means by which God's vision for life, abundant and fulfilling, might be experienced by all.

THE JOURNEY FROM VOLUNTARY TO OBLIGATORY
SILENCE (REFLECTIONS ON PSALM 39 AND QOHELETH)

James L. Crenshaw

The omniscient narrator in the prologue of the book of Job exonerated a scrupulous father from any spoken offense against *yhwh*, leaving open the possibility of rebellious thoughts. It did not take readers long to provide what the narrator neglected to do; in the eyes of some early rabbis, Job was guilty of thinking unseemliness of *yhwh*. In a delicious bit of irony, the narrator actually has Job harbor the fear that his children have gone astray and blessed[1] *Elohim in their thoughts* while in a sinful state. In Job's view, sin's pernicious tentacles extended beyond the deed to the thought that later expressed itself in action. The poet who composed Ps 39 determined to avoid both types of offense,[2] but in the end abandoned his voluntary silence for speech that ultimately echoes Job's plea to be left alone to die (Job 7:16; 10:20; cf. 9:27 and 14:6).

---

1. The existence of antithetic meanings for the verb *bārak* in the prologue to the book of Job rests on the two instances in which the antagonist assures *yhwh* that an afflicted servant will curse him to his face. The other five uses of the verb (four in the prologue and one in the epilogue) are better explained as the usual "bless." Only two of these are considered problematic. The wife urges Job to bless God and die, just as a condemned Achan was instructed to give glory to God, and Job thinks his children may have sinned inadvertently and then blessed *yhwh* without having atoned for the offense. This understanding of his words is more charitable than the suspicion that they have deliberately transgressed.

2. In addition to the standard commentaries, the following special studies of Ps 39 address specific issues: Otto Kaiser, "Psalm 39," in *Gottes und der Menschen Weisheit* (BZAW 261; Berlin: de Gruyter, 1998), 71–83; Richard J. Clifford, "What Does the Psalmist Ask for in Psalms 39:5 and 90:12?," *JBL* 119 (2000): 59–66; W. A. M. Beuken, "Psalm 39," *HeyJ* 19 (1978): 1–11; Ellen F. Davis, "Prisoner of Hope," in *The Art of Reading Scripture* (ed. E. F. Davis and Richard B. Hays; Grand Rapids: Eerdmans, 2003), 300–305.

Focusing Biblical Studies

Warnings against loose speech abound in international wisdom.[3] The danger of being suspected of disloyalty to the ruling administration was real, as was punishment for false accusation and lies in general within a kinship society. Teachers compared a spoken word to an arrow that, once released, could not be recalled. They also warned that a spoken word could be carried by a bird to unintended ears. In the imagination of teachers, the tongue's power over an individual resembled a ship's rudder. In each instance a tiny instrument wielded control over something many times its size. The teachers' realism gave rise to such gems as the description of a gossiper who could not resist the latest tasty morsel.

In their zeal, however, teachers even sought to monitor the thought that lay behind words and deeds. Sometimes they attributed irreligious reasoning to practical atheists, whom they labeled "fools."[4] At other times, they adopted a pedagogy of uttering the unthinkable and thereby allowing untraditional views wider distribution in the same way some early rabbis employed the principle of uttering the impermissible and medieval philosophers introduced forbidden ideas into discourse as things to be rejected.[5] The introductory formula varied—"Do not say";[6] "Were it possible to say"; or "Heretics claim"—but the result was similar. Students widened their intellectual horizons by reflection on ideas that society found suspect.

The poet whose angst is exposed in Ps 39 chafed from the inescapable situation that this worldview created. Two realities impinged upon him: (1) the brevity of human existence, and (2) the heavy hand of *yhwh*. The

3. "Conceal your heart, control your mouth" (Ptahhotep 618); "A man may be ruined by his tongue/Beware and you will do well" (Any 7, 8); "Do not sever your heart from your tongue…" (Amenemope 10, 16; cf. Insinger 25, 21); "Keep firm your heart, steady your heart, do not steer with your tongue; If a man's tongue is the boat's rudder/The Lord of All is yet its pilot" (Amenemope 18, 3–5); "You may trip over your foot in the house of a great man; you should not trip over your tongue" (Ankhsheshonq 10, 7). Similar advice can be found in Mesopotamian wisdom and in Ahiqar.

4. On the biblical attitude to those who acted as if God were not, see James L. Crenshaw, *Defending God: Biblical Responses to the Problem of Evil* (Oxford: Oxford University Press, 2005), 27–40, 203–8.

5. James T. Robinson, *Samuel Ibn Tibbon's Commentary on Ecclesiastes* (Texts and Studies in Medieval and Early Modern Judaism 20; Tübingen: Mohr Siebeck), 112–41, explains the way Ibn Tibbon used dialectic to good effect.

6. I examined the formula ʾal tōmar and its peculiar relationship to theodicy in "The Problem of Theodicy in Sirach, On Human Bondage," *JBL* 94 (1975): 49–64, which was later published in James L. Crenshaw, *Urgent Advice and Probing Questions: Collected Writings on Old Testament Wisdom* (Macon: Mercer University Press, 1995), 155–74.

second of these two, punishment for sin, rendered the first one intolerable. The poet's provisional solution, a silence that was tantamount to withdrawing from life, brought further agitation. His extraordinary request for relief was fueled by his understanding of the human condition as *hebel*,[7] an assessment that placed him in a camp alongside Qoheleth. In the following close reading of Ps 39, we shall be attentive to intertextual associations in theme and in syntax, with special attention to Qoheleth.

Psalm 39:2–14

2. I resolved that I would guard my way
    From sinning with my tongue;
    I would keep a muzzle to my mouth
    while the wicked one was in my presence.
3. I was completely silent;
    I refrained[8] from good
    But my pain intensified.
4. My mind was hot within me;
    A fire raged in my thoughts.
    I spoke out.
5. *Yhwh*, tell me my end
    and what is the measure of my life;
    I want to know how fleeting I am.
6. Look, you have set my days at handbreadths,
    and my span is nothing in your sight;
    surely every person standing[9] is total emptiness.
7. Surely one walks as an image;[10]
    surely they hustle about—a breath;[11]
    He amasses but does not know who will gather in.

---

7. The search for the primary meaning of *hebel* continues in Dominic Rudman, "The Use of הבל as an Indicator of Chaos in Ecclesiastes," in *The Language of Qohelet in Its Context: Essays in Honour of Prof. A. Schoors on the Occasion of his Seventieth Birthday* (ed. A. Berlejung and P. Van Hecke; OLA 164; Leuven: Peeters, 2007), 121–41; Ethan Dor-Shav, "Ecclesiastes, Fleeting and Timeless," *Azure* 18 (2004): 67–87, opts for "vapour" or "mist" (74).

8. BDB, 364, lists "shew inactivity" as a meaning for the *hiphil* of *hāśâ*.

9. That is, even the person who can stand transfixed is actually no more than a vapor.

10. As MT stands, the picture is that of a phantasm, an image that quickly slips away. I understand the *bet* as *essentia* (as an image).

11. The elliptical style of the poet reaches a high point here. Its meaning conveys the utter futility of human enterprises that ultimately amount to nothing, for possessions succumb to time just like people.

8. And now, Lord, what can I anticipate?
   My hope is in you.[12]
9. From every rebellion deliver me;
   lay not on me the reproach of a fool.
10. I had been silent, not opening my mouth,
    for *you* did it.[13]
11. Remove your blow from me;
    I am dying from the rebuke of your hand.
12. With punishment for iniquity you chastise a person,
    and you consume his treasure like a moth.
    Surely everyone is a breath.
13. *Yhwh*, hear my prayer,
    and listen to my outbursts;
    do not ignore my tears,[14]
    for I am a resident alien with you,
    a sojourner like all my ancestors.[15]
14. Look away from me so that I can smile
    before I die and am not.

Psalm 39 is unique in that it begins with the verb *ʾāmartî*. In the Psalter, the closest thing to it is Ps 82:6, which has *ʾanî-ʾāmartî ʾelōhîm ʾattem* ("I had thought you were gods") to indicate previous disposition in the same way *ʾāmartî* does in 39:2. The translation above is relatively straightforward except for v. 6. I take *niṣṣāb* to suggest fixity, like one standing erect, but it may be a musical notation like *selâ* at the end of this verse and six verses later[16] or certainty about the human condition. The harsh tone and ambiguity of *kî ʾattâ ʾaśîtā* in the tenth verse prompted a later translator to render the clause in Greek less offensively,

12. "This double expression of existential complaint offers an exact frame to the core verse, 'My hope is in thee' (v 8b)... [T]his core verse functions like the prow of a ship in high seas" (Samuel Terrien, *The Psalms: Strophic Structure and Theological Commentary* [Grand Rapids: Eerdmans, 2003], 330–31).

13. Although some interpreters understand this verse as present, it seems better to take it as the poet's reflecting back on a previous condition and offering a justification for silence, one that points straight to *yhwh*.

14. According to *Ber.* 32b, supplication moves on an ascending scale (prayer, crying aloud, tears). The last of these, tears, can pass through any door, for the gates of tears are always open. The Psalmist, however, is less sanguine than some rabbis.

15. Robert Alter, *The Book of Psalms* (New York: Norton, 2007), 140 sees this verse as an "instance of the so-called breakup pattern in which a hendiadys ('sojourner and settler' meaning 'resident alien') is split up with each of the component terms set into one of the two parallel versets."

16. Amos Hakam, *The Bible Psalms with the Jerusalem Commentary*, vol. 1 (Jerusalem: Mosad Harav Kook, 2003), 308 n. 4, attributes this view to some commentators, although he thinks *niṣṣāb* means "certain, established."

ho poiēsas me ("for you made me"). This slight change transformed an accusation into acknowledgment of *yhwh* as personal creator. The occasion for the poet's charge of heavy handedness on the part of the deity may be the silence referred to in vv. 3–4. Hence the pluperfect translation in v. 10 rather than an improbable present tense.

Structure

The structure of the poem is unclear, for clues point to different ways of dividing its individual units. First, three vocatives (two uses of the Tetragrammaton and a single use of *ʾadonāi*) suggest a tripartite prayer (vv. 5–7, 8–12, 13–14) that is introduced by vv. 2–4. Second, the two refrains that conclude vv. 6 and 12 and universalize the assessment of human existence as transience may indicate a two-part psalm with a final plea in vv. 13–14. Whoever added the two *selâs* apparently viewed the poem as a composition comprising two units.

Both readings are predicated on the assumption that the poem was composed by a single author, but Otto Kaiser has reached an entirely different conclusion on the basis of theme alone.[17] The concentration on *hebel* in vv. 5–7 and 12 led him to postulate an older didactic poem that a redactor fashioned into a "school text" resembling Job 28; Qoh 3:1–8; Ecclus 24:1–22; and Wis 2:1–9. By excising the first *kol* and *niṣṣab* in v. 6, as well as *ʿal ʿāwôn* six verses later, Kaiser attributes greater uniformity to an original poem than its present form exhibits. The four uses of *ʾak* in vv. 6, 7, and 12 may reinforce his interpretation, if they are seen as isolating the short poem from its larger context.

Because the original poem that Kaiser has separated from the larger psalm lacks distinctive markers that point to a date, one could argue that it is a *late* insertion.[18] Its theme, life's transience, seems more at home in post-exilic texts than in earlier ones. Viewing this unit about life's transience as a late insertion is subject to the objection that *dibbartî bilšônî* requires something other than *weʿattâ*. The expression "and now" ordinarily marks strong transition,[19] whereas "I spoke out" should be

17. Kaiser, "Psalm 39." He also relies heavily on uniformity of consonants in each colon.
18. Any attempt to ascertain the date of a biblical psalm requires decisions about so many unknowns as to render the conclusion highly tenuous, on which see James L. Crenshaw, *The Psalms: An Introduction* (Grand Rapids: Eerdmans, 2001), and idem, "Foreword: The Book of Psalms and Its Interpreters," in *The Psalms in Israel's Worship*, by Sigmund Mowinckel (Grand Rapids: Eerdmans, 2004), xix–xliv.
19. H. A. Brongers, "Bemerkungen zum Gebrauch des adverbialen *weʿattāh* im Alten Testament," *VT* 15 (1965): 289–99.

followed by something that explains why the poet abandoned an earlier resolve to remain quiet. As the psalm stands now, the poet moves from the awareness of personal *hebel* to the generalization that everyone's existence is *hebel* before asking, "What can *I* expect?" in a world that lacks real substance.

Content

Psalm 39 is a supplication for relief from an unspecified affliction that is interpreted as punishment for an infraction of divine rule. The prayer consists of three separate petitions (the last one reinforced by cohortatives [vv. 13–14]) and is introduced by an autobiographical snippet. Whereas the usual lament introduced by ᶜ*ad matay* or ʾ*ad ᶜānâ* inquires about the duration of present suffering, this one asks about the number of days remaining before the grim reaper's scythe does its work.[20] In the absence of response, the psalmist determines to shorten those days by foregoing *yhwh*'s presence.

The exposure of the poet's inner feelings[21] echoes those of Jeremiah, who also chafed from conduct that he considered inappropriate for *yhwh*. In both instances, adopting a policy of silence resulted in mental agitation that overcame the resolve to keep quiet. Two things about this personal revelation in vv. 1–4 conceal more than they reveal. First, who is the evil one, and second, why did the poet abstain from good?

Apparently, the *rāšāᶜ* is nearby, but why was refraining from speech an effective response to the presence of a wicked one? We know that sages wrestled with this issue, for they have preserved an answer in sayings juxtaposed to one another in Prov 26:4–5. Depending on the situation, one should either answer a fool to expose his stupidity or refuse to dignify a remark by responding. Was the poet afraid that he might say something that would encourage the *rāšāᶜ*, perhaps an expression of envy for prosperous evildoers like that laid bare in Ps 73:3–14?[22] Or does the opening verb ʾ*amārtî* in the sense of "resolve" point to cases like Pss 14:1 and 53:2 where this verb is followed by *belibbî (ô)*? In

20. John Goldingay, *Psalms*. Vol. 1, *Psalms 1–41* (Grand Rapids: Baker Academic, 2006), 557–58, implausibly translated *hôdîᶜēnî* by "acknowledge" and thinks the poet is asking for strength to accept a short life.

21. Alter, *The Book of Psalms*, 137, thinks the dominance of triadic versets, as opposed to the usual dyadic, expresses a powerful psychological tension, introducing an element of surprise and destabilizing what has gone before it.

22. The numerous studies of this psalm have not exhausted its riches, on which see Crenshaw, *The Psalms*, 109–27.

other words, is the psalmist afraid of voicing doubt that might strengthen practical atheists?

The second issue in the personal data that remains unclear is the statement that the poet refrained from good. One way of resolving the difficulty is to understand the expression as elliptical,[23] its meaning being "to do nothing," either good or bad. The verb would then have the sense of showing inactivity, as in Judg 18:9 and 1 Kgs 22:3.[24] If the poet neither spoke nor did anything, there was less possibility of giving offense, for both words and deeds are often ambiguous. Another approach to the problem is to interpret the response to the presence of a wicked person against the background of the sages' warning against helping sinners. Charity, in other words, must be closely monitored lest one strengthen those bent on wrongdoing.

Curiously, the poet's good intentions only intensified the angst, creating a raging inferno within the mind and the seat of emotions. Humans, he learned, need something other than the instrument that effectively controls the mouths and behavior of domesticated animals. That discovery did not prevent a later teacher, Ben Sira, from using different symbolism in a prayer that a guard and a seal be placed on his mouth to prevent harmful speech (Sir 22:27–23:3). In addition, he requests that whips be set over his thoughts lest enemies exult over his misfortune.[25] Ben Sira's petition is immediately followed by a section in the Greek text identified as "discipline of the tongue" (Sir 23:7–15).

When the psalmist says he refrained from *ṭôb*, he obviously implies that he believed one capable of doing the good. That view was not universally shared, for a few thinkers considered goodness beyond the capacity of humans. In the reasoning of some, the mind is more devious than anything else (Jer 17:9a),[26] and consequently no one is able to do

23. This is not the only instance of ellipsis in the psalm (cf. v. 6, "they hustle— a breath," and vv. 2a and 5b). On the basis of *mēhamôn* in Ps 37:16 and *hehāmôn* in 1 Chr 29:16, one could construe *yehemāyûn* as a distortion of an original reference to wealth.

24. Alter, *The Book of Psalms*, views the *mem* on *miṭṭôb* as one of deprivation, but this interpretation is unlikely since the silence is voluntary.

25. As late as 4Q412 15, the poet advises doors of protection for the tongue, and The Epistle of James compares the tongue to a fire and considers it an instrument of poison (vv. 6–8), a small member that controls humans the way rudders guide ships. Here, too, the idea of bits in the mouths of horses is mentioned in the context of keeping the tongue in check.

26. James L. Crenshaw, "Deceitful Minds and Theological Dogma: Jer. 17:5– 11," in *Prophets, Sages, and Poets* (St. Louis: Chalice, 2006), 73–82, 222–24, also

good (cf. Ps 62:10, "Surely humans are *hebel*, mortals a lie; on scales for weighing, together they weigh more than a breath [*hebel*]"; cf. also Ps 116:11). Or is that opinion restricted to fools as in Ps 14:1? Apparently not, for this low view of humans is also attributed to *yhwh* in the next two verses. Such hyperbole stands in tension with the mention of the righteous (*bedôr ṣaddîq*) in v. 5, unless righteousness is judged to be less demanding than *ṭôb*. In that case, *ṭôb* would be a habitus and *ṣaddîq* a temporary achievement.

The first prayer that shatters the self-imposed silence seeks information that is hidden from most people: the precise time of their death. The poet chooses his language carefully, opting for the Hebrew noun *qēṣ* that Amos used to refer to the end of a nation. This desire to know one's ultimate destiny fueled an entire enterprise that promised secret knowledge about the future.[27] The psalmist bypasses these professionals and goes directly to *yhwh*. Others may have calculated human longevity as one hundred and twenty years[28] or as the more realistic seventy to eighty years, but the poet refuses to enter into a mythic explanation for a human life span. Instead, he shifts from duration to the quality of existence,[29] which he describes as total emptiness, a mere image devoid of substance despite every hustle and bustle. Ironically, he sees his own brief existence as nothing in *yhwh*'s presence, presumably because the deity is not subject to time's erosive power.

The second prayer alternates between trust and accusation. The poet's only hope lies in the Lord, but this taskmaster exacts a heavy toll on mere humans. The language of painful discipline dominates this section, but so does that of death-dealing punishment. No wonder the poet boldly

published in Ehud Ben Zvi, ed., *Utopia and Dystopia in Prophetic Texts* (Helsinki: Finnish Exegetical Society; Göttingen: Vandenhoeck & Ruprecht, 2006), 105–21; and P. J. Tomson, "'There Is No One Who Is Righteous, Not Even One': Kohelet 7, 20 in Pauline and Early Jewish Interpretation," in Berlejung and Van Hecke, eds., *The Language of Qohelet in Its Context*, 183–202.

27.   Practitioners of various divinatory techniques sought to read the future and in doing so to gain both prestige and monetary profit. Apocalyptic literature takes a much wider sweep by focusing on changes of universal magnitude.

28.   A text from Emar, Enlil and Namzitarra, reckons life to be 120 years (cf. Gen 6:3). Like Qoheleth, this author sees life as fleeting; the closing lines read that "the days of man are approaching, day to day they verily decrease, year after year they verily decrease. One hundred twenty years are the years of mankind—verily it is their bane" (Jacob Klein, "The 'Bane' of Humanity: A Lifespan of One Hundred Twenty Years," *Acta Sumerologica* 12 [1990]: 57–70).

29.   This shift mirrors that from silence to speech, perhaps also from trust to sharp attack.

accuses the Lord even while explaining his earlier mutism. His emotions evoked the same extreme words, "For you did it," that the destruction of Jerusalem generated in the composer of Lam 1:21. Comparing *yhwh* to a destructive moth, the psalmist reduces existence to a single breath, a rare concrete sense of *hebel*.

The third prayer, or rather outburst,[30] employs the language of disenfranchisement to describe the poet's powerlessness. The resident alien and the sojourner, *gēr* and *tôšāb*,[31] were protected by provisions that were believed to have been established by *yhwh*. The powerful reminder that Abraham and all Israel's ancestors were but pilgrims on a brief journey invokes special consideration, the hospitality extended to visitors. Nevertheless, the poet abandons all hope and requests that *yhwh* hasten the *qēṣ* by looking away.

Affinities with Other Psalms

The four occurrences of *ʾak* in Ps 39 are two fewer than the six in Ps 62, where *hebel* is said to be the human essence in that an individual weighs less than a breath (Ps 62:10). In both psalms, the exclamatory particle *ʾak* reinforces a low assessment of humankind, as if the judgment would not stand on its own. The psalmist who composed Ps 144:4 compared people to a breath, but the weaker observation does not require any emphasis. Moreover, the initial statement in Ps 62:2 employs the same adjective *dûmiyyâ* that the poet uses in Ps 39:3 to characterize himself as silent. The sixth verse in Ps 62, nearly identical with v. 1, has the imperative *dōmmî* plus a reference to hope, like Ps 39:8. Verses 2–5 and 6–9, the two literary units in Ps 62 that *precede* the comment about human transience, are each set off by the musical notation *selâ*, unlike its appearance in Ps 39 *following* a refrain about humans as *hebel*.

The author of Ps 90 chose a different way to express the brevity of human existence. He compares people to grass that flourishes briefly and then dies. In his view, the irrevocable decree that relegates humans to dust in v. 3 becomes more oppressive in light of the seventy or eighty years allotted to humans, especially when *yhwh*'s chastisement for

---

30. *HALOT*, 1443.

31. 1 Chr 29:15 brings together several ideas that appear in Ps 39, specifically resident alien and sojourner, all our ancestors, days like a shadow, and absence of hope. Heb 11:13 applies the category of sojourners to a long list of biblical heroes. According to Lev 25:23, the earth belongs to *yhwh*, its inhabitants being sojourners and resident aliens.

offenses makes daily existence unbearable. The comparison of humans to a flower in Job 14:2 may be more elegant,[32] but flowers also wither and die. Both images, grass and flowers, are combined in Ps 103:15–17 and in Isa 40:6–8, which contrast their brief flourishing to *yhwh*'s steadfast love and word respectively. In Isa 40:6–8, the divine breath changes vitality into its opposite, like the desert winds. The word for breath is *rûaḥ*, for *hebel* never applies to *yhwh* though it does describe idols.

Resemblances to Qoheleth

Whereas these texts move from human transience to divine immutability, Qoheleth emphasizes the anthropological angst resulting from life's brevity, anxiety made worse by its unfairness. Etymologically, the root *hebel* signifies "breath," breeze," or "vapor"; this concrete use occurs in the Bible only occasionally (e.g. Isa 57:13 [|| to *rûaḥ*] and Pss 39:12; 62:10).[33] In context with *rûaḥ*, it hovers in the background of Jer 10:14–15 (= 51:17–18) but usually has a metaphorical sense, especially in polemic against the worship of idols and/or foreign gods.[34] Frequently, *hebel* indicates futility (Job 9:29; Ps 94:11; Isa 30:7; 49:4; Lam 4:17), a meaning that Qoheleth interchanges with the sense of ephemerality. Outside Qoheleth, *hebel* has this latter nuance in Job 7:16; Pss 39:6; 78:33; and 144:4.

Affinities between Ps 39 and Qoheleth go beyond a common theme, life as *hebel*. There are also some close syntactical relationships. Both authors refer to individuals who labor to accumulate things but cannot know who will gather them in. This particular problem expressed itself for Qoheleth in the context of inheritance (Qoh 2:18–23). He complains that he had used both wit and energy to acquire goods only to pass them along to a stranger who may lack intelligence altogether.

32. See James L. Crenshaw, "Flirting with the Language of Prayer (Job 14:13–17)," in *Worship and the Hebrew Bible: Essays in Honor of John T. Willis* (ed. Patrick Graham, Rick Marrs, and Steven McKenzie; JSOTSup 284; Sheffield: JSOT, 1999), 110–23, repr. in Crenshaw, *Prophets, Sages, and Poets*, 6–13, 201–3.

33. Rudman, "The Use of הבל as an Indicator of Chaos in Ecclesiastes," 121–22 and 133, does not include Ps 39:12, limiting the concrete use to two, and even then, he writes, "a figurative use is evident."

34. Deut 32:21 has *hebel* in parallelism with *lōʾ ʾēl*, suggesting that idols have no real vitality. Several examples of *hebel* emphasize the powerlessness of idols (Jer 10:3, 8, 15; 14:22; 16:19; Jon 2:9). According to 2 Kgs 17:15, Israelites who turned to *hahebel* became worthless themselves (*wayyehbālû*).

By dividing the consonants *bṣlm* differently in Ps 39:7, the picture changes from walking as an image to walking in a shadow,[35] which occurs in Qoheleth. For him, a shadow prefigures the emptiness of life rather than providing relief from the hot sun.

Thus far the affinities between Ps 39 and Qoheleth have been striking. Three others, somewhat less persuasive, are worth considering. The psalmist worries about extinction with these words: *beṭerem ʾēlēk weʾênennî* ("before I go and am no more"). Two things in this phrase recall Qoheleth: first, the verb for dying, which Qoheleth uses in its participial form *hôlēk*,[36] and second, the negative particle *ʾênennî* that denotes extinction.[37] The former is an abbreviated reference to going to be with dead ancestors, a euphemism for dying. The additional particle simply reflects the usual belief among Semites that a shadowy existence in Sheol was no real life. Hence the psalmist anticipates personal annihilation, at least on earth. The image of returning to dust is apt, for what distinguished a person no longer remains once the ravages of time have done their ruinous work. The third similarity between Ps 39 and Qoheleth is the rare use of the verb *ḥāšâ* for voluntary silence (Qoh 3:7; Ps 39:3).[38] Qoheleth does not move from a recognition of transience and rampant injustice to prayer. His response to the danger of loose speech is less extreme than the psalmist; although the occasion for guarding the tongue differs greatly. Qoheleth's justification for limited speaking is the distance separating *Elohim* from humans, not the fear of a human

---

35. The *mem* thus becomes the participial prefix to the verb *hālak*. Other interpreters think the word *beṣelem* derives from a root *ṣlm* and means "shadow."

36. The exquisite poem in 1:4–11 begins with the clause *dôr hôlēk wedôr bāʾ* ("a generation dies [literally 'goes'] and another comes"). Similarly, 6:4 says that the stillbirth "comes in futility and departs, its name covered by darkness."

37. On this negative particle, see James L. Crenshaw, "Qoheleth's Quantitative Language," in Berlejung and Van Hecke, eds., *The Language of Qohelet in Its Context*, 1–22; Antoon Schoors, *The Preacher Sought to Find Pleasing Words: A Study in the Language of Qohelet* (OLA 41; Leuven: Peeters, 1992), 151–52; and Bo Isaksson, *Studies in the Language of Qoheleth with Special Emphasis on the Verbal System* (Acta Universitatis Upsaliensia: Studia Semitica Upsalensia 10; Stockholm: Uppsala, 1987), 172–74.

38. Goldingay, *Psalms, Book I*, 556, writes that "*ʾālam* never occurs to describe voluntary silence except as an attribute to *Yhwh*'s servant who is silent under attack (Isa 53:7), though Job also apparently kept silence for a week (2:13). The parallel verb *ḥāšâ* is likewise never used to describe voluntary silence except in Ecclesiastes' meditation (3:7)." The relevance of Job 2:13 escapes me, for it does not employ the verb *ʾālam*.

enemy.[39] For the psalmist, suffering leads to a concept of *hebel* but does not generate a desire to enjoy life as it does for Qoheleth.[40]

Another significant difference is the way each thinker expresses inner resolve. The psalmist uses *ʾamartî* alone, but Qoheleth adds *belibbî* to verbs of speaking. This linguistic expression occurs most often in Qoheleth and Psalms, although it can be found elsewhere.[41] The verbs range from *ʾāmar* and *dābar* to *hitbārēk* in Deut 29:18 ("Everyone who exalts himself inwardly, thinking 'I shall be safe although I follow my rebellious mind.'") The usual *ʾāmar* and *dābar* plus the reference to the mind can be nuanced variously as "resolved," "prayed," "thought," "mused," and imagined." Here is an example of each use:

Gen 8:21   *Yhwh* resolved, "I will never again destroy the earth because of humankind, for the human imagination is pernicious from youth"...

Gen 24:45   Before I had finished praying, Rebekah approached...

1 Sam 27:1 David thought, "I shall now perish by Saul's hand"

Gen 17:17   Abraham fell on his face; laughing, he mused, "Can a child be born to one who is a hundred years old?"

Deut 7:17   If you imagine, "These nations are more numerous than we; how can we dispossess them?"

About two thirds of these expressions occur in Genesis, Deuteronomy, Psalms, and Qoheleth. The latter's uses are noteworthy, given the brevity of the book when compared with the other three.

39. Antoon Schoors, "God in Qoheleth," in *Schöpfungsplan und Heilsgeschichte. Festschrift für E. Haag* (ed. R. Brandscheidt and T. Mende; Trier: Paulinus, 2002), 251–70, and "Theodicy in Qohelet," in *Theodicy in the World of the Bible* (ed. A. Laato and J. C. de Moor; Leiden: Brill, 2003), 375–409.

40. The role of joy in Qoheleth is widely debated, with Norman Whybray and Norbert Lohfink leading the way to a positive understanding of joy as a divine gift. Others, like me, cannot reconcile the prevailing mood of the book and its haunting refrains that emphasize life's emptiness with anything approximating joy. For the opposite view, see Whybray, "Qoheleth, Preacher of Joy," *JSOT* 23 (1982): 87–98; Lohfink, "Qoheleth 5, 17–19—Revelation by Joy," *CBQ* 52 (1990): 625–35; and Ludger Schwienhorst-Schönberger, "Gottes Antwort in der Freude. Zur theologie göttlicher Gegenwart im Buch Kohelet," *BK* 54 (1999): 156–63. On the problem, see Hans-Peter Müller, "Theonome Skepsis und Lebensfreude—Zu Koh 1, 12–3, 15," *BZ* 30 (1986): 1–19.

41. Gen 8:21; 17:17; 24:45; 27:41; Deut 7:17; 8:17; 9:4; 15:9; 18:21; 1 Sam 27:1; 1 Kgs 12:26; Pss 10:6, 11, 13; 14:1; 53:2; 77:7; Qoh 1:16; 2:1, 15; 3:17, 18; Isa 14:13; 47:8, 10; Jer 5:24; 13:22; Zeph 1:12; Obad 3; Esth 6:6. Qoh 9:1 has *nātattî ʾeth libbî*.

The unusual *ʿim lebābî ʾaśîḥâ* in Ps 77:7 introduces the idea of accompaniment, as if the mind joins the psalmist in the thought process ("I meditated with my mind"). On the basis of the Egyptian concept of communing with one's *ba* or soul, Michael V. Fox interprets Qoheleth's language about speaking *belēb* as conversation between two separate and independent entities.[42] He does this despite a solitary use of *debartî ʾanî ʿim libî* in Qoh 1:16. Fox's reading of Qoheleth rests on the assumption that the usual prepositional *be* has the sense of accompaniment rather than expressing location. If Qoheleth had wished to indicate dialogue between him and the mind as the seat of cognition, he could have done so by exclusive use of the preposition *ʿim* after verbs of speaking. That he did not do so suggests that he was not influenced by an Egyptian idiom when combining verbs of speech with *belibbî*.

Still, the personification of the *lēb*, at least metaphorically, does take place in the Hebrew Bible. According to Prov 14:10, the *lēb* possesses the power of perception, "knowing" its own bitterness, and Ps 27:8 attributes speech to it ("My heart says to you, 'Seek my face'"). In both instances, the cognitive aspect seems to give way to the emotive, and one cannot rule out a purely symbolic understanding of this language.

The contexts containing the language about speaking *belēb* are overwhelmingly negative. To many moderns, the fool is perhaps the most sympathetic one who engages in this practice ("The fool reasons: 'There is no god,'" Pss 14:1; 53:1; "The fool boasts: 'I cannot be moved...God has forgotten; he hides his face [and] never looks; ...You will not inquire,'" Ps 10:6, 11, 13). The fiction of an omniscient narrator permits readers to grasp the innermost thoughts of others, especially when the intention is devious. Even a tendency to see oneself in the very best light is exposed in Esth 6:6 ("Haman thought; 'To whom would the king want to do a kindness more than to me?'").

A temporary suspension of justice encourages the wicked to presume an inactive deity ("Those who say, '*Yhwh* will do neither good nor evil,'" Zeph 1:12). In the interest of humility, the newly freed Israelites are warned to give credit to *Yhwh* ("Do not boast: 'My strength and might acquired this wealth for me,'" Deut 8:17). The most extreme instance of *hubris* in the Bible evokes this disparaging comment: "You thought: 'I will ascend to heaven above *El*'s stars, set up my throne, sit in the mount

---

42. Michael V. Fox, *A Time to Tear Down and a Time to Build Up: A Rereading of Ecclesiastes* (Grand Rapids: Eerdmans, 1999), 176. ("Note how his heart is treated as a distinct 'person' in 1:17 and 7:25," presumably in addition to 2:1.) In his discussion of the heart in Qoheleth's thought, Fox refers to a similar concept in the Egyptian "Memphite Theology" (77–78).

of assembly in the abode of Saphon, mount the back of a cloud, [and] be like *Elyon*'" (Isa 14:13–14). Nations, too, are reminded that they are subject to *yhwh* ("Who say: 'I am, and there is none besides me,'" Isa 47:10; "Who think; 'Who will bring me down to earth?,'" Obad 3).

A positive use of this expression is rare, like *yhwh*'s determination to show a favorable face despite the inherent flaw in human nature. In Jer 5:24 the negative introduction does not rule out an attempt in a positive direction ("They do not say: 'Let us fear *yhwh* our God who gives rain...'"). One characteristic of the good person who makes a cameo appearance in Ps 15 is the inner acknowledgment of truth (*wedōbēr ʾamet bilbābô*, v. 2). The rare use of a participle in this expression implies that truthfulness is habitual, just as a similar one in Obad 3 suggests an arrogant state of mind.

Qoheleth uses the expression under discussion eight times. In 2:1, 15; 3:17, 18 it takes the form *ʾāmartî ʾanî belibbî*, changing to *debartî ʾanî belibbî* in the second of two occurrences in 2:15. In 1:16, as stated earlier, it has a different preposition, *ʿim* standing alone. In 9:1 the verb *ntn* is followed by the preposition *ʾel* ("to"), yielding "For all this, *I committed to my mind*..."[43] Similarly, 8:16 has "When *I set my mind* to know wisdom..." As was true of Gen 27:41, in which Esau contemplated murder, the expression is not rigid, for there a subject falls between the verb and *belibbô*. Qoheleth varies the preposition, using the prefix *be* as well as free-standing *ʿim* and *ʾel*. He also prefaces the expression with a direct object following a causative or emphatic *kî*. In Qoheleth's case, the expression is self-revelatory, its autobiographical form differing from the others, which are instances of imaginary mind-reading.[44]

Conclusion

At best, the preceding exercise in intertextuality[45] demonstrates that Qoheleth was not alone in viewing existence as *hebel* and that others

43. Arguing that this and related expressions (*nātan lelibbî*) imply intentional movement, Pierre Van Hecke, "The Verbs *rāʾâ* and *šmăʿ* in the Book of Qohelet: A Cognitive-Semantic Perspective," in Berlejung and Van Hecke, eds., *The Language of Qohelet in Its Context*, 203–20 (215 n. 51), considers it less likely that listening, a passive state, is meant. He overlooks the possibility that listening as an intellectual activity is highly intentional.

44. The extent of detachment in Qoheleth has assumed fresh perspective as a result of Fox's interpretation of the frame narrative as a device that distinguishes a speaker, Qoheleth, from the narrator who keeps at a safe distance because of Qoheleth's radical teaching.

45. The claim that the historical paradigm has been replaced by a literary one may be exaggerated, for even the current interest in reception history combines both

took note of the lack of justice where reward for labor was concerned. Above all, a close reading of Ps 39 shows that at least one independent thinker who was in some ways like Qoheleth risked an intimacy with *yhwh* that exposed his weakness and temerity. The psalmist journeyed from voluntary to obligatory silence, in between these hoping in vain[46] to be granted the status of *gēr* and *tôšāb*. In the end, he opted for non-existence, but it nonetheless freed him from chastisement.[47]

history and literature. The extensive intertextual studies by André Robert in the first half of the twentieth century were inspired by an interest in the influence of earlier literature on successive generations, not by Julia Kristeva.

46. Hope, that is, can be sustained only as long as there is life. The psalmist's final words of death and non-being emphatically authenticate the claim that human existence is fleeting, like breath itself.

47. In this analysis of Ps 39, I have omitted the superscription that mentions Jeduthun, like Ps 62 which also distinguishes words and thoughts (v. 5). According to 2 Chr 5:12, Jeduthun, a Levite singer along with Asaph and Heman, was present when Solomon dedicated the temple.

HOW DO EXTRABIBLICAL SOCIOPOLITICAL DATA ILLUMINATE OBSCURE BIBLICAL TEXTS? THE CASE OF ECCLESIASTES 5:8–9 (HEB. 5:7–8)

Norman Gottwald

Introduction

My lengthy title intends to state the problematic of the present study as clearly as possible. It assumes that sociopolitical information is valuable in illuminating biblical texts, but to what extent and in what ways? There are some widely recognized instances of a significantly close "fit" between extrabiblical data and biblical texts, as with the Moabite Stone and the Assyrian inscriptions. But most of our uses of sociopolitical data are less clear-cut and many of them are precarious and disputable. I have in mind biblical texts with historically unidentified referents and syntactic obscurities, texts that do not intersect with extrabiblical social data in any unambiguous way. Thus I have chosen Eccl 5:8–9 as an exemplary case. Is this text clarified by the known details of Ptolemaic administration of Coele-Syria, as many have claimed? My conclusion is that the sociopolitical data do not resolve the interpretive issues specific to this text, but they do supply a sociopolitical context for Ecclesiastes that illuminates the situation of the author and helps to account for his perspective on life.

The Text as Text

The translation of v. 8 is reasonably straightforward: "If you see oppression of the poor and denial of justice and right in the *medinah* [province or state?], don't be surprised by the matter since a *gavoah* [high one? person with power over others? official?] is watched by a higher one and higher ones watch over them."

The locus of oppression and injustice is the *medinah*, providing a seemingly political context, whether the political entity is a province or the state at large. Those who are the source of oppression and injustice are simply called "high ones," presumably those with the status and power to wrong others, but their office or occupation is not stated, and, while they are usually taken to be under governmental appointment, some interpreters see a more generic reference to anyone with coercive power, including wealthy landowners and merchants. The salient fact that these high ones are pictured in at least three successive tiers may imply a network more suited to layers of officialdom than to assorted powerful individuals acting on their own.

A further uncertainty is how the watching of the high ones is to be construed. Interpreters generally agree that they are not simply "observing." But are they "scrutinizing" one another's work by carefully double- and triple-checking to make sure that the oppressive and unjust actions are thoroughly carried out in a foolproof system? Or are they "spying" on one another as they jockey for power at one another's expense and willing to behave capriciously and arbitrarily out of self-interest? Whatever the nuance here, the watching is a hostile one from the viewpoint of the poor who are on the receiving end of their actions. What is unmistakable is that victimization of the poor is carried out by those with overwhelming cumulative power that cannot be escaped.

By contrast, the meaning of v. 9, which seems to extend the thought of v. 8, is totally "up for grabs" (described by Gordis as "an insuperable crux"[1]), chiefly because of its puzzling syntax. Every effort at a translation has to make large assumptions as to how the words, more or less individually clear, fall together to give a sense that articulates with the injustice of the high ones in v. 8. Very literally the words in order read, "And/but the profit or gain of a land in all that a king for a cultivated field."

For the most part translators take it as a single sentence that identifies the king as profitable for cultivated land, as in the RSV, "But in all, a king is an advantage to a land with cultivated fields," or in the NRSV, "But all things considered, this is an advantage for a land: a king for a plowed field." A similar translation is found in the NAB. The REB restricts the scope of the king's jurisdiction by reading, "The best thing for a country is a king whose own lands are well tilled." The NIV breaks the verse into two parts, "The increase from the land is taken by all; the king himself profits from the fields"; similarly in the NLB. Some translations remove the king from the verse. C. L. Seow in the AB redivides consonants and treats *kol* as a probable noun from the verb *kul*, cognate to Aramaic

1. Robert Gordis, *Koholeth: The Man and His World* (New York: Bloch, 1955), 240.

kayla, with the sense of "measure/provision," thereby reading, "But the advantage of the land is in its provision, that is, if the field is cultivated for provision."[2] The JPS Tanakh offers the surprising translation, "Thus the greatest advantage in all the land is his: he controls a field that is cultivated," to which it adds the note "i.e., the high official profits from the labors of others; but meaning of verse uncertain." It takes the pronoun *hu* as a possessive whose antecedent is the "high one" of the previous verse and appears to repoint the noun *melek* as a verb translated as "he controls." A number of translations provide alternative readings in footnotes. We could easily go on with examples of other translations that resort to various lexical and syntactical maneuvers to extract meaning from this puzzling sequence of words.

If we stay with the most commonly construed meaning, the verse says that the king is in some way profitable for agriculture. But in what way? Does he actually increase the productivity of the land? Or does he, standing at the apex of the "high ones" of v. 8, insure that the flow of surplus from agriculture is sustained and coordinated for state purposes without necessary regard to the needs of the cultivators? The *yitron* of the land is commonly translated as "advantage" or "benefit," on the surface suggesting that the statement has a positive coloration: the king's management of agriculture is good for all. However, given the negative tone of the preceding statement about "the high ones," and considering the book's frequent theme that in the end there really is no "profit" or "gain" in human labor, it is likely that the verse completes the harsh assessment of "the high ones" by tracing their practices to the very highest political authority.

The Text in the Context of the Book

When our text is read against the entirety of Ecclesiastes, are any of its ambiguities and uncertainties clarified? It must be admitted at the outset that we search the book in vain for any specific historical or socio-political referents beyond the fiction of Solomonic authorship with which it opens.

The term *gavoah/gevohim*, for "the high one/s" of 5:8 occurs in 7:8 in the phrase "high [i.e. proud] of spirit," in contrast to "patient or humble of spirit," which follows immediately on a reference to oppression and bribery but in generalized aphoristic form that is not applied to any social or political status or office. Elsewhere in the Hebrew Bible, *gavoah*

2. C. L. Seow, *Ecclesiastes: A New Translation with Introduction and Commentary* (AB 18C; New York: Doubleday, 1997), 201, 204.

as applied to the status or attitude of persons, displays a uniformly derogatory usage for proud or arrogant persons whose power is the object of criticism and judgment. This strengthens the interpretation of "the high ones" of 5:8 as arrogant wielders of unjust power. It does not, however, specifically identify them as bearers of political office.

The wielders of political power that are named in Ecclesiastes apart from kings are called either *sallitim* or *moselim*. Both are terms specifying political authorities, in one instance made a bit more precise by reference to "ten *sallitim* in a city." These authorities are uniformly devalued or critiqued by Qoheleth. Wisdom is declared to be more powerful then the ten *sallitim* (7:19), and one of the evils noted by the author is "an error or misjudgment issuing from a *sallit* (10:5), which occasions the further dour comment that "folly is set in many high places." This misrule of authorities is explained or illustrated by the rapid rise and fall in the fortunes of political appointees: "I have seen slaves on horses, and princes or officials walking on foot like slaves" (10:7). Also, the author remarks that "the words of the wise heard in quiet are superior to the shouting of a *mosel* among fools" (9:17). Nevertheless, Qoheleth warns that one must be respectful of a *mosel*'s power, for if his anger should flare up against you, it is best to show him quiet deference (10:4).

In treating the rule of kings, the writer is more guarded and indirect. He tells an example story of a "great *melek*" who besieged a city but was foiled by the wisdom of "a poor wise man" with the attendant message that, although "wisdom is better than might," its practitioner is readily despised or forgotten (9:13–16). A woe is addressed to any land that has an immature parvenu as its *melek*, whose courtiers are allowed to carouse, and a blessing is declared on any land whose king is of noble birth and maintains court decorum (10:16–17). In spite of these allusions to effete kings, readers are warned, "Even in your thought, do not curse the king, nor in your bedroom curse the rich, for a bird of the air will carry your voice, or some winged creature tell the matter" (10:20). Thus, regard for the king is not grounded in his sanctity or righteous rule but in his power to enforce his will with the help of loyal informers.

Finally, in limning the portrait of himself as Solomon, the writer gives a laundry list of his accomplishments in the pursuit of pleasure: building houses, planting vineyards, gardens, and orchards, constructing pools for irrigation water, acquiring household slaves, singers, concubines, great herds and flocks, and feasting on the plunder and tribute of other kings and their lands which became provinces of his empire (2:4–8). In most respects this list of the achievements of the author's Solomonic persona follows the Solomonic credits in 1 Kings, going so far as to say "I have acquired great wisdom, surpassing all who were over Jerusalem before me" (1:16). But there is this major difference: in 1 Kings Solomon's wisdom is given to him as a singular unqualified gift from which his works flow seamlessly, whereas Qoheleth's pseudo-Solomon undertakes his works as a "test" of his confidence that wisdom is guiding him but in the end fails to find satisfaction in what he has accomplished. The only wisdom he emerges with is that his life has been one of unsatisfying toil, the whole of it a mere "vapor and chasing the wind," in which there has been "no *yitron*," no gain or profit when all was said and done.

It appears, then, that the assessment of the royal apex of political power, although somewhat more guarded, is no less negative than Qoheleth's critical allusions to lesser political authorities. The implication for a reading of the role of the king in 5:9 is that the advantage or profit in the royal management of agriculture is either wistfully nostalgic or subtly ironic in tone, possibly even going so far as to turn the *yitron* on its head by viewing it, not as positive gain, but as the agrarian surplus that the king extracts from the land in company with "the high ones" who either serve in his chain of command or profiteer on their own initiative. In 4:1, it is baldly stated that "on the side of the oppressors there was power, and there was no one to comfort them [the oppressed]." No exception is made for the king as the presumably ultimate power authorizing or permitting the oppression.

With all that said, however, the exact offices and procedures involved in this oppressive exercise of power are not named or described. The rhetoric of the book remains at the level of generalities and heavily stereotypical language. Norbert Lohfink has examined the terminology of *melek*, *sallit*, and *mosel* and concludes that *melek* refers to Hellenistic kings, while *sallit* and *mosel* are lesser officials who represented the Hellenistic rulers in Palestine, possibly including persons of the likes of Zenon, who was the regent of the Ptolemies in overseeing royal estates in Palestine, or the Tobiad Joseph, who outbid others to become the paramount tax farmer for the province of Coele-Syria.[3] Lohfink's proposals are suggestive, but remain speculative, in part because the Hebrew terms and their sketchy treatment do not correspond to any of the known Greek names and functions for the several layers and branches of Ptolemaic administration and in part because the synoptic view of the Ptolemaic administration of foreign provinces may not have been as schematic as

---

3. Norbert Lohfink, "*Melek, sallit* und *mosel* bei Kohelet und die Abfassungszeit des Buchs," *Bib* 62 (1981): 535–42.

frequently claimed and was subject to changes over the decades.[4] The LXX of Ecclesiastes gives us no help at this point, since apart from *basileus* for *melek*, it consistently uses forms of the verb *exousiazo*, "to have the right or power over things and persons to do as one sees fit," thereby lumping together the Hebrew terms for lesser officials under the general category of "authorities" rather than identifying them with any of the Greek titles for administrative officers employed by the Ptolemies.

The Text as an Expression of Social Placement and Social Ideology

While the sum total of our textual study has not been altogether "vapor and a chasing of the wind," it has not yielded a specifiable historical and political setting directly connected to extrabiblical sociopolitical data. While Ecclesiastes cannot be later than the Ptolemaic period, and in my view fits most comfortably in the third century, it cannot be ruled out that it belongs to the late fifth- or fourth-century Persian period. C. L. Seow, arguing from the Aramaic flavor of the book and from the occurrence of socioeconomic terms and practices attested in the Elephantine papyri in particular, places Qoheleth in the Persian political economy. I do not find his case compelling, if only because a perusal of Ptolemaic administrative documents turns up many practices similar to those cited from Elephantine, although necessarily minus the terminological connection to Ecclesiastes because of the official language change from Aramaic to Greek.[5] Nevertheless, in the absence of any evidence that securely dates the book, Seow is persuasive in keeping the temporal horizon of its composition open to question. Even as many of us prefer a Ptolemaic setting, it has to be acknowledged that the Ezra–Nehemiah texts show a similar embroilment of political figures in the social tensions and oppressions of Persian Palestine, although in their case the angle of vision is that of the officials themselves.[6] So what light does the considerable sociopolitical data we have about the impact of Persian and Ptolemaic rule on Palestine throw on the social placement and ideology

---

4. Roger S. Bagnall, *The Administration of the Ptolemaic Possessions Outside Egypt* (Leiden: Brill, 1976), and *Reading Papyri, Writing Ancient History* (London: Routledge, 1995).

5. Roger S. Bagnall and Peter Derow, *Greek Historical Documents: The Hellenistic Period* (Atlanta: Scholars Press, 1981).

6. Norman K. Gottwald, "Expropriated and the Expropriators in Nehemiah 5," in *Concepts of Class in Ancient Israel* (ed. M. R. Sneed; Atlanta: Scholars Press, 1999), 1–19.

of Qoheleth? As for social placement, Qoheleth is a highly literate intellectual who, if we are to believe the colophon to the book, was a collector and arranger of wise sayings that he pondered and shared by teaching others. Whether he was also a scribe attached to an institutional setting cannot be determined, nor is there any certain sign, despite the Solomonic fiction of authorship, that he held a political office of any sort. There is only a glimmer of such a possibility in his remarks on the rough and tumble of courtly politics.

The extent of his wealth is unclear. His clichéd references to "the poor" do not suggest a truly impoverished person. It is not difficult, however, to imagine him as one of those landowners victimized by "the high ones" without redress. At any rate, his dismay at the rapid change of fortune that can come through unexpected loss or gain is the mark of one who has had, or presently holds, enough goods to feel vulnerable and insecure in the socioeconomic order. While he constantly insists that there is nothing "new under the sun," that dismal view concerns the macrocosm of human experience, but not the microcosm of personal life where the unpredictable "new" may upset the life conditions of any particular person for good or ill at any moment. While it is difficult to say which parts of the book may be born of direct personal experience, once the Solomonic fiction is given up, Qoheleth looks at life from the angle of those who suffer from the power of kings and magnates rather than the disillusionment of the powerful with which he launches the book.

Qoheleth's bleak assessment of the enduring experience of human pain and loss, much of it due to the arbitrary actions of social and political forces, leads him to retreat into a modest private enjoyment of such goods and supportive social ties as he presently possesses. This split between the uncontrollable public sphere and the modestly manageable private sphere was one of the hallmarks of the Hellenistic age, and it need not have required any direct knowledge of Hellenistic texts for Qoheleth to have experienced that yawning gap due to the pervasive impact of foreign rule in Palestine. Peter Green characterizes "the over-riding mood of the Hellenistic age" as "dynastic autocracy in public affairs, commercial or intellectual disengagement in private life."[7] Qoheleth finds no dependable public ethic to restrain people from "lording it over" one another in a competitive struggle for limited goods (8:9). Certainly Seow is correct in believing that this public/private split was

---

7. Peter Green, *Alexander to Actium: The Historical Evolution of the Hellenistic Age* (Berkeley: University of California Press, 1990), 35.

already felt under Persian rule, although greatly intensified by Ptolemaic exploitation of Palestinian resources.

The net effect of placing Qoheleth in this vulnerable setting makes him appear much less as a misanthropic crank and much more as a man with understandable grievances for which he saw no redress other than private resignation. Yet his book and his alleged teaching career proved to be a channel for him to turn personal grievance into generalized commentary on sociopolitical and economic life around him, believing that his chastened wisdom—unable to unlock the secret of life's workings—was at least more satisfying than mindless hedonism, lust for wealth, and exercise of arbitrary political power.

Theology of the Author

There is a close correlation between Qoheleth's views of arbitrary social and political authorities and his views of God, conceived as the ultimate sovereign whose intentions and reasons for shaping human life are as impenetrable as the capricious acts of human authorities. Indeed, divine intentions are more inscrutable than the intentions of the authorities who at least can be seen to aim at enhancing their personal glory and power. But what are the aims of a deity who already possesses all imaginable power and yet declines to share his designs with humans? In such circumstances, notwithstanding the occasional mouthing of piety, as in the final admonition "to fear God and keep his commandments," Qoheleth adopts a stance toward God as guarded as his stance toward human authority. He advises that one "play it cool" before God, neither being overly righteous nor overly wicked, presumably because a middle course will draw less attention to oneself and will entail less of a downfall should God decide to change one's "lot" (7:16–18). When a person participates in temple worship, he cautions to avoid making rash vows, for God will strictly punish those who break their vows (5:1–7).

The "fear of God" counseled in these contexts has a very different tone than the Torah-oriented piety counseled at the close of the book. It is a fear based on careful calculation to avoid the attention of an inscrutable deity whose whims are as likely to bring more ill than good to his naive worshipers. Both divine and human sources of authority and power are far removed from the actual concerns of those whose life conditions they largely control. A similar distancing from civic deities emerged in the Hellenistic world, accompanied by cynicism among intellectuals and by the growth of private cults attuned to the personal needs of their followers. Qoheleth, in a forbidding monotheistic milieu that puzzles and alienates him, offers no "private" form of religion that might bring solace, even so much as the personal piety of many of the psalmists.

Tentative Conclusion

Ecclesiastes 5:8–9 is one of the more explicit articulations of the arbitrary social and political oppression that elsewhere pervades the book. Without our being able to say that the text alludes to Persian or Ptolemaic administration as such, it indicates a harsh and tightly knit system of oppression in which powerful officials and magnates collaborate to extract agricultural surplus unjustly, unrestrained by the king who himself benefits from the surplus. What it describes is in keeping with imperial political economy in the century or two when Ecclesiastes, primarily on linguistic grounds, is likely to have been written. These verses, together with others in the book that display the arbitrary and oppressive policies and behavior of rulers, echoed in the inscrutable distance of God from the human plight, helps to clarify the bleak outlook of Qoheleth and his determination to secure a private space where he can survive from day to day. At this point the relative helplessness of his position in life merges with an ideology of guarded cynicism and resignation, around the edges of which he manages to embroider a teaching and writing career to generate a measure of meaning that he is unable to find anywhere else in his world.

In answer to the question of the present study's title, I would say that extrabiblical sociopolitical data contribute to an understanding of biblical texts by postulating explanatory options that can be fed into the array of textual information generated by the several methods of inquiry customary in biblical research. The "explanations" evoked are definitely not all of one sort. Some concern social systems and processes, while others attain greater specificity, allowing us to make more direct spatio-temporal correlations between social world and text. The social clarification of Eccles 5:8–9 proposed here is clearly of the first type, concerning systems and processes and their role in shaping textual ideology.

The value of the social-scientific inquiry is not dependent on showing close correlations in all or most cases. The question of the level and degree of correspondence between social world and text should be a problematic that is allowed to "simmer" or "percolate" as we scrutinize the world and the text in repeated forays into their many facets. The papyrologist Roger Bagnall notes perceptively the way philological and exegetical studies of ancient texts are "interactively" and "recursively" linked to the forming and testing of hypotheses about the historical, cultural, and social matrix of documents.[8] If it is also the case, as Terry Eagleton formulates it, that "...the text exists in the 'hollow' it has scooped out between itself and history,"[9] presenting itself in a particular ideological formation that is responsive to and expressive of social conditions, it follows that any insights into the network of ideas and practices that connect the ideological and social formations will in one way or another enlarge and deepen our understanding of texts.

8.   Roger S. Bagnall, *Reading Papyri, Writing Ancient History* (London: Routledge, 1995), 1–8.

9.   Terry Eagleton, *Criticism and Ideology: A Study in Marxist Literary Theory* (London: Verso, 1976), 80.

THE CHRONICLER BURIES SAUL

Jennifer L. Koosed

1. *The Telling of Saul's Decease*

The task of the narrator is not an easy one, he said. He appears to be required to choose his tale from among the many that are possible. But of course that is not the case. The case is rather to make many of the one. Always the teller must be at pains to devise against his listener's claim— perhaps spoken, perhaps not—that he has heard the tale before. He sets forth the categories into which the listener will wish to fit the narrative as he hears it. But he understands that the narrative is itself in fact no category but is rather the category of all categories for there is nothing which falls outside its purview. All is telling. Do not doubt it.

—Cormac McCarthy[1]

The Hebrew Bible contains four different versions of Saul's death and/or burial (1 Sam 31; 2 Sam 1:1–16; 2 Sam 21:12–14; and 1 Chr 10). Not only do the Samuel stories fail to cohere, but the differences between the versions in Samuel and the one in Chronicles are also multiple. Analyses of the discrepancies between Samuel and Chronicles have focused on questions of source and history,[2] finding value primarily in the flakes of "factual" gold panned from the "fictional" mud. However, narrative and history are more difficult to sort than this method allows, and meaning adheres even in the dirt. The story replicates as it moves through time and space, as the storyteller makes "many of the one," and each tale of the teller contains a world of import.

---

1. When I reflect upon Doug Knight's influence on my work, I think of many different stories, classes, conversations, books. I also remember a piece of advice: always be reading a novel. Cormac McCarthy's *The Crossing* (New York: Knopf, 1994) is the novel I am reading at the time of writing this piece. The epigram above comes from p. 155 of *The Crossing*.

2. For a concise summary of the scholarship comparing Chronicles and Samuel's accounts of Saul's death, see Craig Y. S. Ho, "Conjectures and Refutations: Is I Samuel XXXI 1–13 Really the Source of I Chronicles X 1–12?," *VT* 145 (1995): 85–96. Against the prevailing opinion, Ho argues that the Chronicler had a different, more historically accurate source than 1 Sam 31.

The Chronicler's work is dated anywhere from after the Babylonian Exile, through the Persian period, to the beginnings of the Hellenistic period, with the majority of scholars settling on the "mediating position" of a late Persian-period date.[3] Beginning with W. M. L. de Wette (1806) and further solidified by Martin Noth (1943), most Chronicles scholarship also works from the hypothesis that the Chronicler had a version of Samuel–Kings, albeit one not necessarily identical to the Masoretic text (MT).[4] In addition to Samuel–Kings, the Chronicler also appears to have some account of the Torah,[5] and explicitly mentions 31 other sources.[6] It is possible that some of these sources did not actually exist, but their mention is testimony to the increasing authority of textuality in the Persian period.[7] The Chronicler's reliance on sources, either virtual or real, reveals the author's creativity shaped by his or her ideological agenda.[8] The various ideologies of Chronicles are well documented,[9] and they include the elevation of the genealogical line of Judah, the idealization of David, the creation of a Temple liturgy, and the centralization of the priesthood.

The story of Saul's death and burial is particularly laden with ideology in both the books of Samuel and Chronicles. In Samuel, the writer is an apologist, at pains to demonstrate that David did not usurp the throne.[10]

3. Kai Peltonen, "A Jigsaw Without a Model? The Date of Chronicles," in *Did Moses Speak Attic? Jewish Historiography and Scripture in the Hellenistic Period* (ed. Lester L. Grabbe; JSOTSup 317; Sheffield: Sheffield Academic, 2001), 225–28.

4. Ho, "Conjectures and Refutations," 82–83. See also Steven L. McKenzie, *The Chronicler's Use of the Deuteronomistic History* (Atlanta: Scholars Press, 1985).

5. Marc Zvi Brettler, *The Creation of History in Ancient Israel* (New York: Routledge, 1995), 22.

6. As listed in Jacob M. Myers, *I Chronicles* (AB 12; Garden City, N.Y.: Doubleday, 1965), xlvi–xlviii. The Chronicler may be using nominal variations for some of the same sources.

7. Donald C. Polaski, "What Mean These Stones? Inscriptions, Textuality and Power in Persia and Yehud," in *Approaching Yehud: New Approaches to the Study of the Persian Period* (ed. Jon L. Berquist; Atlanta: SBL, 2007), 37–48.

8. I am indebted to Doug Knight for sensitizing me to the ideologies that shape biblical law and narrative.

9. See, for examples, Myers, *I Chronicles*, xxxii–xl, lxiv–lxxxv; Sara Japhet, *The Ideology of the Book of Chronicles and Its Place in Biblical Thought* (trans. Anna Barber; New York: Lang, 1989); Jonathan E. Dyck, "The Ideology of Identity in Chronicles," in *Ethnicity and the Bible* (ed. Mark G. Brett; New York: Brill, 1996), 89–116.

10. Baruch Halpern, *David's Secret Demons: Messiah, Murderer, Traitor, King* (Grand Rapids: Eerdmans, 2001); Steven L. McKenzie, *King David: A Biography* (New York: Oxford University Press, 2000).

Saul is mortally wounded in a battle against the Philistines on Mount Gilboa. According to 1 Sam 31:4–5, Saul asks his armor-bearer to kill him rather than let the Philistines find him wounded. The man refuses and Saul falls upon his own sword—a double death, one at the hands of the Philistines, one by his own hand. In 2 Sam 1, an Amalekite from Saul's camp comes to David and tells another story, presumably a fabrication in order to garner favor: Saul is mortally wounded and asks the Amalekite to kill him. He complies with Saul's request, kills him, and then takes the dead king's crown and armlet to present to David—another double death, but this time the second is by the hand of the Amalekite. In just a few chapters, Saul has been killed in two different ways, with three different wounds, none of them inflicted by David. The telling multiplies as death becomes a story.

The report of the demise of Saul and his sons does not end with the accounts of their deaths. According to the end of 1 Sam 31, the Philistines find Saul's body. They cut off his head and display his body on the wall of Beth-shean, a Philistine stronghold; no mention is made of the fate of his severed head. They strip off his armor and display it in the temple of Astarte. The strong men of Jabesh-gilead hear of the desecration of Saul's body and take it back, along with the bodies of his three sons also killed in battle. The men then burn the bodies in Jabesh. After the flesh is incinerated, they bury the bones under a tamarisk tree (1 Sam 31:9–13).

Later, Saul's body is dug back out of the ground and into the episode between David and the Gibeonites. In 2 Sam 21, a famine in the land is ascribed to God's punishment on behalf of the Gibeonites—apparently, Saul had violated a treaty between the Gibeonites and the people of Israel by attempting to "wipe them out" (2 Sam 21:2). However, this story is riddled with inconsistencies. In Josh 9, Joshua contracts this treaty with the Gibeonites under false pretenses and counter to God's original command to kill all of the people who inhabited the land (Josh 9:15). The Gibeonites are allowed to live, but they are cursed because of their deception (Josh 9:22–27). It seems strange that God would come to their defense now. And in any case, there is no biblical account of Saul attempting the genocide of the Gibeonites. The story of the Gibeonites' complaint against Saul's house seems tailor made to provide David an excuse to execute the remainder of the royal male descendents, his rivals to the throne. He hands over the seven men and they are impaled. At the end of the episode, Saul's and Jonathan's bones (but not the bones of the other two sons killed on Mount Gilboa?) are un-interred and reburied in the tomb of Saul's father (2 Sam 21:14) along with the bodies of the seven sacrificed relatives.

Saul is still not permitted to rest in peace. The Chronicler resuscitates him in order to kill and bury him one more time. 1 Chronicles 10 opens as the battle on Mount Gilboa is nearing its bloody end. The text records that Saul "and his three sons and all of his house died together" (1 Chr 10:6), implying that more than just three sons were killed on that fateful mountain. Consequently, all of David's rivals to the throne are eliminated without the necessity of the convoluted tale of the Gibeonites' bloodguilt (2 Sam 21), which is, in fact, absent from the Chronicler's history. The Chronicler, then, displays Saul's armor in the "temple of their gods," hangs his head in Dagon's temple, and does not reveal the location of the rest of his body, for which it uses an unusual word. The men of Jabesh-gilead rescue the body anyway from some undisclosed location, and bury the bones under an oak rather than a tamarisk tree, without preceding the burial by immolation. The tale of the possibly prevaricating Amalekite and his subsequent fate (2 Sam 1) is eliminated altogether. The death of Saul fits the Chronicler's agenda on multiple levels. The focus of the narrative is on David and David's legitimate rise to power. Even more forcibly than the Deuteronomic Historian, the Chronicler lays the blame for Saul's demise on Saul's own actions and God's judgment upon them (1 Chr 10:13–14).[11]

2. *Sorrowing Saul*

> He sighed and seemed himself weary and cast down. He said that while one would like to say that God will punish those who do such things and that people often speak in just this way it was his experience that God could not be spoken for and that men with wicked histories often enjoyed lives of comfort and that they died in peace and were buried with honor. He said that it was a mistake to expect too much of justice in this world. He said that the notion that evil is seldom rewarded was greatly overspoken for if there were no advantage to it then men would shun it and how could virtue then be attached to its repudiation? It was the nature of his profession that his experience with death should be greater than for most and he said that while it was true that time heals bereavement it does so only at the cost of the slow extinction of those loved ones from the heart's memory which is the sole place of their abode then or now. Faces fade, voices dim. Call their names. Do this and do not let sorrow die for it is the sweetening of every gift.
>
> —Cormac McCarthy[12]

---

11.   Saul Zalewski, "The Purpose of the Story of the Death of Saul in I Chronicles X," *VT* 39 (1989): 466.

12.   McCarthy, *The Crossing*, 288.

The story of Saul's death in 1 Chr 10 has long puzzled commentators. The passage serves as the narrative link between the extensive genealogies and the story of David's reign—the primary focus of the Chronicler. Yet, there is no subtle segue here; the genealogical lists end and the narrative begins abruptly. The Chronicler omits the other stories about Saul (although he is mentioned in the genealogies, without any indication of his royalty), assuming that the reader already knows who Saul is and how he got to that fateful moment on Mount Gilboa.[13] As enumerated above, the differences between Samuel and Chronicles are multiple. Not only is the Chronicler's story an unnecessary repetition—if the reader is familiar with the story of Saul, as the Chronicler seems to assume, then the reader already knows how Saul met his demise—but the repetition is not exact. The story masquerades as a repetition, but comparison reveals difference not identity. Concerning another foundational figure in the history of Israel, Sigmund Freud writes in his final work, *Moses and Monotheism*,

> almost everywhere noticeable gaps, disturbing repetitions, and obvious contradictions have come about—indications which reveal things to us which it was not intended to communicate. In its implications the distortion of a text resembles a murder: the difficulty is not in perpetrating the deed, but in getting rid of its traces.[14]

Saul's death and burial is replete with such "noticeable gaps, disturbing repetitions, and obvious contradictions," a specter is haunting Israel, the specter of Saul. The Chronicler's telling of the death of Saul bares all the marks of trauma remembered.

Trauma is a word first employed to describe bodily wounds and injuries. By the end of the nineteenth century, the word had also been applied to the emotional pain and suffering caused by catastrophic experience.[15] In the field of psychology, the catastrophic experience or "traumatic stressor" has been further defined as "events involving 'actual or threatened death or serious injury, or a threat to the physical integrity

---

13. See Zalewski, "The Purpose," 449–50, for a brief survey of the scholarship on the Chronicler's decision to begin with Saul's death.

14. Sigmund Freud, "Moses and Monotheism," in *The Standard Edition of the Complete Psychological Works of Sigmund Freud* (ed. James Strachey et al.; London: Hogarth, 1939), quoted in Jay Geller, "Trauma," in *Handbook of Postmodern Biblical Interpretation* (ed. A. K. M. Adam; St. Louis: Chalice, 2000), 266.

15. Ian Hacking, "Memory Sciences, Memory Politics," in *Tense Past: Cultural Essays in Trauma and Memory* (ed. Paul Antze and Michael Lambek; New York: Routledge, 1996), 75–76.

of self and others' that produce 'intense fear, helplessness, or horror.'"[16] Traumatic memory, in particular, has attracted the attention of historians, sociologists, psychologists, psychiatrists, writers of fiction and memoir, literary critics, philosophers—in short, memory studies have exploded in the wake of the brutalities of the twentieth century. A substantial portion of these studies focuses on the relationship between trauma and representation.[17] Trauma disrupts representation and distorts narrative. The story of Saul betrays multiple levels of trauma: the primordial matricide, the murder of Saul himself, the pain of the Babylonian war, and the disassembling experience of exile.

Even though it is precisely chronology that is disrupted when trauma is remembered, I want to begin my analysis of the Chronicler at the beginning and work my way forward. First, I regress the Chronicler back to the birth of culture itself—the murder of the mother. Julie Kelso's book on Chronicles is the only work of biblical criticism that explores the text through psychoanalytic theories of trauma and repression. Kelso's book is about absences, the absence of women characters in Chronicles and the absence of women readers of Chronicles. For Kelso, "the book of Chronicles silences women in specific ways, most radically through their association with maternity."[18] As Freud points out, noticeable gaps hide unspoken and unspeakable events. According to Freud's theories of repression and disassociation, the traumatic event cannot be assimilated into normal, narrative memory. As expressed by two contemporary psychologists, "Traumatic memories are the unassimilated scraps of

16. Richard J. McNally, *Remembering Trauma* (Cambridge, Mass.: Harvard University Press, 2003), 79, citing from the DSM-IV.

17. In the study of trauma and its psychological effects, there are two prevailing theories: first, "horrific experiences are engraved on the mind, never to be forgotten"; second, "the mind protects itself by banishing traumatic memories from awareness, making it difficult for many people to remember their worst experience until many years later" (ibid., 1). Both theories attempt to explain the phenomena associated with the aftershocks of trauma which include nightmares, flashbacks, emotional numbing, and sleep disturbances. The debate between the two theories extends at least as far back as the differences between Freud and Wittgenstein's understanding of the effects of trauma on memory and representation, and extends into the conflicts—physiological, psychological, and legal—between the proponents of Recovered Memory and those of False Memory Syndromes. See K. M. Fierke, "Bewitched by the Past: Social Memory, Trauma and International Relations," in *Memory, Trauma and World Politics: Reflections on the Relationship between Past and Present* (ed. Duncan Bell; New York: Palgrave, 2006), 116–34, and McNally, *Remembering Trauma*, 1–26.

18. Julie Kelso, *O Mother, Where Art Thou? An Irigarayan Reading of the Book of Chronicles* (London: Equinox, 2007), 1.

overwhelming experiences, which need to be integrated with existing mental schemes, and be transformed into narrative language."[19] They are therefore banished from consciousness, but their affects do continue to be felt by the individual. Whereas Freud posits the murder of the father as the traumatic crime covered up by culture, Kelso, following Luce Irigaray's critique of Plato, Freud, and Lacan, pushes past patricide to an even more ancient matricide.[20] No matter the quality of one's relationship, it is difficult to kill one's mother.[21] It is even more difficult to dispose of the body, and the originary matricide has left its traces in the books of Chronicles.

Kelso reads in an Irigarian mode as an analyst does an analysand[22]— she puts Chronicles on the couch, asks it questions, allows it to speak. On her couch, Chronicles transforms from the dry genealogical lists, the sanitized David, and the sterile regurgitation of Kings to a dynamic text of hidden complexities. Demonstrating the principle that the repressed always returns, the Chronicler's attempt to exclude women is ultimately unsuccessful because "Chronicles depends on the absence and silence of women for its imaginary coherence."[23] Kelso argues that the genealogies in the first nine chapters of Chronicles—some of which simply list male names without the intervention of a word let alone a woman—betray the repression of the mother and the fantasy of monosexual reproduction not only where women are absent but also when women are present. Chronicles largely lacks any mother–son or mother–daughter connections, but when they do appear they are eruptions of the unrepresentable that disrupt the syntax of the text, the logic of the grammar, even realism itself.[24] Next, Kelso argues that the repression of the mother is also

19. Basel van der Kolk and Otto van der Hart, "The Intrusive Past: The Flexibility of Memory and the Engraving of Trauma," in *Trauma* (ed. Cathy Caruth; Baltimore: The Johns Hopkins University Press, 1995), as quoted in Geller, "Trauma," 263.
20. Kelso, *O Mother, Where Art Thou?*, 22.
21. A deeper repression implies a deeper pain. Perhaps the trauma of matricide goes deeper than even the trauma of patricide because inadvertent matricide was quite common before the advent of modern Western medicine. Many infants murdered their mothers during the process of birth.
22. Roland Boer also uses this language in his reading of Chronicles as utopia; see his *Novel Histories: The Fiction of Biblical Criticism* (Playing the Texts 2; Sheffield: Sheffield Academic, 1997), 157.
23. Kelso, *O Mother, Where Art Thou?*, 1.
24. Ibid., 127–78.

"readable through the description of…certain male bodies in the narrative," especially through the body of Saul.[25]

Kelso builds her argument on several of the peculiarities of language in the Chronicler's version of events. In the heat of the battle, Saul is pierced by an arrow (v. 3) and reacts in a way unclear in the Hebrew. The final phrase of v. 3 can be translated "and he was wounded" or "he became frightened of the archers" or "he writhed in fear from the archers."[26] Saul begs his armor-bearer to run him through so that the uncircumcised Philistines are not able "to act arbitrarily" or "to deal wantonly" or "to humiliate" him. The verbal root (עלל) can also mean "to insert or to thrust in."[27] Taken together, Kelso suggests that Saul is worried that the Philistines will rape him.[28] The verses that follow highlight a continued anxiety over penetration. Saul is penetrated by the Philistines, begs his sword-bearer to penetrate him before he can be further penetrated, and finally penetrates himself when his sword-bearer refuses. The text betrays masculine anxiety over becoming feminized, and in the end recalls the paradigmatic biblical story of the vulnerable female body—Saul worries that the Philistines will do to him what the Benjaminites did to the Levite's concubine (Judg 19:25 and 20:5).

Chronicles further feminizes Saul's body and specifically links that body to maternity through its use of an unusual word for Saul's body. The men of Jabesh-gilead take the נופה of Saul back to their city (1 Chr 10:12).[29] This word appears nowhere else in the Hebrew Bible and

> is a strange word that has a semantic range that includes hollowness and closed-ness (נוף). In other words, the word you [the Chronicler] choose here to represent the bodies of Saul and his sons is a word that evokes the *male* body as an enclosed, empty container, an exterior shell encasing an empty space… But more than this, this hollow, contained body, under threat of penetration from the enemy men, evokes the maternal body— that container for the father's seed.[30]

The Chronicler substitutes male for female by narrating Saul's death as a substitute for the murder of the mother. This fundamental substitution is disclosed by other male to female substitutions in the Chronicler's

---

25.　Ibid., 168. The other male bodies Kelso reads are those of Jehoram, Asa, and Uzziah.

26.　Ibid., 172.

27.　Ibid.

28.　This is also suggested by Myers, *I Chronicles*, 78.

29.　The word is used twice in 1 Chr 10:12 in feminine construct form. It replaces the typical word for "body" used in 1 Sam 31:12.

30.　Kelso, *O Mother, Where Art Thou?*, 173.

account. The temple of the God Dagon replaces the temple of the Goddess Astarte (1 Chr 10:10 vs. 1 Sam 31:10); a ghost or necromancer (both masculine) replaces the woman of Endor (1 Chr 10:13 vs. 1 Sam 28:7–25).

The Chronicler recalls Saul's conjuring of Samuel's ghost and attributes Saul's loss of divine favor to his trespass into the spirit world at the very point where Saul himself becomes a ghost by dying yet living on. Trauma disrupts, not just in the moment of the event; traumatic events extend into the future, and the Chronicler, living centuries after Saul, is still haunted by the circumstances of his death. Jacques Derrida uses the figure of the ghost or specter to name that which is past but continues to exercise effects in the present.[31] This "persistence of a present past"[32] is manifest in the Chronicler's narrative repetitions, repetitions that are not simple recounting of the story but repetitions that are themselves new stories, as if Saul's first, second, and third wounds are not enough really to kill him; as if the brutal rending of his body by the Philistines, its burning by the men of Jabesh-gilead, their burial of him and then his second burial by David is not enough really to keep him dead. "As in the work of mourning, after a trauma, the conjuration has to make sure that the dead will not come back: quick, do whatever is needed to keep the cadaver localized, in a safe place, decomposing right where it was inhumed…"[33] The Chronicler is not content to allow the body simply to decompose, nor to let the Deuteronomic Historian's brutal destruction of Saul's body stand. The Chronicler stabs him again, tears him apart again and buries him again, this time under an oak.

Kelso analyzes the Chronicler with special attention to disassociative symptoms from which she infers the trauma of matricide buried deep in the unconscious. It is not necessary to delve so deeply into the unconscious of the text, so deeply into the past, to locate another traumatic stressor. The Chronicler is also dealing with the actual death of Saul. Saul's death may cover over the murder of the mother, but it is also a murder of a father—as the first king of a unified state of Israel, Saul is

---

31. Jacques Derrida, *Specters of Marx: The State of Debt, the Work of Mourning, and the New International* (trans. Peggy Kamuf; New York: Routledge, 1994). Derrida's own concept of the specter is influenced by although not identical to Nicolas Abraham and Maria Torok's psychoanalytical theory of the phantom, which in turn is grounded in Freud's own proposals about trauma and mourning. See Colin Davis, "État Présent: Hauntology, Spectres and Phantoms," *French Studies* 59 (2005): 373–79.

32. Derrida, *Specters of Marx*, 97.

33. Ibid.

the father of the nation. This father's death is particularly poignant because Chronicles is written at a time when the entire royal line as well the very institution of monarchy has been completely destroyed. Saul's death is a figure for the death of all Israelite and Judahite kings; Saul's death is a figure for the death of monarchy itself. Saul's death and burial also gives birth to the Chronicles' narrative as well as the focus of that narrative—David's reign. David may be the beloved one, the hero in both Samuel–Kings and Chronicles, but the demise of Saul and his house keeps emerging in the story like a bad dream, unresolved and unresolvable. "The tradition of all the dead generations weighs like a nightmare on the brain of the living."[34] David's glorious reign is predicated on a horror show.

Chronicles scholarship frequently focuses on the possible historical accuracy of the account vis-à-vis Samuel's narrative; however, such questions may be immaterial. Jay Geller notes that even Freud's theories were less about any actual event and more about "the unsaid of conflicted desires and guilt, of feeling and fantasy, of identity-subverting knowledges that the community fears to recognize."[35] After all, it is not the Chronicler, whoever he or she may be, who is remembering a personal trauma. Rather, the Chronicler is expressing and shaping collective memory. Building upon the work of the French sociologist Maurice Halbwachs, K. M. Fierke writes, "collective memory is ahistorical in so far as it simplifies and is impatient with any kind of ambiguity, reducing events to mythic archetypes."[36] Such memory is always in the service of the present, forging collective identity.

Social memory, in particular, must be able to be articulated because it relies on transmission—multiple people in multiple generations must have the memory, by definition.[37] Fierke puts Freud and Wittgenstein in conversation about the ability to represent traumatic events. She concludes,

> The literal experience of trauma may be beyond representation, but in the imitation or acting out of the traumatic event, the victim reproduces the linguistic boundaries of the past experience. Trauma is consequently part of a cultural package involving a range of speech acts, patterns of relationship and assumptions. The key difference between traumatic memory and

34. Karl Marx, *The Eighteenth Brumaire of Louis Bonaparte*, as cited by Derrida, *Specters of Marx*, 108.

35. Geller, "Trauma," 265.

36. Fierke, "Bewitched by the Past," 116; see also Antze and Lambek, eds., *Tense Past*, xx–xxii.

37. Fierke, "Bewitched by the Past," 125.

declarative memory is thus not one of the presence or absence of language but rather the degree of *perspicuity* with which the traumatic event is expressed. Acting out is a phenomenon by which the traumatized individual or group continues to live within the linguistic boundaries of a past world. This can be distinguished from a narrative account that reflexively identifies the past as past.[38]

Chronicles is involved in the acting out of the past in the present, a repetition of multiple traumas, repressed, displaced upon one another. "In this respect, the habit of remembering is also a habit of forgetting in that the memory becomes tied to a specific narrative that focuses selectively on elements of the past."[39]

The Chronicler forgets in order to remember. The Chronicler forgets that Saul was chosen and anointed before he was forsaken and destroyed. The Chronicler forgets that some of Saul's descendents survived the battles, only to be assassinated later by David's machinations. The Chronicler mis-remembers the witch of Endor and the role of Astarte and the tamarisk tree that marks Saul's first burial. The Chronicler forgets that Saul's body was burned. The re-telling of the sorrow reveals in what it includes and what it excludes, in what it repeats and what it alters. Every remembering is also a forgetting but every re-telling calls out Saul's name and revives the sorrow.

3. *The Darkening*

He said that even the sepulturero would understand that every tale was a tale of dark and light and would perhaps not have it otherwise. Yet there was still a further order to the narrative and it was a thing of which men do not speak. He said the wicked know that if the ill they do be of sufficient horror men will not speak against it. That men have just enough stomach for small evils and only these will they oppose. He said that true evil has power to sober the smalldoer against his own deeds and in the contemplation of that evil he may even find the path of righteousness which has been foreign to his feet and may have no power but to go upon it. Even this man may be appalled at what is revealed to him and seek some order to stand against it. Yet in all of this there are two things which perhaps he will not know. He will not know that while the order which the righteous seek is never righteousness itself but is only order, the disorder of evil is in fact the thing itself. Nor will he know that while the righteous are hampered at every turn by their ignorance of evil to the evil all is plain, light and dark alike. This man of which we speak will seek to impose order and lineage

38. Ibid., 121.
39. Ibid., 122.

upon things which rightly have none. He will call upon the world itself to testify as to the truth of what are in fact but his desires. In his final incarnation he may seek to indemnify his words with blood for by now he will have discovered that words pale and lose their savor while pain is always new.

—Cormac McCarthy[40]

Death's disorder disrupts even the most careful of narratives. Chronicles begins with an exuberant fecundity, nine chapters tracing lineages, focusing on the bountiful branches of the Israelites. On the surface, the genealogies chronicle life, but every birth notice is also an obituary deferred, as the son is produced to take the place of the father when he dies. These lines run on through and beyond the exile and then the narrative interrupts time and doubles back to tell the murder of Saul at the hands of the Philistines. The Chronicler's telling is a narrative shaped by trauma—the trauma of both matricide and patricide. But the Chronicler is also dealing with a more recent and accessible memory: the memory of the Babylonian destruction and exile. When Saul's body is buried, he is merged, literally and figuratively, with the Land of Israel. Saul's death and burial, then, becomes the locus of the Chronicler's process of assimilating the trauma of the Babylonian destruction and transforming it into narrative. Examining Saul's corpse also is an analysis of an aspect of the Chronicler's utopian geography.

Roland Boer has argued that Chronicles can be read as utopian literature: "In this light, Chronicles may be understood as a document that draws on memory of the past in order to construct the picture of a possible and hoped for future."[41] Integral to this vision is a unified people of Israel, living in a land of Israel, centered on Jerusalem, the Temple, and the proper priestly worship that happens therein. Ideal identity is intertwined with utopian space, but on closer examination, both lack the stability the Chronicler attempts to achieve. In terms of the land, the map the Chronicler verbally draws of Israel is impossible to draw physically. There are multiple problems with the Chronicler's topography.[42] What Boer suggests is that these problems are not interpretive puzzles to be

40. McCarthy, *The Crossing*, 292–93.
41. Boer, *Novel Histories*, 139.
42. See also Douglas A. Knight, "Joshua 22 and the Ideology of Space," in *"Imagining" Biblical Worlds: Studies in Spatial, Social and Historical Constructs in Honor of James W. Flanagan* (ed. David M. Gunn and Paula M. McNutt; JSOTSup 359; London: Sheffield Academic, 2002), 51–63. Knight notes that the texts of the Persian period use "territory to convey ideology" (63).

solved, but rather they are "a manifestation of the issue of conjunction and disjunction in utopian narrative."[43] Utopias are always haunted by their corresponding dystopias.

As a whole, Chronicles suppresses the Israelites' troubled relationship with the land. In Chronicles, the time in Egypt, the exodus, the conquest, and the Assyrian and Babylonian invasions are downplayed. This is not the amnesia of repressed memory; it is the refusal to remember, born of a debilitating pain. This refusal to remember marks even the opening chapters of 1 Chronicles. As Sara Japhet notes about chs. 1–10, "There is a direct line from Israel the patriarch to Israel the people, and the line is one of natural growth and multiplication, taking place in the natural environment of the land of Israel."[44] Ephraim and Manasseh are born, live, and die in Israel not Egypt; Joshua never has to conquer the land because he is already there; Saul's body is not desecrated in Beth-shean because that area was not occupied by Philistines.[45]

However, such major events as the sojourn and captivity in Egypt, the exodus, the conquest, the Assyrian and Babylonian invasions, cannot be wholly forgotten. The collective anxiety about the fragility of the bond between people and land is deflected, and the collective anxiety about the ability of foreign armies to destroy is redirected. The repressed returns and is acted out on the body of Saul. "Every *revenant* [French: 'ghost' or 'specter'; literally, 'that which comes back'] seems to come from and return to *the earth*, to come from it as from a buried clan destiny (humus and mold, tomb and subterranean prison), to return to it as to the lowest, toward the humble, humid, humiliated."[46] Saul is a figure for the land. His body is multiply penetrated, hewed into pieces, put on humiliating display, and finally returned first to his people and then to his land as the men of Jabesh-gilead rescue his body and bury it under an oak tree. Responsibility for Saul's death is triply ascribed—the Philistines draw first blood, then Saul himself administers the final blow. Yet, ultimately, "it was the Lord himself who put Saul to death"[47] (1 Chr 10:14). Who is responsible for the land's penetration, fragmentation, humiliation? Foreign invaders, the Israelites themselves, or God? The ideal Israel may be inviolable and in harmony with its God, but the ordeal of Saul's body betrays the collective anxiety of those who were living on in a world still

43. Boer, *Novel Histories*, 144. See pp. 144–45 for a fuller description of the topographical problems at the beginning of 1 Chronicles.
44. Sara Japhet, "Conquest and Settlement in Chronicles," *JBL* 98 (1979): 218.
45. Ibid., 215.
46. Derrida, *Specters of Marx*, 93 (emphasis original).
47. Zalewski, "The Purpose, 465.

damaged and different because of the Babylonian destruction and the Persian occupation.

At the beginning of *The Crossing*, the protagonist captures a pregnant wolf. Instead of following the instructions of his father—to kill her—he decides to take her home, over the border, back into Mexico. "Doomed enterprises divide lives forever into the then and the now"[48] and the journey is, indeed, a doomed enterprise. The wolf is killed, and the babies in her belly die with her. After burying them, the teenager crosses back into Texas only to discover that his mother and father have been murdered and their horses stolen while he was away. He finds his little brother in foster care, and together they cross back into Mexico to recover their horses—another doomed enterprise marked by blood and loss. His third border crossing is to find his brother, whether dead or alive. He locates his grave, disinters him, and carries his bones back home.

There are only three tamarisk trees (*eshel*) in the Hebrew Bible. Abraham plants one at Beer-sheba as a witness, the memory of an agreement he makes with the Philistine Abimelech (Gen 21:33). Saul stands under one in 1 Sam 22:6, perhaps as a foreshadowing of the one he is finally buried under in 1 Sam 31:13. In Chronicles, Saul is buried under an oak, an *elah*. Oaks appear more frequently in the textual landscape and they are often associated with important events.[49] In addition, the oak, the *elah*, evokes the Valley of Elah where the boy David first triumphed over the Philistines, proving himself more capable than Saul and his armies (1 Sam 17), foreshadowing his eventual triumph over them all. What is the ideology of a tree, especially one whose roots will curl around a king's bones, breaking them apart, drinking them in, transforming them into leaf and sap and bark? The grave is the last space a body will occupy, a unique space because it is one that will ultimately consume the body. The land of one's ancestors *is* the land composed of their decomposed flesh. This is not a metaphor. As the leaves of the tree unfurl, evergreen or changing hue; as the soil covers over, "faces fade, voices dim"; as the grave closes, the light dies and the dark descends. Trees remember while hearts forget. Every tree is a telling; this tree is told for Saul.

---

48. McCarthy, *The Crossing*, 129.
49. Ho, "Conjectures and Refutations," 95–96.

THE CONSERVATISM OF PSEUDO-SOLOMON

David Penchansky

The three books of Hebrew wisdom, Job, Proverbs, and Qoheleth, made a unique and positive contribution to Israelite religious literature because (a) they emphasized observation as a reliable source of religious knowledge rather than direct revelation from God;[1] (b) they remained open to questions and doubt; and (c) they listened to and incorporated the religious ideas of other cultures and ethnicities. The Wisdom of Solomon came afterwards, when the influence of Hellenism had changed forever the ways that the Israelite sages thought.

Although Pseudo-Solomon (what we call the author) wrote the book in Greek rather than Hebrew, the Wisdom of Solomon is unmistakably part of the biblical wisdom corpus. The author uses wisdom vocabulary and literary images which he borrows from the earlier Hebrew texts, but he transforms the wisdom tradition to suit the new cultural context: (a) whereas the older sages appealed to their own careful observation as a source of divine truth, Pseudo-Solomon appeals to the sacred history, particularly the stories in Genesis and the Exodus; (b) whereas the more ancient wisdom traditions explored the possibilities of sacred doubt and questioning, Pseudo-Solomon appealed to authority and tradition to shut down debate. For the first time in the wisdom tradition, doubt became a sin; and (c) Whereas the ancient wisdom traditions borrowed freely from other cultures, Pseudo-Solomon regarded the surrounding Hellenistic culture as a threat. He wrote to promote Israelite exceptionalism and nationalism and to protect young people from the dangers of Greek thinking and Greek values. He does however move easily in the rarified atmosphere of Hellenistic philosophy and metaphysical speculation, introducing new concepts to the Israelite discussions of God, concepts he likely learned through his contact with Greek writings and Greek teachers.

---

1. Although Job received a direct revelation from God, the author of Job disparaged God's direct revelation, elevating instead Job's wise judgment, which came from observation.

Pseudo-Solomon, while employing these Greek concepts, does so in the service of a conserving impulse. He tries to hold back the Hellenistic flood, which to his mind threatened to wash away Israelite religious identity.

The first section[2] (chs. 1–5 or 1–6) concerns the problem of evil. The sages frequently considered the tension between the world as it should be and the world as people actually experienced it. Pseudo-Solomon recognized that in this life a righteous person may die unfairly. But he promises reward and compensation for such a righteous person in an afterlife.

Early in his career, in 1966, Alexander Di Lella published a compelling and influential article in the *Catholic Biblical Quarterly* contrasting the books of Sirach and the Wisdom of Solomon. He characterized Sirach as "conservative" and the Wisdom of Solomon as "progressive" in their response to the larger Hellenistic culture.[3] He defines "conservatives" as those who preserve the ancient way. "Progressives" are those who introduce new ideas into the tradition.

Both the Wisdom of Solomon and Ben Sira receive and pass on the ancient Israelite wisdom tradition which they received from the Hebrew books of Job, Proverbs, and Qoheleth.[4] But these newer sages, Ben Sira and Pseudo-Solomon, came in a time when Greek culture dominated the Diaspora Jewish community.[5] These books both respond to the profound intellectual challenge offered by the Hellenistic culture, which remained a heavy presence in the region throughout the period of their composition. Sirach came considerably earlier,[6] and probably faced a dramatically less

---

2. The other two sections do not impress. The second describes and celebrates Lady Wisdom, and the third consists mostly of poetic expansions and reflections from the books of Genesis and Exodus.

3. Taking a somewhat different perspective, Metzger asserts that "...the Wisdom of Solomon...is concerned to unite the conventional piety of orthodox Judaism with the Greek philosophical spirit current at that time in Alexandria" (Bruce M. Metzger, *An Introduction to the Apocrypha* [New York: Oxford University Press, 1957], 66). As will become clear, I am closer to Metzger, who firmly roots Pseudo-Solomon in conventional piety.

4. There probably existed a guild of sages, which preserved and disseminated these writings, but I do not care to argue that here. See R. N. Whybray, *The Intellectual Tradition in Israel* (Berlin: de Gruyter, 1974), for an alternate explanation.

5. There are theoretical difficulties that accompany words such as "Greek" and "Hellenist." I use them in their accepted, "common-sense" definitions.

6. The Hebrew version dates from 180 B.C.E., while his grandson translated the work into Greek in 130. Wisdom books are notoriously difficult to date, and in many cases it appears that they were deliberately left devoid of chronological reference

volatile situation, not having experienced the persecution against the Jews by Antiochus IV (king of Syria between 175 and 163 B.C.E.). However, both books show the significant Hellenistic imprint upon the lives of the Jewish communities of the eastern Mediterranean.

Di Lella defines conservatives as those who held to the essential elements of their ethnic Judaism by supporting the ancient ways. Progressives were those who explored Hellenistic ideas even at the risk of their Jewish identity. Most scholars claim that Pseudo-Solomon wrote for apostate Jews who had rejected their Jewish roots and practices in favor of Hellenistic culture and philosophy. A description in 1 Maccabees coming from a roughly similar time mentions apostate Jews who reject Jewish practice and even try to undo their circumcisions: "Thereupon they built a gymnasium in Jerusalem according to the Gentile custom. They covered over the mark of their circumcision and abandoned the holy covenant; they allied themselves with the Gentiles and sold themselves to wrongdoing" (1:14–15). Pseudo-Solomon reports on a similar faction who despised the law. He describes the ungodly saying that the righteous one "reproaches us for sins against the law" (2:12). Therefore, it is reasoned, Pseudo-Solomon's audience was those who disparaged the Jewish law.

Di Lella calls Pseudo-Solomon progressive because he introduced the idea of immortality and the afterlife as a response to the problem of evil. Pseudo-Solomon says, "For God created us for incorruption (ἀφθαρσία), and made us in the image of his own eternity (ἀϊδιότητος)" (2:23). This idea of life after death was only newly introduced to the Jewish community. One finds some bare hints of immortality in the books of Daniel and 2 Maccabees: "Many of those who sleep in the dust of the earth shall awake, some to everlasting life, and some to shame and everlasting contempt. Those who are wise shall shine like the brightness of the sky, and those who lead many to righteousness, like the stars forever and

points as a way to universalize the message. Along with Collins, I prefer to stay agnostic on the dating of the Wisdom of Solomon, and move on to other issues. I note especially what Collins says about the ambiguity of dating this material: "Whether the book can be tied to such specific events [as David Winston does in "Solomon, Wisdom of," *ABD* 6:120–27] remains questionable, since it never alludes to these events explicitly. Moreover, we shall argue that the account of the persecution of the righteous [one of the arguments for specific dating] has the character of a quasi-philosophical argument about the profitability of justice, rather than of a veiled historical commentary, and the apocalyptic scene that it evokes was traditional by the Roman period. It cannot be taken as a reliable guide to the circumstances in which the book was composed" (John Collins, *Jewish Wisdom in the Hellenistic* Age [Louisville: Westminster John Knox, 1997], 179).

ever" (Dan 12:2–3); "…the king of the universe will raise us up to an everlasting renewal of life… One cannot but choose…to cherish the hope God gives of being raised again by him….the Creator of the World…will in his mercy give life and breath back to you again" (2 Macc 7:9, 14, 23).

"How is it fair that the righteous suffer?" the sages had always asked. Pseudo-Solomon assures them not to worry. After they die, the righteous will receive their reward and recompense in heaven. "Their hope is full of immortality" (2:4b), he asserts. "The faithful will abide with [God] in love" (2:9b).

In contrast to the Wisdom of Solomon, Di Lella observes, the book of Sirach was the more traditional of these two late wisdom books. It held faithful to ancient Israelite ideas. Ben Sira believed in an insensate Sheol, a place where the dead had no true consciousness or feelings. Pseudo-Solomon, on the other hand, embraced these new ideas regarding immortality, and these new methods of reasoning which he learned from the surrounding dominant Hellenistic culture.[7]

Di Lella argues that the wisdom tradition had reached a stalemate in their deliberations upon the problem of evil. The sages believed in a moral universe where good was rewarded and evil punished. If one lived according to the principles of wisdom, it invariably resulted in a long and prosperous life. But the human experience of suffering and injustice told them otherwise. People who were good suffered horribly, while evil, oppressive figures lived comfortable lives of prosperity and ease. Pseudo-Solomon seeks to mediate these two positions. Di Lella states, "…only the progressive Pseudo-Solomon provides an adequate and satisfying solution to the vexing problem of retribution."[8] Pseudo-Solomon declared that rewards and punishments are distributed *after* death. Di Lella observes, "the consoling truth of blessed immortality [is] the *ultimate* answer to the problem of retribution."[9]

All of the Hebrew wisdom writings up to this point struggled over this disconnect between human experience (which includes justice not requited) and belief in a balanced universe. Pseudo-Solomon argued that God's punishment of the wicked, though delayed, is sure to come and that those who suffer in this life will receive compensation in life after death.

---

7. Alexander A. Di Lella, "Conservative and Progressive Theology: Sirach and Wisdom," *CBQ* 28 (1966): 139–54 claims more of a Hebrew pedigree for Pseudo-Solomon's discussions of immortality.

8. Ibid., 151.

9. Ibid.

In the afterlife God would reward human righteousness. God had not adequately compensated the upright in the present world and would thus bring things into balance in the next life. This raw and unproven idea moves Pseudo-Solomon to new structures of thinking. He did not set out to write a treatise on immortality, but rather to address this age-old question: How can we assert the goodness of God in the presence of evil and suffering? This question (and its unsatisfactory divine answer) had silenced Job. This question had moved Qoheleth to subvert all the basic assumptions of traditional piety. Perhaps the Israelites reflected upon this question more deeply than any other culture or religion, but they ultimately came up empty. However, they had never seriously considered how something that happens after death could change their perspective.

The surrounding cultures thought about the dead all the time. The early Israelite community taught against the prevailing belief that the dead, one's ancestors, were deeply involved and invested in the lives of the living. They rejected the notion that their people should both feed and placate their departed family members. Israelite religion rarely made explicit claim regarding the fate of these ancestors but prohibited the summoning of the dead for any purpose. "Do not turn to mediums or wizards; do not seek them out, to be defiled by them" (Lev 19:31).[10] Mosaic law declared the realm of the dead and dead bodies (of both human and animal) unclean and defiling.

> Command the Israelites to put out of the camp…everyone who is unclean through contact with a corpse. (Num 5:2; see also 9:6–10)

> These are unclean for you…whoever touches one of them when they are dead shall be unclean until the evening. And anything upon which any of them falls when they are dead shall be unclean… (Lev 11:31–32)

By the first century, only the demon-possessed and predatory animals inhabited the burial sites, located outside the common living space. Therefore, the earlier Israelite sages did not consider that the fate of the dead contributed anything to the problem of evil.

Pseudo-Solomon crossed over and explored this forbidden realm, the realm of the dead. In his view of immortality, the righteous receive immortal life as a gift, while the wicked are punished with death.[11] This

---

10. See also Lev 20:6, 27; Deut 18:11. (The incident with King Saul and the medium at Endor [1 Sam 28:1] is the exception that proved the rule.)

11. A problem obvious to anyone who reads the Wisdom of Solomon is a contradiction that apparently did not disturb Pseudo-Solomon, its author: if God punishes the wicked by causing them to die, why then do all die? Why must the righteous die with the wicked if it is a punishment for the unrighteous? (see Michael

idea becomes part of how Christianity and Islam explain the presence of evil and the unfairness of death.[12] It is an important teaching in Judaism as well.[13]

This is why Pseudo-Solomon is a conservative rather than a progressive: Pseudo-Solomon delivers his new idea (divine retribution in the afterlife) to shore up the old notion of divine retribution. He turns people back from what he regards as the abyss of doubt, so they could once again express confidence in divine competence and faithfulness. Instead of embracing religious ambiguity as did the ancient Hebrew sages, Pseudo-Solomon condemns doubt. He regards "putting God to the test" as an act of "distrust" (1:2). Those who doubt are guilty of "perverse" (1:3) and "foolish thoughts" (1:5). "[God] is found [he writes] by those who do not put him to the test" (1:2a).

The law of retribution argued that the universe was "fair and balanced." But it has consistently failed to explain day-to-day human experience. Pseudo-Solomon covered up this explanatory failure with a *deus ex machina*, which has always been a sloppy plot device, the last resort of a playwright bereft of ideas. At the very end, he says, God arrives to make everything turn out well. The Jewish teaching regarding the justice of God had nearly failed because of the sufferings of the exilic community of Israel. Pseudo-Solomon's narrative breathed new life into this timeworn doctrine. Because later Jews and especially Christians accepted most of Pseudo-Solomon's narrative in their later teachings, the influence of retributive theology remains the dominant narrative used,

Kolarcik, *The Ambiguity of Death in the Book of Wisdom 1–6* [AnBib 127; Rome: Pontifical Biblical Institute], 76–78). The fate of the unrighteous remains vague in the Wisdom of Solomon, similar to the ambiguity one finds in the Hebrew Bible, and unlike the confident assertions in the New Testament.

12. These are some of the areas of compatibility between the Wisdom of Solomon and later traditional notions of the afterlife: (a) a righteous person will transcend death, defeat or overcome it; (b) the righteous receive a great reward in heaven—this compensates for their unfair suffering in life; (c) the unrighteous are excluded from blessed reward and experience death. However, the distinction between the first death (mortality) and the second death (eternal punishment) is not clearly made by Pseudo-Solomon. This distinction is very important in traditional Christian theology.

13. The book was popular with Christians, but not because of its major themes. Rather, they liked it because of certain isolated verses which suggested to them a Christological interpretation. For instance, see the discussion of Sophia as logos, the persecuted righteous one, the mention of the blessed wood that brings righteousness (concerning Noah's ark) and the mention of God's divine word coming down to judge the earth (referring to the death of the firstborn in Egypt). See Metzger, *Introduction to the Apocrypha*, 75–76.

and continues to prevail over most other attempts to explain the evil and unfairness of life.[14] Pseudo-Solomon *conserves* an ancient tradition.

Di Lella argues that Pseudo-Solomon, coming upon an intractable theological problem, "thought outside the box," and thus developed an innovative way to solve the dilemma. How can one reconcile the goodness of God with the presence of innocent suffering, while the guilty escape unscathed? By asserting that God metes out his justice in the afterlife, Pseudo-Solomon changed the way his community understood suffering. For Di Lella, this makes him a progressive.

On the contrary, the distinct character of Pseudo-Solomon's contribution comes clear when we compare the Wisdom of Solomon to two of his wisdom forebears, the books of Job (briefly) and Qoheleth (at length). If we define (again using Di Lella's terms) conservatives as those who seek to preserve older ways and to prevent change, how might we categorize the Wisdom of Solomon when compared to these books? Job questions God's justice, while Pseudo-Solomon finds new reasons to accept it.[15] Job's reckless declaration of his own innocence at YHWH's expense shatters the ancient traditional affirmations. Pseudo-Solomon supports these affirmations at every juncture. Job raises questions while Pseudo-Solomon suppresses them. The book of Job represents a more progressive approach to the questions of innocent suffering than the Wisdom of Solomon. The Wisdom of Solomon uses a new idea (reward and punishment in the afterlife) to shore up a very old and oppressive idea, the law of retribution.

To compare Job and the Wisdom of Solomon, one must juxtapose the two books and ask them similar questions. However, Pseudo-Solomon closely reproduces teachings of the Hebrew sage known as Qoheleth. While not quoting, some of his writing resembles the world-weary attitude of the author of the much older book. Pseudo-Solomon tells a story of wicked men in their conflict with a solitary righteous man.[16] The scene opens when these wicked men discuss among themselves life's meaning. "Short and sorrowful is our life," one laments, "and there is no remedy when a life comes to its end" (2:1). How should they conduct themselves

14. The essence of retributive theology is not that the retribution occurs *in this life*. Rather, that is incidental to its teaching. The real teaching is that all iniquity is punished by God, inevitably.

15. See my *Betrayal of God: Ideological Conflict in Job* (Louisville: Westminster John Knox, 1990), particularly Chapters 3 and 4.

16. I have used the words "ungodly" and "wicked" to describe this group. The author scarcely identifies them, using ἀσεβεῖς in 1:16, "But *ungodly men* by their words and deeds summoned death; considering him a friend, they pined away, and they made a covenant with him, because they are fit to belong to his party."

in the light of this hopeless pronouncement? One of them advises that if this is all life offers, they must take pleasure in it to the fullest. "Come, therefore, let us enjoy the good things that exist," he says (2:6).

The position of the ungodly strongly resembles some of the arguments found in the book of Qoheleth. These are quotes from the Wisdom of Solomon: "Short and sorrowful is our life, and there is no remedy when a life comes to its end, and no one has been known to return from Hades" (Wis 2:1); "For our allotted time is the passing of a shadow, and there is no return from our death, because it is sealed up and no one turns back" (2:5); "Come, therefore, let us enjoy the good things that exist, and make use of the creation to the full as in youth" (2:6). Note the similar sentiment in Qoheleth: "There is nothing better for mortals than to eat and drink, and find enjoyment in their toil" (Qoh 2:24; also 8:15); "For there is no enduring remembrance of the wise or of fools, seeing that in the days to come all will have been long forgotten" (Qoh 2:16; see also 3:20; 9:10).

This conversation among the ungodly takes a sinister turn when one of them suggests that because God does not see and cannot punish them, they should feel free to attack the weak and powerless: "Let us oppress the righteous poor man; let us not spare the widow or regard the gray hairs of the aged" (Wis 2:10).

At this point, the righteous man enters the narrative. This person had criticized the behavior and belief system of the wicked men, and they hate him for it: "He reproaches us for sins against the law, and accuses us of sins against our training" (Wis 2:12). He has bragged to them of his trust in God and his confidence that God will always defend him: "He calls the last end of the righteous happy, and boasts that God is his father" (2:16). The ungodly feel guilty because of the constant presence and pressure of this righteous man: "The very sight of him is a burden to us," they say (2:15). Therefore, they decide to make him an example to disprove his false claims: "Let us beset him with insult and torture, so that we may find out how gentle he is…for, according to what he says, he will be protected" (2:19–20). Thus they prove (as they believe) that their philosophy of life is superior to his. Even though he was righteous, God did not protect him. They tortured and killed him, but there was no divine intervention. However, the narrator observes,

> Thus they reasoned, but they were led astray,
> for their wickedness blinded them,
> And they did not know the secret purposes of God,
> nor hoped for the wages of holiness. (2:21–22)

These texts contain more than one voice. There is the voice of the implied author, Pseudo Solomon. Pseudo-Solomon tells a story, and the story has characters who speak. These are the additional voices. Pseudo-Solomon sets up these fictive voices as examples of faulty and sinful thinking. When one of these "unrighteous" declaims of God's inattention to human wickedness, that is not Pseudo-Solomon's voice. Rather, it is a voice Pseudo-Solomon expects us to reject with loathing. Pseudo-Solomon disapproves of these characters and what they say. This same speaker who questions the meaningfulness of life goes on to say, "let us oppress the righteous poor man; let us not spare the widow or regard the gray hairs of the aged" (2:9). Pseudo-Solomon asserts that the people who question the meaningfulness of life (as do some in the earlier wisdom tradition) are also the ones who act with oppressive violence. Therefore, Pseudo-Solomon in this context, regarded people like Qoheleth the skeptic (writing hundreds of years earlier) as purveyors of dangerous, sinful ideas, ideas which he, Pseudo-Solomon, links with violence and implicates in oppression. For Pseudo-Solomon, the voice that questions divine faithfulness, saying, "For we were born by mere chance" (2:2a), is dripping with evil intent: "Let us lie in wait for the righteous man, because he is inconvenient to us and opposes our actions" (2:12).

Pseudo-Solomon responds to Qoheleth's skepticism, or perhaps a skeptical "school" within the community of the sages. He faults them, because neither the ungodly in Pseudo-Solomon's narrative, nor Qoheleth, had taken into account what an afterlife would mean for their moral and intellectual choices. By impugning the motives of those who raise questions (because they use their philosophizing as an excuse for evil behavior), Pseudo-Solomon believes he can pull his students back from the abyss of their own questions.

This story, which covers part of ch. 1 and all of ch. 2, does not continue until ch. 5, and there things have changed considerably. Pseudo-Solomon describes the scene:

> Then the righteous will stand with great confidence
> In the presence of those who have oppressed them
> And those who make light of their labors. (5:1)[17]

This company of the righteous has passed through death to some manner of existence on the other side. Do the ungodly see their victim back from the dead in some horrific vision, or because they too are dead, assembled in some final judgment? Pseudo-Solomon does not explain. Collins describes this as "an apocalyptic scene."[18] In either case, the

---

17. The NRSV translation reflects the sense that ὁ δίκαιος might have become here a collective noun, "the righteous ones."

18. Collins, *Jewish Wisdom in the Hellenistic Age*, 179.

ungodly see that the righteous have received their reward. They have become "numbered among the children of God,[19] / their lot among the holy ones" (5:5). They have become members of the divine council, joined to the company of angels.[20] These wicked ones had not considered that their victim would get such a reward *after* they killed him.

Finally, Pseudo-Solomon declares that these wicked individuals who so obsessed over the brutal reality of human death would die indeed, would experience the death they expected. Nickelsburg observes:

> In all these things they [the ungodly] were wrong, but in one way they were right. They face the extinction they anticipated. This is so because they themselves summoned death (1:16), and now it claims them. Their nihilistic belief led to sinful actions, and these are punished by the annihilation they had posited in the first place. On the other hand the righteous will live forever (5:15–16). Theirs is the gift of immortality in which they had believed.[21]

These wicked men would "become dishonored corpses and an outrage among the dead forever" (4:18).

There are the various theories as to what Pseudo-Solomon actually meant with regard to death and immortality in this passage. The two most common are:

1. The death of the wicked refers to eternal death, not the death which all experience. Immortality (ever-lasting life after physical death) is a reward God gives to the righteous. This interpretation agrees with the standard rabbinic and first-century Christian notions of the afterlife.

2. Death for the wicked constitutes non-existence, or a shadowy existence in the netherworld of Sheol. Whereas the older Hebrew writing consigned all people to this shadow existence, Pseudo-Solomon sends the unrighteous there as a punishment. The righteous enjoy eternal heavenly life.[22]

---

19. The terms ἐν υἱοῖς θεοῦ and ἐν ἁγίοις both commonly refer to angels. See the discussion in Chapters 3 and 4 of my *Twilight of the Gods: Polytheism in the Hebrew Bible* (Louisville: Westminster John Knox, 2005).

20. Ibid.

21. George Nickelsburg, *Jewish Literature Between the Bible and the Mishnah* (Philadelphia: Fortress, 1981), 177–78.

22. Ernest G. Clark claims that for Pseudo-Solomon, death and eternal life have to do with the *quality* of life, but that the sage says nothing about life *after* death. See Clark's *The Wisdom of Solomon* (Cambridge: Cambridge University Press, 1973), 11–12.

These two great, muscular efforts by later traditions sought to compel Pseudo-Solomon to agree with either one external standard (first-century Jewish and Christian orthodoxy) or another (ancient Israelite beliefs regarding Sheol). I suggest a third explanation for this sage's muddle:

Interpreters cannot succeed in conforming Pseudo-Solomon to either the way Israelites believed in earlier periods, or the way later Christians and Jews believed. The text remains ambiguous and ill-fits these other thought-systems. On this issue, Pseudo-Solomon is confused. On the one hand, he embraces the popular Hellenistic thinking regarding the immortality and preexistence of the soul. On the other hand, he is a child of the Hebrew Bible. Its terms and concepts shaped and structured his thinking. Therefore, his ideas hang together poorly. Either he has not realized that the ancient Israelite agnosticism regarding Sheol differs from Greek notions of the immortal soul, or he realizes it, does not know what to do with it, and dumps the problem in the reader's lap.

Earlier sages urged their readers and students to attend to and to trust the validity of their human experience over against theological affirmations concerning the nature of God. Pseudo-Solomon tells his readers (contrary to this earlier wisdom tradition) not to believe their own experience of life. He tells them instead to trust him, the final sage. He assures them that the wicked have long, miserable, unproductive lives, while the godly will gain immortality in the next world. Both of these assertions are unprovable, and only available by means of revelation, or many layers of inference. One cannot confirm the existence of an afterlife through human perception or experience. Perception and experience had served the sages as the primary sources of divine knowledge. Whatever may or may not happen in the afterlife, it is not available to human perceptual knowledge or human memory. It becomes a matter of faith and optimism.

When the sages experienced suffering, they questioned the justice of God. They attempted to resolve this dilemma in different ways. Different ones within the sapiential community would claim one or more of the following:

1. All suffering is deserved. People suffer as a result of sin.
2. Suffering is purgative.
3. Suffering is instructive.
4. There is no adequate answer to the problem of suffering.
5. God is unjust.[23]

---

23. See James L. Crenshaw's introduction to *Theodicy and the Old Testament* (Philadelphia: Fortress, 1983).

The sages never came to consensus, but within their discourse they accomplished the following things: by their emphasis on experience and judgment (because they did not appeal to special revelation or religious authority), they gave worth and dignity to the independence of the human spirit. Each individual's perspective or voice must not be ignored, but must remain as an angle of vision that stands against the most authoritative religious pronouncements. Pseudo-Solomon offers a different approach when he claims that the magnitude of the innocent suffering pales against the prospect of their future reward.

The earlier Hebrew sages taught the Israelites to deal with and find benefit in theological ambiguity. They asserted that binary answers (yes or no; good or bad; in-group or out-group) seldom sufficed for real world difficulties. By their rhetoric and their teaching they allowed that truth often lies at the collision of two or more contradictory ideas. The Hebrew sages nurtured and kept alive the ancient Israelite tradition of sacred doubt.

The "school" that produced the books of Job and Ecclesiastes was characterized by their openness to ideas from beyond the Israelite society, their willingness to entertain seditious thoughts about their traditions, their ruthless honesty in self-examination, their willingness to confront the powerful, the high level of their literary accomplishments, and their embrace of ambiguity. Pseudo-Solomon changed key elements of that tradition in the service of his own theological project. He sought to protect God from accusation of unfairness, and claimed that the law of retribution still worked, in spite of evidence of human experience. He introduces a whole new source of knowledge, but one which was unavailable to observation. Humans must trust in a future eschatological rectification in heaven for all the injustice on earth. One may work for justice in this life, but ultimately it will only come from God, after death.

The Wisdom of Solomon is conservative in its stance, perspective and outlook: Pseudo-Solomon supports the ancient piety which claimed that the righteous are always rewarded and the wicked punished. Rich people use this belief to justify their accumulation of wealth and to excuse themselves from responsibility for the sufferings of the poor. God enforces justice in the universe. If one is evil, one suffers at some point. If one is righteous, at some point they will receive a reward. The reverse is also true. If one is rich, it is because one is righteous. If one is poor, sick, or suffering, it must be because of some sin. Pseudo-Solomon asserts that this holds true. He argues its reliability as a fundamental principle of life.

Pseudo-Solomon assures his readers that God will ultimately rectify all wrongs. The powerless, therefore, must wait passively until their redemption arrives. This "pie-in-the-sky" patient waiting discourages people from complaining about their conditions or trying to change them.

Pseudo-Solomon falls under the sway of extreme nationalism and hatred of the ethnic other. In his poem praising divine mercy, he describes God's near limitless patience. He gives the wicked Canaanites a lot of time to reform their ways: "But even these you spared, since they were but mortals...you gave them an opportunity to repent" (12:8, 10). But Pseudo-Solomon confides to the reader the impossibility that the Canaanites would ever submit to God.[24] He says, "their origin was evil and their wickedness inborn, and...their way of thinking would never change. For they were an accursed race from the beginning" (12:10–11).

Pseudo-Solomon maintained a stance fanatically anti-Canaanite. The language of Canaanite hatred served well to mask his hostility towards Greek domination. His attitude reflects an extreme nationalism and a deep hatred and distrust of the foreign other. He has transformed the earlier wisdom tradition of universalism, for he seeks to establish the superiority of the Jewish religion.

Thus, Pseudo-Solomon moves the wisdom tradition away from that which made it so dangerous and transgressive, its elevation of the human voice over the divine voice.

---

24. The Canaanites might have represented the Greeks to Pseudo-Solomon, as the ancient (for him) Egyptians represented the contemporary Egyptians, two different groups of Gentiles symbolized very differently in Pseudo-Solomon's writing. See Collins, *Jewish Wisdom in the Hellenistic Age*, 218.

WAS THE JUDAISM OF THE DEAD SEA SCROLLS A MYSTERY RELIGION?

Peter J. Haas

One of the central features of the religious life described by the community rules of the Dead Sea scrolls is the sacred meal and drink. These have been interpreted as a symbolic reflection of the Temple sacrifices on the one hand and as forming an historical bridge to later Judaic and Christian rituals on the other. While such diachronic associations are useful for constructing a history of Judaic religion in Roman times, I intend in this essay to take a synchronic approach. That is, I want to see not so much where these rituals stand in the evolution of later religious traditions, but rather to see where they stand in relation to other religious models of their time. It seems to me that many of the features of the religious cult described in the community documents of the Dead Sea scrolls find a parallel in what we know of Greek and Greco-Roman mystery religions. My argument in what follows is that one way of looking at the religious community described in the scrolls is to see it as a sort of Judaic mystery religion. Although largely ignored, the notion of some Hellenistic Judaisms taking on the form of a mystery cult was already suggested by Erwin Goodenough. As I shall show below, this kind of comparison helps explain many of the distinctive features and unprecedented liturgical and ritual elements expected of the practitioners. My discussion will focus primarily on the community rules of the "Community Rule" (4QS; originally published as the "Manual of Discipline") and the "Damascus Document" (4QD; also called "The Zadokite Document").

It is now well known that when the first scrolls were published, the translation and commentary were largely in the hands of Catholic scholars. In their widely accepted view, the religious community was based in the ruins at Qumran and was a kind of pre-, or even proto-, Christian monastic "order" that, much like medieval monks, spent their lives living by rules of celibacy, prayer, holiness, and scholarship. It was even thought by some that there was a direct historical link to formative Christianity insofar as the scrolls defined a religious life that was either Pharisaic or Essenic, and which may have influenced, or even included, John the Baptist, who passed these practices on to Jesus.[1] The extent to which these speculations bear closer scrutiny is beyond the scope of what I want to do here. My point, rather, is that this reading of matters sees the community of the Scrolls as a more or less self-contained phenomenon within the world of Judaism as it was making its transition to "Middle Judaism" and early Christianity. In other words, the religious world of the scrolls was seen as distinctly separate from the surrounding "pagan" cultures.

This exclusivistic view has come under increasing question as more of the Scrolls became known, and especially after a new generation of scholars came to have access to the entire corpus of materials. One of the harshest critics of the "received view" was Norman Golb. In addition, much work in the area of Hellenistic and Greco-Roman Judaism, textual as well as archeological, has shown that the Jews and Judaisms of the period did not exist in their own cultural bubble but were in deep conversation with the surrounding world. We are now well aware that the boundaries between what were subsequently to become early Christianity and formative rabbinic Judaism were vague to the point of non-existent in the early centuries of the first millennium, and that the boundaries of these "Judaisms" in turn were remarkably fluid and open to the surrounding cultures.[2] In short, we have over the last few decades come to see the Judaic religions of the Hellenistic world to be extraordinarily diverse and in fact part of the multi-ethnic and syncretistic mix of religious practices that characterized Greco-Roman civilization in Late Antiquity. It is in the framework of this new understanding that a comparison of the Dead Sea Scroll religion with the widespread model of mystery religions finds its place.

Before proceeding to the scrolls themselves, it will be worthwhile to survey briefly what we do and do not know about the mystery religions of this time. One of the difficulties in this area is that, of course, the mystery religions were "mysterious" precisely because their lore, myth, and ritual were to be secret. Thus we have very little information about

---

1. See, for example, Carl Hermann Kraeling, *John the Baptist* (New York: Scribner, 1951), and Matthew Black, *The Scrolls and Christian Origins* (New York: Scribner, 1961).

2. Shaye J. D. Cohen, *The Beginnings of Jewishness* (Berkeley: University of California Press, 1999), and Erich S. Gruen, *The Reinvention of Jewish Tradition* (Berkeley: University of California Press, 1998).

their inner workings and what we do know often comes from critics who cannot, obviously, be assumed to be giving an accurate and sympathetic picture. Nonetheless, enough of a picture emerges from our various sources to draw some reasonably accurate outlines of what it meant to be a mystery religion.

We have in fact information on a number of mystery religions, including those based on the myths of Dionysius, Orpheus, Isis, and Mithras. Probably the one that is most fully documented, however, is that of the Elysian mysteries. This seems to have been a fairly widespread tradition and we have numerous bits and pieces of evidence for its myths and rituals, from initiates, outsiders, and archaeological evidence. Ancient writers who refer to the Eleusian mysteries include, for example, such initiates as Sophocles, Herodotus, Aristophanes, Plutarch, and Pausanias, as do the later Christian critics Clement of Alexandria, Hypolytus, Tertullian, and Astorias. For this reason I propose to use it as a model for interpreting what may be behind the rules of the two community rule scrolls under consideration here.

The basis of the Elysian mystery cult was the myth of Demeter and her daughter Persephone. Although there are several versions of this myth, what I am presenting here is based largely on the Homeric "Hymn to Demeter," which seems to have most of the common and persistent themes despite variation of details. Demeter was, of course, the goddess of grain and so of the harvest more generally. The operative part of the myth for the mystery cult begins with the abduction of her daughter, Persephone, by the god of the underworld, Hades. Demeter, struck by grief, began a long search for her daughter, torch in hand, during which she neither ate nor drank. At one point she encountered a man named Celeus, who takes her in and gives her drink, sometimes identified as barley water. According to one version, Celeus was a king of Eleusis and had her seated on a chair draped with a ram's fleece. While at the house (or castle), the goddess takes a liking to Celeus' son and attempts to endow him with eternal life. However, as she is placing the child in a flame as part of the ritual, the mother walks in and the proceeding is aborted. Some versions have the child die, and in compensation Demeter gives special knowledge to the surviving son, Triptolemus. Such knowledge may have included the sacred hymns and rituals which make up the subsequent mystery cult. In any case, it is this child who later on establishes a shrine to Demeter at Eleusis. In the end Demeter, by withholding the harvest, was able to involve Zeus in restoring Persephone. In response to the lack of sacrifices, Zeus worked out a compromise by which Persephone was to be returned to earth with the proviso that she had not partaken of food in the netherworld. As matters turned out, however, Persephone had indeed tasted food in Hades (according to some accounts it was pomegranate seeds) and so she was not able to return to earth permanently. Thus it came to be that she was to spend part of each year in Hades, during which times Demeter withholds the harvest, and part of the year on earth, during which time flora and fauna flourish.

The mystery religion based on this myth had by all accounts two stages or levels. The "lesser mysteries" involved preparatory ritual cleansing with water while sitting on a chair covered with a ram's skin. The "greater mystery," open only to sworn initiates, involves some complex series of rituals including a nine-day fast, the drinking of a type of grain and water mixture (*kykeon*), travelling with lit torches, and the manipulation of various sacred objects such as the *kiste* (some sort of sacred chest) and the *Kalathos* (a lidded basket), each apparently containing some sacred or symbolic objects. One of our most detailed accounts of the actual ceremony is from the much later Clement of Alexandria, who reported that participants recited a formula which he gives as follows: "I fasted; I drank the *kykeon*; I took from the *kiste* (a cylindrical reliquary); having done my task, I placed in the basket, and from the basket into the *kiste*."[3] There has been some speculation, based on Clement and other later writers, that the ceremonies also included a *hieros gamos* or sacred marriage resulting in the birth of a new child. Whatever the details, it seems clear that the participants of the great mystery were reenacting those portions of the Demeter myth dealing with the search, discovery, and return of Persephone. The end result was probably the attainment of eternal life in some form, based on the goddess's actions in the house of Celeus and of course the return (or rebirth) of vegetation each spring.

As noted above, we have information on a number of other mystery cults, those of Osiris, Orpheus, and Mithras in particular, although none of the information on these is nearly as ample as what we have for the practices at Eleusis. Yet in each case the general structure seems to be the same. The participant or hierophant undergoes a ritual that reenacts the central myth of the deity, and usually results in the gaining of wisdom or insight achieved by replicating the experience of the deity. At least for the accounts preserved by later Christian writers, this usually involved acquiring some insight, or more importantly, control over what will happen to the practitioner after death.

3. Clement of Alexandria, *Protreptikos* II, 18; in *Clement of Alexandria with an English Translation by G. W. Butterworth* (LCL 92; Cambridge, Mass.: Harvard University Press, 1953), 43.

* * *

With these thoughts in mind, I wish now to turn to the central rituals described in the two Dead Sea scrolls under consideration. I begin with the Community Rule. It opens with the "master" telling the "holy ones" (hierophants?) that if they freely proceed with pure hearts and minds, they will be able to enter the "covenant of kindness" (the Hebrew is *brit tsedek*, Vermes has "Covenant of Grace").[4] Once the community has been formed, the priests and Levites recite the various blessings of the Lord as well as an accounting of the sins of the people and the curses to befall those who have joined the minions of the evil one. After each such recitation, the congregation responds with "amen" or some similar formulae. This, we are told near the bottom of the second column (lines 19–25), is to be done

> year after year all the days of Belial's dominion. The priests shall enter the Rule foremost, one behind the other, according to their spirits. And the Levites shall enter after them. In third place all the people shall enter the Rule, one after another, in thousands, hundreds, fifties and tens so that all the children of Israel may know their standing in God's Community (*byhd ʾl*) in conformity with the eternal plan (*lʿst ʿwlmym*)… For all shall be in a single Community of truth, of proper meekness, of compassionate love and upright purpose, towards each other in the holy council, associates of an everlasting society [*byhd ʾmt wʿnwt twb wʾhbt hsd wmhšbt sdq [ʾy]š lrʿhw bʿst qwdš wbny swd ʿwlmym*].[5]

The point of all this is so that "by the spirit of the true counsel concerning the paths of man," the participant "by the spirit of holiness which links him with his truth he is cleansed of all his sins."[6] The end result is that

> God, in the mysteries of his knowledge (*brzy sklw*) and in the wisdom of his glory (*wbhkmt kbwdw*), has determined an end to the existence of deceit and on the occasion of his visitation he will obliterate it forever. Meanwhile, truth shall rise up forever in the world which has been defiled in paths of wickedness during the dominion of deceit until the time appointed for judgment.[7]

4. Geza Vermes, *The Dead Sea Scrolls Translated with an Introduction and Commentary* (New York: Heritage, 1967).

5. Florentino García Martínez, *The Dead Sea Scrolls Translated* (Leiden: Brill, 1994), 5. The Hebrew text is from A. M. Habermann, *Megilloth Midbar Yehuda: The Scrolls from the Judean Desert* (Tel Aviv: Machbaroth Lesifruth, 1959), 62.

6. García Martínez, *The Dead Sea Scrolls*, 5; Habermann, *Megilloth Midbar Yehuda*, 62.

7. García Martínez, *The Dead Sea Scrolls*, 7; Habermann, *Megilloth Midbar Yehuda*, 63.

The central point of this ceremony is captured in column V, lines 7ff.:

> Whoever enters the council of the Community enters the covenant of God in the presence of all who freely volunteer. He shall swear with a binding oath to revert to the Law of Moses with all that it decrees, with whole heart and whole soul, in compliance with all that has been revealed concerning it to the sons of Zadok, the priests who keep the covenant and interpret his will and to the multitude of the men according to his will. He should swear by the covenant to be segregated from all the men of sin who walk along paths of irreverence. For they are not included in the covenant since they have neither sought nor examined his decrees in order to learn the hidden matters in which they err by their own fault and because they treated revealed matters with disrespect...

After some discussion of the priesthood, the document returns our attention to the community itself. Column VI, lines 18–20 tells us that every person who pledges to join the community shall be examined and if "the lot results in him joining the foundations of the community (*lqrwb lswd hyhd*) according to the priests and majority of the men in the covenant, his wealth and his belongings will also be included at the hands of Inspector of the belongings of the Many..." Upon admission, the novitiate is to wait one full year before touching the "pure meal" (*thrt rbym*, literally "the purity of the many"; see also column V, line 13) of the congregation, nor shall he drink of the "pure drink" (*mšqh hrbym*, literally "the drink of the many"). Near the end of the document (column IX), we are told that

> When these exist in Israel in accordance with these rules in order to establish the spirit of holiness in truth eternal, in order to atone for the fault of the transgression and for the guilt of sin and for approval for the earth, without the flesh of burnt offerings and without the fats of sacrifices—the offerings of the lips in compliance with the decree will be like the pleasant aroma of justice and correctness of behavior will be acceptable like a freewill offering—at this moment the men of the Community shall set themselves apart...[8]

This portion of the scroll is followed by a series of rules and regulations to govern community life (bottom of column VI through the first few lines of column X), and then a long hymn (or psalm) that seems to serve as a sort of doxology.

* * *

---

8. García Martínez, *The Dead Sea Scrolls*, 13.

Before proceeding, a few words need to be said about the translation. The following is based on the assumption that a few passages, properly understood, offer deep insight into the presuppositions and intellectual structure of the religious ritual being described.

The first is the question of the nature of the agreement in which these initiates are entering. The Hebrew has *bryt ḥsd*—a covenant of *hesed*. The meaning of the word *hesed* is unclear. Vermes has given it a more Christian translation as "grace"; García Martínez has "kindness," though further down he renders it as "compassionate" in the phrase "compassionate love." Other traditional English translations have included "loving-kindness" and "favor." Nelson Glueck, in his *Hesed in the Bible*, argues that it means something like fulfilling one's obligations of rights and duties to another, especially in the context of a covenant. Assuming that all these translations are at least partially correct, we can say that what the initiate here is entering is an agreement with the deity in which each side takes on duties and obligations toward the other. What results is what the document labels a *yahad* and which is most often translated as "community." While the word "community" here is not wrong per se, it does connote something more open and fluid than I think the Hebrew intends. What we do have is more like an "association" or a "guild" or "collegium." The phrase translated "eternal plan" is also less clear in the Hebrew. The word *atzah* can mean "counsel," "advise," or "plan." *Olamim* can mean "eternal," but is also the plural of "worlds." So the allusion here may be not so much to simply an eternal plan but to the arrangements of the cosmos more generally.

This brings us to the long phrase in lines 24 and 25. A discussion of the proper translation of this line could probably constitute a monograph on its own. I would thus like to focus attention on the last phrase, "towards each other in the holy council, associates of an everlasting society" (*[ʾy]š lrʿhw bʿst qwdš wbny swd ʿwlmym*). The holy council, as noted above, could also be rendered as "holy plan." The next phrase, however, is clearly translated badly. It in fact means something like, "the affiliates (literally children) of the secret of the *olamim* (so, "eternal secret" or "secret of the cosmos"). This is one of several places in the scrolls in which *sod* ("secret") is taken to be *yᵉsod* ("foundation" or "establishment") and so translated as some synonym of society. Assuming that the text is saying what it means, we are dealing with some sort of secret, a theme that permeates these scrolls. Since the "secret" is in fact not eternally hidden insofar as that it has been revealed (to the Zadokite priesthood, possibly through the "Teacher of Righteousness" or the "Righteous Teacher," and of course to the appropriate initiates into this sect) and since the plan is about to unfold in public, I think the intent is less on the eternity of the secret and more on its application to all the realms or dimensions of the cosmos.

Probably the most egregious translations are those of "pure meal" (*ṭhrt rbym*), and "pure drink" (*mšqh hrbym*). The two Hebrew phrases are, in fact, as noted earlier, "purity of the many" and "drink of the many." The first feature to notice is that in neither case does the word "sacred" appear in the original Hebrew. To be sure, given other passages in these scrolls, and the religious connotations of the concept of "purity," the adjective "holy" is not entirely out of place. On the other hand, it is not what the text says. The text makes reference to what is shared by the "commonality," not to what is sacred per se. More important, however, is that the first phrase does not specify that it is referring to a "meal." Again, the inference from other descriptions of the ritual life of the society offer support for the inference that this is a meal or at least some food, but the text, I think significantly, does not actually say this. Further, the Hebrew word used does not mean partake or eat but rather "touch" or "approach." I bring this up because I want to leave open the possibility, as does the scroll itself, that the subject here is not a meal that is eaten but some other communal object the full initiates can touch or approach.

* * *

These considerations of the original text allow us to draw some tentative conclusions about the nature of the "association" under discussion. What we have in these passages is a series of rituals which in many suggestive ways seem to parallel structures in the Elysian (and other) mystery rituals. First we have an invitation for true believers to enter into the community. After they have been dutifully advised of their rewards if they join with the proper intention, a sort of initiation ceremony takes place. The members are read the riot act, as it were, made to hear a recitation of blessings and curses by the priests and Levites. At the end of each such ritualistic recitation, the community of commoners responds with "amen" or some similar formula ("We and our fathers before us have sinned…"; "God has judged us and our fathers also"). This ritual of covenant affirmation is not unprecedented. It is in fact reminiscent of the final admonition given by Moses as told in Deut 27–28. This ritual of covenant renewal having been accomplished, the community then organizes itself "in their Thousands, Hundreds, Fifties, and Tens…" Again, this method of organization is familiar. It is the one adopted by Moses, on the advice of Jethro, in Exod 18:25. What all this amounts to is, I wish to suggest, a kind of a reenactment of the way the community was originally constituted. In other words, as in the case of the Eleusian Mysteries, we have here a community that is symbolically and ritualistically undergoing the experience of the founding myth of the original association. In so doing, of course, the initiates are also symbolically constituting or reconstituting the community of believers in its original purity. They have become in effect the new Israel, or maybe more accurately, the old Israel revivified at least for the duration of the ceremonial period.

So far we have been discussing what might be called the "lesser" ritual of the community. All members participate in this part and emerge purified and part of the true and uncontaminated community. The next stage is open only to those who have persisted in the community for a year. Only at this point may the member participate in the "greater" ritual, that of partaking of the "purity of the many" and drinking of the "drink of the many." Exactly what these are is not made clear in the text. In fact, as we noted, the traditional translations are misleading. Nonetheless, it is hard to avoid associating the sacred drink here with the *kykeon* of the Demeter ritual in the Eleusian mysteries. Further, it is hard to avoid thinking of the "purity of the many" as possibly referring to some sacred object that is handled during the ceremony, much like the *kiste* or *kalathos* in the Eleusian mysteries. This should not, of course, be taken to mean that the drink and purity of the scroll community were necessarily barley water and a lidded basket. Most interpretations see that "meal" and drink alluded to here as some sort of reminiscence of the Temple offerings. I see no reason why this cannot have been the case. My only point again is that there does seem to be a parallel to the way in which popular Greco-Roman mystery religions are reported to have operated.

To summarize my argument so far, I wish to claim that what we have in the "Community Rule" is a description of a Judaic religious group that has modeled itself to some significant degree on the common Hellenistic religious paradigm of the time, namely, that of a mystery religion. What we see is a select group of potential initiates who re-enact the founding "myth" of the "true" community, who then undergo a novitiate period to test their dedication and "purity" and who upon becoming full members partake of sacred food (or rituals) and drink. As part of becoming a member, the initiate accepts certain rules of behavior that govern the community and participate in learning or reciting certain doxologies or hymns.

At this point, the narrative of the "Damascus Rule" becomes relevant. In comparison to the "Community Rule," this text seems to give us more insight into the doctrines or teachings of the sect. What is of note here is the opening historical account of the scroll, which seems to give an internal spiritual history of Israel from the particular perspective of the community's sectarian vantage point. To state matters rather baldly, there is the larger community which has virtually from the beginning strayed from the covenant and so has been in continuous rebellion, and the small remnant that has maintained the truth and which is destined to survive through to the end when the great wrath of the divine shall put the wicked to an end. I think this perspective is best summed up at the end of column IV and the beginning of column V:

> ...However David had not read the sealed book of the Law (*bspr htwrh*) which was in the ark, for it had not been opened in Israel since the day of the death of Eleazar and of Jehoshua, and Joshua and the elders who worshipped Ashtoreth had hidden the public (*nglh* = exposed copy) until Zadok's entry into office...[9]

The role of the righteous remnant is explicated further on (near the end of column VI and the beginning of column VII):

> to separate unclean from clean and differentiate between the holy and the common; to keep the Sabbath day according to the exact interpretation, and the festivals and the day of fasting, according to what they had discovered, those who entered the new covenant in the land of Damascus... to keep apart from every uncleanness according to their regulations without anyone defiling his holy spirit, according to what God kept apart for them. For all those who walk according to these matters in perfect holiness (or the perfection of holiness; *btmym qdš*), in accordance with his teaching, God's covenant is a guarantee for them that they shall live a thousand generations.[10]

What this history appears to be telling us is that the divine truth given in the Torah has been obscured or misrepresented by evil persons (or maybe more particularly by an evil and false priesthood). The really true meaning of the revelations, however, has been sealed away and has been guarded by a select group of priests (the Zadokites), who now, near the end of history, are surfacing and reconstituting the true Israel. Those willing and able to accept the truth as taught by the current Zadokite leadership and who are willing to dedicate themselves wholeheartedly to

9. García Martínez, *The Dead Sea Scrolls*, 36; Habermann, *Megilloth Midbar Yehuda*, 79.

10. García Martínez, *The Dead Sea Scrolls*, 37; Habermann, *Megilloth Midbar Yehuda*, 81.

the covenant will enjoy the eternal life promised by the Torah. The others will be left to perish in their sin. The person who has come to reveal the truth now is the "Teacher of Righteousness" (or "Righteous Teacher," more literally, the "Teacher of *Tzedek*") and it is up to him and his Zadokite disciples to bring the true remnant into the eternal covenant with its promise of everlasting life. This true remnant ritually reconstitute the true (Mosaic) community and gain access to its Truth. Again, the parallels with the promise being offered by the Hellenistic mystery cults are striking.

* * *

In the end, of course, our knowledge of both the nature of the mystery religions in general and of the Scroll community in particular is too limited to draw absolute parallels. My goal, rather, has been briefly to lay out a basis for suggesting that the cult described in the Scrolls might in fact reflect a larger mode of religiosity that was commonly known and accepted throughout the Hellenistic world. The scrolls of course contain much that is particular to the Judaic religious tradition, especially in its strong dependence on the biblical literature. It is easy to see how one could draw a straight line from the inherited biblical tradition through the Scroll community and on into later manifestations of Judaism, whether in the form of the early Church or of early Rabbinism. On the other hand, it is easy to see, in a synchronic perspective, that the particular Judaism of the Scroll community is being articulated in a fashion that would make sense to Jews who were living in a world that was heavily influenced by Greco-Roman culture. It is a truism that various Judaisms from within always see themselves as being the true religious descendants of the Mosaic revelation. It is also a truism, however, that each generation of Jews, in whatever way that is defined, structure their Jewish lives in ways that are in accord with the cultural and social givens of their day. In the community of the Scroll, I wish to argue, we see a good Hellenistic example of this as a community of Jews living in a confusing time of great change has adopted a religious model widely understood in their time to use as a vessel for expressing their particular ethnic and religious heritage. If I am correct, then what we have in these two community scrolls is a remarkable look into the inside of a particular Hellenistic mystery religion written by the adherents themselves.

CONCLUSION:
THE FUTURE FOCUS OF BIBLICAL STUDIES

Jon L. Berquist

The Rise of Persian and Hellenistic Studies

Biblical studies, such as the excellent essays in this volume, now frequently focus on the Persian and Hellenistic periods. Such was not always true. This volume serves not only as a testimony to this shift in the emphasis of biblical studies but also as a pointer along the way toward a sharper focus of our work.

Twenty years ago, biblical scholars rarely mentioned Yehud or the Persian period. It was widely presumed that the fifth and fourth centuries B.C.E. were a "dark age" in ancient Israelite and Judean history, a post-monarchical time in which very little of import happened and about which very little could be known through historical or textual investigation. Even the more extensive treatments of the period's Israelite religion and society would characterize the time as a "silver age" in comparison to the luster of the previous golden years. Such an assessment may have improved upon Wellhausen's estimation of Israelite culture and worship in consistent decline and constant devolution since the lofty heights of the eighth century, but these appraisals of the Persian and Hellenistic period only served to continue the denigration of these later centuries in biblical scholarship and to ward off serious and fair consideration. The history of biblical scholarship's treatment of the Hellenistic period traces a different arc. More than a century ago, the Hellenistic period received great attention, and the Maccabean period was thought to have generated a number of biblical texts. However, most of twentieth-century scholarship discarded and ignored these theories, and the Hellenistic period lost the interest of scholars of ancient Israel and the Hebrew Bible.

By contrast, the end of the twentieth century and the beginning of the twenty-first have seen a sharp increase in the historical and social consideration of the Persian and Hellenistic periods. Many of the contributors to this volume have been among the scholars to lead this development.

Whereas these latter eras were once considered the unknown periods, many scholars would now understand that there is more direct archaeological, historical, and textual evidence for the Persian and Hellenistic periods than for the preceding centuries. Although scholarly consensus on the dating of biblical texts still proves elusive, a strong and vocal group of scholars would date a number if not most of the Hebrew Bible's texts to these times, or would at least emphasize the creative role of these periods in the collection and redaction of the texts. The change in the last twenty years of scholarship has been remarkable, and scholars should recognize this shift as one of the most rapid and pervasive developments in the history of modern biblical scholarship.

Many of the reasons for this change of scholarly perception have been documented. Advances in archaeological understanding downplayed the historical certitude of the Hebrew Bible's telling of the monarchy; not only did Genesis and Judges seem less historically accurate, but many scholars questioned the verisimilitude of texts such as Samuel and Kings. Also, new archaeological findings demonstrated the historical realities present during the later periods. At the same time, scholars recognized the extensive contributions of historians working in the Achaemenid and Hellenistic periods, which grew in their value to biblical studies. As scholars adjusted their terminology from the "postexilic" nomenclature to Persian/Achaemenid and Hellenistic studies of Yehud, scholarship assigned an enhanced value to the period itself (as opposed to defining it by its predecessor), as well as a growing recognition that the period represented a time when Yehud/Judah was a colony or a peripheral social formation within larger world empires. This change of focus allowed scholars to perceive the historical context, fitting Yehud into a greater pattern of historical events and providing a setting for understanding Yehudite culture, society, and religion.

However, a number of other factors contributed to the increase of Persian and Hellenistic studies in biblical scholarship. First is the growth of social-scientific studies of ancient Israel and the Hebrew Bible. Such approaches asked different questions than the previous historical-critical paradigms, despite sharing a diachronic and historical interest. Initially, social-scientific studies focused on the pre-monarchical and monarchical periods of Israel's history, but through the 1980s these approaches began to work toward later time frames. Here, Douglas Knight's influence on the growth of Persian and Hellenistic studies is particularly noteworthy, because of his role in encouraging social world approaches in the Society of Biblical Literature, in his own doctoral teaching, and in the Library of Ancient Israel series of monographs that he edited. In these contexts,

Knight has provoked and challenged both senior and junior scholars to attend to social world concerns. Many of this volume's contributors began their exploration of social-scientific methods either under Knight's tutelage or in the context of Knight's collegiality. As the number of biblical scholars with social-scientific orientations has grown, there has been an enhanced opportunity for the investigations that opened the Persian and Hellenistic periods to greater and more productive exploration.

Knight has influenced Persian and Hellenistic biblical studies in a deeper way. Beginning with his own dissertation, Knight not only recovered but also forged original and ongoing links between American and Scandinavian biblical scholarship. This collaboration has proved extraordinarily fruitful in the foundations for Persian and Hellenistic studies. Knight's collaborative emphasis continues to embrace Israeli archaeology and also American Jewish scholars. As a result, this volume includes scholarly contributions from these several vectors, all of which too often still remain separate and isolated in their scholarship. It is hard to imagine how Persian and Hellenistic biblical scholarship could have flourished as it has without the generative interchange of ideas across these national, cultural, and religious boundaries.

The Next Challenges

Given these gains in biblical scholarship through the last quarter century, what can we suggest as a future focus for biblical studies that continues these trajectories and builds constructively upon these advances? I would suggest five future foci, and then three ways in which these developments may well influence the wider field of biblical scholarship.

First, scholarship has attained a broad consensus about the general shape of Yehudite and surrounding society in the Persian and Hellenistic periods, but more attention here is needed. In particular, archaeological investigations are now demonstrating sharper detail within these periods, with advances in the chronological differentiation throughout the period but even more so in the geographic distinctions and the social differences within the periods. Scholars need to integrate these new findings with sociological, political, and historical understandings to produce an analysis of the culture, society, history, and religion of Yehud and surrounding areas. Our goal should be an exploration of the periods that is not only more complete but also more sensitive to the diversity within the period and the internal differences. This recognition of diversity is present in some of the best scholarship in the field right now, as demonstrated by several of the essays in the present volume. This work is likely to propel historical reconstruction forward as much as the initial social-scientific forays into the Persian and Hellenistic periods of the last twenty years.

Second, the collaboration of American, European, and Israeli scholars that has been so fruitful in the scholarly advances regarding the Persian and Hellenistic periods must continue, now in new generations of scholars. Herein lies a great risk in the success of Persian and Hellenistic biblical scholarship; now that this work is established as a field of study in its own right, there is a temptation for scholars to work more individually and more conventionally. By resisting this tendency, new collaborations can achieve deeper results, especially because some of the best work is now being conducted outside the US–Europe–Israel conjunction of scholarship. Furthermore, the geographic and interreligious cooperation must continue and expand, including scholars from more continents and perspectives. In this way, Persian and Hellenistic biblical studies will have access to a greater array of information, examples, and worldviews, which will only serve to enhance the models at work in our scholarship.

Third, scholarship needs to proceed at the intersection of Persian and Hellenistic studies and approaches such as empire-critical studies, postcolonial studies, and world-systems approaches. The periods at hand demonstrate the realities of large, bureaucratic empires, in which Yehud functioned as a small periphery. Scholars have recognized this by adopting the terminology of empires and colonies to reflect these historical situations and by using social-scientific analyses of empires. In the years ahead, scholarship can progress significantly through the critical use of the tools of these newer methods to expand the investigation. Postcolonial studies in particular have gained a strong and influential foothold in biblical scholarship, but as yet the integration of this approach with Persian and Hellenistic studies has only begun.

Fourth, scholarship needs to continue its exegetical work of texts that represent the Persian and Hellenistic periods. Such scholarship forms one of the greatest contributions of this present volume, in which scholars use a variety of exegetical approaches to deal with different parts of the Hebrew Bible to elucidate various aspects of the Persian and Hellenistic periods. Whereas scholarship from just a few years ago attended to such texts with a narrow set of methods (mostly social-scientific), the wider range of approaches can only improve our understanding of the nature and function of biblical texts within this time period.

Fifth, scholarship should pay greater attention to the use of earlier texts within the Persian and Hellenistic period. Again, several essays within this volume advance scholarship in this direction and point the way to further work. Scholarship recognizes that many Hebrew Bible texts were first composed in earlier periods but gained their current form and significance in the Persian and Hellenistic periods. These texts should not be interpreted only as examples of composition and later redaction, but also in terms of their recasting, resignification, or reuse in a later period. Redactional theories have usually underemphasized the creativity in the Persian and Hellenistic periods, and this represents significant ground for further research.

Refocusing Biblical Studies

To support these scholarly advances and to communicate their developments to a new generation of students and other readers, I would call scholars to endeavor toward three larger synthetic works as well. In light of an emerging consensus of Yehudite history in the Persian and Hellenistic periods, we will need a new critical history of Israel, Judah, and Yehud, to move beyond the historiography of scholarship's recent past. A focus on the history of these later periods should be foundational, and this historical investigation can then be the groundwork for the more speculative historical reconstructions of earlier periods. The integration of the last decades of study into the later periods can reinvigorate the broader task of historical description of ancient Israel, by refocusing attention away from the apologies about what is not known about the earlier times to concentrate on what is now known about the later periods. A new history and a new way of teaching history will establish a healthy basis for the next generation of scholarship.

Building upon such new historical reconstruction, scholarship's second synthetic goal should be a new critical history of the Hebrew Bible as literature. This will expand upon the exegetical advances and variety of recent years, as well as a fresh understanding of the function of texts and language in the Persian and Hellenistic periods. A new focus on the later periods of textual production can move beyond the older paradigms of creation that leads to appropriation, showing instead the constant traditioning process at work in every generation and the creative work done at each step. A new theory of the literature's expression and change would be a significant contribution to biblical scholarship, rooted in the Persian and Hellenistic studies of the recent generation.

Lastly, the diversity of religious practices and understandings in the Persian and Hellenistic periods can empower the recognition of the multiple innovations in ideology, worldview, and religion. Scholarship needs to move beyond the genetic theories of unified origins, in which many practices spring from a singular cause; instead, biblical scholars need broad synthetic understandings of multiplicity of religious expressions in the midst of pluralistic cultures. In so doing, scholarship can rightly focus on the diasporic diversity of this religious heritage, resisting the monolithic interpretations that result in contemporary implications of restriction. Whether scholars think of this in terms of a new history of Israelite religion, a new breadth of theologies of the Hebrew Bible, or an analysis of worldviews surrounding the text, the benefits are significant not only for the understanding of the ancient society and its texts but also for the contemporary expressions and ethics from around the world that trace themselves back to ancient Israel.

If the focus of biblical studies looks in these directions, the future seems promising indeed. Such scholarship will flourish as a legacy to Douglas Knight, whose work offered an example, encouragement, and impetus to explore the Persian and Hellenistic periods using social-scientific and other methods within a broad global collaboration.

INDEXES

INDEX OF REFERENCES

INDEX OF AUTHORS